OUR LIFE AMONG THE IROQUOIS INDIANS

Rev. Asher Wright.

OUR LIFE AMONG THE
IROQUOIS INDIANS

BY

HARRIET S. CASWELL

FOREWORD BY Jack T. Ericson
NEW INTRODUCTION BY Joy A. Bilharz

University of Nebraska Press
Lincoln and London

Foreword © 2007 by Jack T. Ericson
Introduction by Joy A. Bilharz © 2007 by the Board
of Regents of the University of Nebraska
All rights reserved
Manufactured in the United States of America
∞
First Nebraska paperback printing: 2007

Library of Congress Cataloging-in-Publication Data
Caswell, Harriet S., b. 1834
Our life among the Iroquois Indians /
Harriet S. Caswell; foreword by Jack T. Ericson;
new introduction by Joy A. Bilharz.
p. cm.
Reprint. Originally published: Boston and Chicago:
Congregational Sunday-School and Publishing
Society, 1892.
Includes bibliographical references.
ISBN 978-0-8032-5999-7 (pbk.: alk. paper)
1. Seneca Indians—Missions. 2. Seneca Indians—
Social life and customs. 3. Wright, Asher, 1803–1875.
4. Wright, Laura M. (Laura Maria), 1809–1886.
5. Missionaries—New York (State). I. Title.
E99.S3C3 2007
974.7004'975546—dc22
2007017856

FOREWORD

On December 2, 2006, Joy Bilharz and I attended a memorial service for Abby Laura Pierce Wheeler (1914–2006) at the Asher Wright Memorial Presbyterian Church, Cattaraugus Territory. Many years ago Laura, a good friend, urged me to see a new edition of *Our Life among the Iroquois Indians* into print. Laura wanted present-day Senecas and Cayugas to be aware of the missionary labors of Laura Sheldon Wright, for whom she was named. This is now accomplished.

Some changes were made to Harriet S. Caswell's 1892 publication in preparing this new edition. A new cover was created by the University of Nebraska Press, several line drawings of western or stereotypical Indians were removed, and a map and six new illustrations were added.

Thanks need to be extended to Calvin E. Lay, former president of the Seneca Nation of Indians, for his continued support of research involving the Asher Wright Memorial Presbyterian Church. Gerri Printup and Todd J. LaQuay of the Seneca Nation of Indians Geographic Information Services's Division of Planning prepared the map. Leonora Brown, interpretive programs assistant at Letchworth State Park, was instrumental in guiding research into the William Pryor Letchworth papers and provided the 1870s photograph of the Thomas Asylum for Orphan and Destitute Indian Children. John H. Conlin, editor of *Western New York Heritage*, gave permission to use the photograph of the Seneca mission house, which appeared in an article I wrote on the Seneca Mission Press. Jare Cardinal, director of the Seneca Iroquois National Museum, aided in research. Janet Ferry and the interlibrary loan staff at Reed Library, SUNY Fredonia, were most helpful in ordering articles and microfilm necessary for the preparation of Joy Bilharz's introduction.

I am not sure Joy will ever quite forgive me for pushing her into writing the introduction to this reprint. However, her developing interest in Asher and Laura Wright's work on the Cattaraugus Territory is very likely to lead to further research and publication. For this I am grateful.

Jack T. Ericson

INTRODUCTION

Joy A. Bilharz

Shortly after her graduation from the State Normal School in Massachusetts in 1853, nineteen-year-old teacher Harriet "Hattie" Clark (Caswell) arrived at the Cattaraugus Reservation of the Seneca Nation of Indians in western New York. Her work among the Senecas was sponsored by the American Board of Commissioners for Foreign Missions, an organization founded by New England congregationalists early in the nineteenth century. The resident missionary was Rev. Asher Wright, who assigned her to a post near Lake Erie. Wright had originally been sent to the Buffalo Creek Reservation in 1831 but had gone with the Senecas to Cattaraugus in 1845. With Wright was his second wife, Laura Sheldon Wright. Upon meeting Caswell, the forty-four-year-old Laura probably recalled her own arrival at the Buffalo Creek Reservation a generation earlier, when as a twenty-three-year-old bride, she accompanied the husband whom she had first met only shortly before their wedding in Vermont two weeks prior. She no doubt welcomed the aid of a younger woman, especially one whose experience of the world was greater than her own.

Our Life among the Iroquois Indians is Caswell's story of the nearly seventeen years she spent among the Senecas. More than just a personal recollection, the book provides a description of reservation life in the turbulent years of the mid-nineteenth century. Her account also contains oral histories of the events leading up to the reservation period as told by old men during long winter evenings and details the process of evangelism and the indigenous responses to it. It also provides valuable insight into the lives of two remarkable individuals, Laura and Asher Wright.

Caswell was not present during the "Seven Years' Trouble," when the Senecas at the Buffalo Creek Reservation, along with a considerable number of Onondagas and Cayugas also living there, lost their land through the Treaty of 1838. Asher Wright was the American Board's missionary to Buffalo Creek during this period; he also visited other mission stations in the region, including those on the Cattaraugus and Allegheny reservations south of Buffalo and the Tuscarora and Tonawanda reservations to the north and east. His first wife had died within months of their arrival, and he married Laura in 1833 after requesting that the missionary board find him a "suitable companion" who could deal with Indian women and would be able to learn Seneca.

A graduate of Dartmouth College and Andover Theological Seminary, Asher Wright was trained in linguistics and medicine and brought these skills with him as he embarked on a missionary career. Caswell's book tells us little about him, although she briefly discusses his achievements in translation and printing and the political battles he engaged in to overturn the 1838 treaty and replace it with the Compromise Treaty of

1842. He was also involved in the radical socio-political shift that occurred in 1848 as the Senecas withdrew from the Iroquois Confederacy and established a republican form of government, today's Seneca Nation of Indians. Caswell provides no insight into Wright's character or his daily routine as he ministered to the bodies and souls at Cattaraugus.

This is very different from her picture of Laura Wright. Caswell provides us with a detailed description of Wright's life and ideas and especially her daily interactions with the Senecas, as well as an account of the minutiae of daily life on the reservation. What emerges is a portrait of a strong woman, dedicated to the spread of the gospel but whose primary concern appears to have been helping the poorest people, usually pagan women and children, improve their lives. Laura's interest was in the humanitarian effort in contrast to Asher's more political and academic endeavors. In many ways this dichotomy is representative of ideas about appropriate gender roles at a time when the "Cult of Domesticity" prevailed (Bonvillain 2007, 183–87). This ideology maintained that women were "naturally" more nurturing than men and were therefore suited only to the domestic sphere, while the public sphere (which was considered more important) should be the exclusive domain of men, whose more assertive nature justified their dominance of economic and political affairs.

Neither of the Wrights wrote about their experiences in any format other than letters, most of which are not readily available.[1] Contemporary reports from various individuals, often Quakers and other missionaries who stayed only briefly, provide superficial descriptions of reservation life. Caswell's book, therefore, is the closest thing we have to an ethnographic account from this time period that is based on long-term residence among the Senecas. It is also unique in that it is written by a woman and therefore reflects a perspective often absent from contemporary reports. For that reason it also permits the reader to examine how nineteenth-century ideas about gender and the place of women in society were played out when Euro-American women encountered the Iroquois, a society whose cultural tradition demanded gender equality.

The book contains descriptions of traditional Iroquois culture and events, including precontact religious festivals, the creation story, and the founding of the Confederacy. Caswell recounts the story of Mary Jemison, a white woman of the Genesee who was captured as a teenager and spent most of the rest of her life among the Senecas. As an old woman, Jemison was visited shortly before her death by Laura Wright. Caswell's report must have come directly from Wright. There is also a section dealing with Red Jacket that focuses on his attitudes toward Christianity and missionaries and in conclusion states that his initial resistance was eventually overcome. Another section details Seneca hostilities with the Kah-gwas, a group living on the shores of Lake Erie, and the more distant Cherokees. Caswell includes numerous descriptions of individual Seneca men and women and their interactions with her and the Wrights. More than any other part of the volume, these vignettes provide a window into the lives of ordinary people at this time. Not surprisingly, Christian and pagan Indians are described in separate chapters.

Although there is information in *Our Life among the Iroquois Indians* that is useful to an anthropologist or historian, Harriet Caswell was not a social scientist nor was she an unbiased observer. First as a teacher and subsequently as a general missionary, her presence among the Senecas was motivated by her deep desire to convert pagan souls to Christianity. Although she often sounds ethnocentric and moralizing to twenty-first-century sensitivities, her attitudes were a reflection of the prevailing ideology of Protestant missionization and were shared by most people then working in the field. Additionally, she was no doubt acutely aware of the widespread stereotypes of Indians and presented the Iroquois in a way that would be recognizable to the general public. This explains the phrases that are so jarring to twenty-first-century ears (e.g., "happy hunting ground," "wigwam," etc.) that she surely knew were inaccurate. The cover of the original edition shows an Indian sitting in front of a tipi, and there are other equally incongruent images that have been removed from the new edition.

Like Laura Wright, Caswell developed close friendships with individual Senecas and felt so at home on the Cattaraugus Reservation that when she married Lemuel Caswell, a Boston businessman, their wedding was held at the mission church. Although the ceremony was performed by her brother, Dr. J. B. Clark, it was repeated by Rev. Wright in Seneca for the benefit of the

Indians. Her description of the wedding is one of the most interesting passages in the book as she recounts how Mr. Two Guns and his wife walked up the aisle after the ceremony and asked Rev. Clark to baptize their infant son, whom they had named Lemuel Caswell Two Guns. The name *Caswell* appears again later as the middle name of Arthur Caswell Parker, the grandson of Nicholson Parker, the United States Seneca interpreter, and his wife, Martha Hoyt, Laura's niece who was raised by the Wrights. Arthur C. Parker was a noted Iroquoianist and served as curator of the Rochester Museum (Fenton 1968). Even though she returned infrequently after her marriage, Harriet was obviously remembered fondly by many Senecas.

The book is also important for the light it sheds on the missionization process and the responses it engendered among indigenous peoples. The American Board mission to the Senecas was transferred to the Presbyterians in 1870. The Wrights remained as missionaries but reported to different superiors. There was little, if any, impact on the Senecas. Fundamental to Protestant evangelism was the belief that humans were depraved, and the only route to salvation was through divine intervention and acceptance of the gospel; the only options open to pagans were to convert or be damned (Coleman 1980, 44). Caswell's descriptions of the incredible anguish of young children who feared going to hell for some trivial offense, such as whispering during a Sabbath service, and her delight in their trauma as a measure of success illustrate this belief well. There was little she would not do to advance the Christian message; when a family asked her to make lace sleeves for a dress in which they could bury their daughter, she agreed to do so only if she were permitted to preach to the dying child.

It is in this attitude that she differed significantly from Laura Wright, who believed pagans should be approached in a "gentle and persuasive manner."[2] In a letter to William Pryor Letchworth, Wright describes her friend Polly Doxtator, whom she extolls as a virtuous and moral person; only at the end does she state that Polly was a "persistent pagan."[3] For Wright, the formalities of conversion were less important than whether a person lived an honest and honorable life. Wright and Caswell's work diverged: Laura spent more time with Seneca women, particularly non-Christians, to improve material conditions on the reservation while Harriet took over most of the purely religious duties that usually fell to the missionary's wife or to the missionary himself.

Another goal of the missionary effort was to eliminate idleness as the Protestants firmly believed that "the devil finds work for idle hands." Shortly after her arrival at Buffalo Creek, Laura Wright brought together a group of girls for instruction in "useful arts." When drought and the resulting bad harvests increased poverty at Cattaraugus, she found work for Seneca women sewing flannel shirts that were sold to the Indian Department for the use of the western tribes. Women were also encouraged to come together to sew clothing for their families. By teaching useful skills and providing the necessary equipment, Wright hoped to make Seneca women and children less vulnerable to the economic fluctuations that frequently plagued the United States and, concomitantly, to make them more independent.

After her marriage to Lemuel, Harriet Caswell returned to Boston. She worked for the next fifteen years at the North End Mission, where she opened an industrial school for women in the rooms of the mission house (Clark 1911, 50). Although the establishment of such schools had become an important trend among social reformers, Caswell stated, "Before the popular wave of 'industrial education' had begun to sweep over our land, Mrs. Wright had already inaugurated this movement among the Seneca Indians" (1892: 319–20). Her experiences as a young missionary woman under the tutelage of Laura Wright would influence Caswell throughout her life; Caswell, in turn, would also have an impact on her teacher.

After Asher's death Laura became deeply involved in the Thomas Asylum for Orphan and Destitute Indian Children and served as a trustee of that institution. The asylum originated after a typhoid epidemic in 1847, when the Wrights took orphaned children into their home. It was chartered by the state of New York in 1851 and had ten trustees—five Indians and five whites, including Asher Wright. Laura became a close friend and confidante of William Pryor Letchworth of the New York State Board of Charities, and at the time of her death she was working on the development of the Gospel Industrial Institute, which would have included a high school (with gender-specific instruction), a library and reading room, and a YMCA and YWCA that were modeled on Caswell's work in Boston. In fact, Laura hoped that Harriet would return to the reservation to take charge of the project.

Our Life among the Iroquois Indians can be placed in part within a literary genre typical of the mid to late nineteenth century in which the virtues of missionary work and self-sacrifice were extolled, especially for women (Phillips 1969, 291; Wetter 1978, 633). These books were meant to encourage women to take up the missionary challenge, but it had also become clear that American women could raise funds for missionary efforts beyond those obtained by their husbands (Wetter 1978, 632), and so the narratives also served to generate financial contributions. Caswell's book fits squarely within this agenda as she states (1892: 317), "To Mrs. Wright I owe a debt of gratitude which can be redeemed only by passing on the story of her saintly life for the inspiration of other Christian workers."

Gender was a source of tension for Protestant evangelicals. On one hand they accepted the prevailing standard of a public and domestic dichotomy as rooted in the biological natures of males and females. When Howard Mason visited Baptist mission stations in 1830 he described the proper role of a missionary wife: "She must find her principal sphere of usefulness in keeping her husband whole hearted and happy, in being a good housewife; sustaining all the domestic cares; training up her children well" (Phillips 1969, 311). William Dean, who had buried two missionary wives, echoes this sentiment in his 1854 introduction to the missionary memoirs of Lucy Lord when he writes of the proper role of women in the field: "Their principal and usually only duty is to render their home a heaven, and their husband happy by lightening his cares, training his children, soothing his sorrows, sympathizing in his stresses, and lending their counsel and support to his duties" (Lord 1854). It was never considered that a missionary wife might require some of the same solicitude while she struggled with learning a new language, creating and maintaining housing in an alien physical and cultural environment, and coping with teething infants and cranky toddlers.

Despite this separation of gender roles, there was a realization that Christian women were needed to gain access to pagan women, who often wielded so much power that they were inaccessible to male missionaries (Wetter 1978, 630–31). Thus, wives would be required to engage in some activities that brought them out of their immediate domestic environment (Phillips 1969, 273). Awareness of this is demonstrated in an exchange of letters between Asher Wright and the secretary of the American Board in which Wright requests the board's aid in finding a wife, citing the need for a woman to address some vague but obviously gender-specific issues he had encountered at Buffalo Creek.[4]

Furthermore, as women's role as fund-raiser became increasingly important, missions often focused their appeals on issues that were assumed to be of particular interest to women. As feminism began to take hold as a social movement, at least among the more progressive elements of American society, this meant emphasizing the supposed "degraded" status of pagan women; this issue "became one of the chief emotional appeals for foreign missions" (Phillips 1969, 273). Christianity was portrayed as the major mechanism for elevating female status in foreign lands. Laura Wright was apparently sympathetic to the appeal; Caswell quotes from an essay written by Wright when she was at school in 1826 in which she says that American women need to raise the "degraded females of Asia to the same degree of civilization and respectability which they hold themselves" (1892: 11). Focusing on the rights of women in foreign lands may also have been a convenient way for the men who directed the major missionary organizations to sidestep the issue in domestic affairs.

What was ironic, of course, was that in Iroquois society the social inferiority of women that had dominated western convention was traditionally absent. Descent was matrilineal, and this remains the modern-day criterion for enrollment in the Seneca Nation of Indians. Although the roles of men and women were different, the value of the contributions of each gender was seen as equal. In the Confederacy women were responsible for appointing and removing chiefs and determining the fate of captives. Economically, they grew the major crops of maize, beans, and squash and controlled the distribution of all foodstuffs; land and property were owned by the matrilineage. But following the American Revolution, Iroquois gender roles became less equal. Patrilineality in name and inheritance became the rule (Wallace 1969, 312). Men replaced women as farmers because working in fields was defined by the now dominant culture as improper for women, whose role was reduced solely to that of homemaker.

When the Wrights, and later Caswell, went to the Seneca reservations they encountered a society that had endured the effects of epidemics, warfare, land encroachment, the introduction of alcohol, and all of the other malignant effects of "civilization." When an elected government was established in 1848, only males were permitted to vote and hold office. These rules remained in effect until 1964 and 1966 respectively (Bilharz 1995, 110). Nevertheless, the Seneca constitution adopted in 1848 included the stipulation that no land could be sold without the consent of "three-quarters of the mothers of the nation." This was a tacit recognition that land ownership was vested in the matrilineages and also an acknowledgment of the traditional political roles of Seneca women. Ironically, the addition of this phrase to the constitution was suggested by Asher Wright (Abler 1969, 125). Clearly he recognized that Seneca women had not been "degraded" in precontact and pre-Christian times.

Although Laura Wright and Harriet Caswell paid at least lip service to traditional gender roles, both clearly went beyond what was socially expected of them. The relationship between these two women is another interesting facet of *Our Life among the Iroquois Indians*. Although both were trained as teachers, they were a generation apart and came from different social backgrounds. Wright was born in rural Vermont, where her father was a preacher. After the age of seven, she was raised by an older sister and her husband. Caswell was born and raised in Boston, the daughter of a wealthy family with connections at the highest levels of the American Board hierarchy. Wright married in her early twenties and was a widow for eleven years. Caswell first married in her midthirties, was widowed fifteen years later, and married the Reverend Payson Broad, six years her junior, in 1900 (Clark 1911, 113). Neither woman had any biological children.

This release from the more demanding aspects of the domestic sphere, although perhaps not what either had envisioned for herself, may have freed them for more wide-ranging activities. However, Laura and Asher Wright did adopt an Indian boy, who died before the age of three, and they adopted and raised two of Laura's nieces. Surprisingly, Laura's correspondence rarely mentions these children, and letters from other missionaries speak of her having no domestic duties.

Martha Hoyt, one of the adopted nieces, married Seneca interpreter Nicholson Parker and is mentioned frequently as an adult. When he learned that Hoyt was pregnant by Parker, Asher wrote an anguished letter to the American Board because the couple refused to reveal the date of their marriage (which did, in fact, occur more than nine months before the birth). It is clear that Asher's concern was about the impropriety of premarital sex and had nothing to do with the fact that Parker was an Indian. As Michael Coleman points out (1980, 42, 49), racism was not part of the agenda of Presbyterian missionaries, who, despite being "supremely ethnocentric," assumed that Indians were capable of receiving the gospel and becoming Christian citizens. The Wrights were somewhat unusual in that they had fewer ethnocentric attitudes than many other missionaries, and both evidenced a deep interest in Seneca history and culture. Laura was an active participant in Asher's translation work and was responsible for "the first significant Seneca language publication by the Wrights" (Ericson 2005, 36), a Seneca primer whose title translates as "Beginning Book." It was designed to be useful for both Senecas learning English and English-speakers learning Seneca. Although moral tales were interspersed throughout, the Wrights made a concerted effort not to offend non-Christian Indians.

It is obvious that Laura was an equal partner in Asher's missionary effort even though she is usually referred to simply as the wife of the missionary.[5] As Laura moved out of the shadow of her husband following his death in 1875 (Bilharz 2006), she began to demonstrate the assertiveness that was more typical of Harriet Caswell in earlier years. Seeking money for the Orphan Asylum, she asked William Pryor Letchworth, head of the State Board of Charities, to contact William H. Vanderbilt for a contribution, and when Letchworth did not act quickly enough for her she wrote Vanderbilt herself. She showed no hesitation in criticizing both elected and appointed officials in her private correspondence, and she spent a great deal of effort lobbying for the appointment of individuals whom she found suitable (especially those involved in education) and on pending legislation.

Caswell's book leaves several important questions unanswered. The extent to which she understood and spoke Seneca is unclear. Both Wrights were fluent speakers, and it is likely that Caswell developed some facility in the language as she speaks of teaching the Senecas to speak English and learning to speak "Indian" herself. Her book contains long transcriptions of Seneca legends and history as well as conversations; it would be interesting to know if she heard these firsthand and, if so, in which language or whether she was dependent on a translator.

More frustrating is the matter of Laura's letters, which Caswell quotes extensively. The location of the originals is unknown; perhaps they are among the papers of the recipients, whom Caswell does not identify, or possibly they were written to Harriet herself. In addition, she provides excerpts from three essays said to have been among Laura's papers, but where were the papers? How did Caswell gain access to them, and where are they now?

Some of the quoted letters are from Laura to her husband; unless Laura kept copies of those letters, it is hard to determine how Caswell gained access to them. Asher might have shared them with her (which seems unlikely) or they might have been saved in his papers, which would have gone to Laura after his death, at which time she may have shared them with Caswell. It's possible that Laura's papers may have gone to Caswell after her death in 1886, and Caswell herself may have kept extensive diaries, but this is all speculation.

Our Life among the Iroquois Indians was first published in 1892 by a congregationalist press in Boston, where Caswell was living at the time with her brother (who would later write her biography [Clark 1911]). She had not lived among the Senecas for over two decades. This has led Jack Ericson to speculate that the manuscript may have been initially developed years before, using sources made available by Laura, and only prepared for publication in the years between Caswell's marriages. It would be useful to know the details since a manuscript written decades after the experience would reflect later interpretations and agendas and lose some of its firsthand quality. How accurate are the reconstructed conversations, for instance?

Nevertheless, the reissue of this book makes it available once again to a broad audience, who will perceive it very differently from its original readers. I am grateful to the late Laura Pierce Wheeler for planting the idea in Jack Ericson's mind and to Jack for bringing it to fruition.

NOTES

1. Asher Wright sent annual reports to the secretary of war that were necessitated by the receipt of federal funds by the American Board for some of Wright's work among the Senecas. He was also the author of articles documenting the fraud behind the 1838 treaty that were published by the Quakers. While these give information about the "state of civilization" among the Senecas in terms of literacy and so forth, they reveal little about daily life or Wright's own feelings, although some of this can be found in his letters to the American Board.

2. Laura Wright to William Letchworth, July 5, 1876,

Letterbook Thomas Indian School, William Pryor Letchworth Papers, Letchworth State Park, Castile NY.

3. Laura Wright to William Letchworth, November 30, 1877, Letterbook Thomas Indian School, William Pryor Letchworth Papers, Letchworth State Park, Castile NY.

4. Asher Wright to David Greene, November 15, 1832, 18.6.3., no. 38, reel 788, American Board of Commissioners for Foreign Missions, Houghton Library, Harvard College.

5. William Fenton recognized the importance of Asher's "saintly wife Laura" (1956, 568) in her husband's achievements, describing Asher as possessing "intellectual curiosity vigor and moral purpose, *and he had a fine wife*" (1956, 575; emphasis added).

REFERENCES

Abler, T. S. 1969. Factional dispute and party conflict in the political system of the Seneca Nation (1845–1895): An ethnohistorical analysis. PhD diss., University of Toronto.

Bilharz, Joy A. 1995. First among equals? The changing status of Seneca women. In *Women and power in Native North America*, eds. Laura Klein and Lillian Ackerman, 101–12. Norman: University of Oklahoma Press.

———. 2006. After Asher: The emergence of Laura Wright. Paper presented at the annual conference on Iroquois research, Rensselaerville NY.

Bonvillain, Nancy. 2007. *Women and men cultural con-*

structs of gender. 4th ed. Saddle River NJ: Pearson Prentice-Hall.

Caswell, Harriet S. 1892. *Our life among the Iroquois Indians*. Boston: Congregational Sunday-School and Publishing Society.

Clark, Joseph Bourne. 1911. *"Blue Sky" The life of Harriet Caswell-Broad*. Boston: Pilgrim Press.

Coleman, Michael C. 1980. Not race, but grace: Presbyterian missionaries and American Indians, 1837–1893. *The Journal of American History* 67 (1): 41–60

Ericson, Jack T. 2005. The Seneca mission press. *Western New York Heritage* 8 (Fall): 34–39.

Fenton, William N. 1956. Toward the gradual civilization of the Indian natives: The missionary and linguistic work of Asher Wright (1803–1875) among the Senecas of western New York. *Proceedings of the American Philosophical Society* 100 (6): 567–81.

Fenton, William N., ed. 1968. *Parker on the Iroquois*. Syracuse NY: Syracuse University Press.

Lord, Lucy T. and Edward Clemens Lord. 1854. *Memoir of Mrs. Lucy T. Lord of the Chinese Baptist Mission*. Philadelphia: American Baptist Publication Society. Quoted in Wetter 1978.

Phillips, Clifton Jackson. 1969. *Protestant America and the pagan world. The first half century of the American Board of Commissioners for Foreign Missions, 1810–1860*. Cambridge MA: East Asian Research Center, Harvard University.

Wallace, Anthony F. C. 1969. *The death and rebirth of*

the Seneca. New York: Vintage.

Wetter, Barbara. 1978. She hath done what she could: Protestant women's missionary careers in nineteenth-century America. *American Quarterly* 30 (5): 624–38.

Dedicated

to

The Iroquois

and

His Friends

PREFACE.

A FEW hours' ride from the nearest railroad station in a wagon not the easiest, over a road not the smoothest, meeting with narrow escapes as to mud holes and deep ruts, and you will find yourself upon the Cattaraugus Indian Reservation. You might as well be west of the Rocky Mountains for any indications of the pale face that you see here. Indians in the homes, on the roads, working on the farms, and building houses; Indian children with ball clubs, snow snakes, and arrows; Indian babies upon the backs of their mothers; Indian corn bread boiling in the kettles under the trees; Indians here, there, and everywhere. The straight black hair and shining black eyes that mark the race everywhere meet you here. You hear the curious intonations of the strange language all about you, and yet you are only thirty miles south of Buffalo and five hundred miles from New York City. As you ride through the Reservation you note many farms of which Indian owners may well be proud and others of which they should be ashamed. You will see corn, wheat, potatoes, tomatoes, and other products of the farm in better condition than those of the neighboring white man; and you will see the crops of others sadly choked with weeds and perishing for want of care. The owners of these last expect to live next winter upon the corn and beans and potatoes of their more industrious neighbors. Would that for white man and for Indian the ancient law might be enforced, "If a man will not work, neither shall he eat."

A few years ago the old Mission church was rapidly falling into decay. Now you hear the progressive sound of the hammer and saw. This church building, which the Indians are repairing with

their own hands, was erected thirty-five years ago through the
efforts of Father Gleason. Have this people been taught the trade
of the carpenter, the mason, the paper hanger? No. And yet
they can design and build a house, plaster and paint it, and when
out of repair make it over as good as new. This Mission church
is the prettiest church in this part of the country. The walls have
been delicately tinted and ornamented, the pulpit and seats remodeled, and this, with the painting and other repairs, has all been
done by Indians. The only exception is the " graining," which
was the work of a white man, who, having once plied his trade
in plain sight of those sharp eyes, will never more be needed in
Indian land.

Why are Indians of all tribes natural mechanics? How is it
that they use all trades without instruction in any? What a
blessed movement in Indian affairs is this experiment in industrial education now carried on at Hampton, Carlisle, Santee, and
at Lawrence, Kansas!

You decide to spend the Sabbath. It proves to be the rededica-
tion of the newly repaired church. It is a highly satisfied looking
congregation that fills the freshly painted seats. The remodeled
pulpit is occupied by the missionary and his Indian interpreter.
Upon the same platform a fine choir of young men give us
musical selections accompanied by the cornet played by one of the
Indian brass band. The cabinet organ is admirably managed by
an Indian maiden. The music is soul-inspiring. The sermon upon
the text, " The glory of the Lord filled the temple," describes the
experience of the Israelites under similar circumstances. The
preacher believes that the time has come when this Indian church,
having fulfilled the conditions, may expect the glorious experience
of the builders of old. The sermon is well adapted to their needs
and very practical, especially when the hearers are exhorted not
to defile the house of God by the use of tobacco within its sacred
walls. The people bear this sharp thrust at their favorite weed
with their usual dignified composure.

Having lifted the curtain a moment to take a glance at the present condition of these Indians, let us turn back to the beginning of a life which for more than half a century is to be closely interwoven with every dark thread and every bright thread of their history.

INTRODUCTION.

BISHOP WHIPPLE says: "The Indian is not an idolater. His universe is peopled with spirits. He recognizes the Great Spirit; he believes in a future life. I have never known one instance where the Indian was the first to violate plighted faith. Thirty years ago our Indian system was at its worst; it was a blunder and a crime. It established heathen almshouses to graduate savage paupers. In my boyhood a sainted mother taught me to defend the weak. I believed that these wandering red men were children of one God and Father and that he loved them as he loved us. I vowed that, God being my helper, I would never turn my back on the heathen at my door. I have tried to keep this vow."

However stolid and impassive an Indian may look, do not assume that he is stupid. While Bishop Whipple was visiting an Indian mission, the people were holding a scalp dance quite near. The bishop was indignant. He went to the head chief and said: —

"Wabasha, you ask me for a missionary; I give him to you. I visit you, and the first sight is this brutal scalp dance. I knew the man whom you have murdered. He had a wife and children; his wife is crying for her husband, his children are asking for their father. Wabasha, the Great Spirit hears his children cry. He is angry. Some day he will ask, 'Wabasha, where is your red brother?'"

The old chief smiled, drew his pipe from his mouth, blew a cloud of smoke upward, and said: —

"White man go to war with his own brother in the same country; he kill more men than Wabasha can count in all his life.

Great Spirit smiles and says, 'He good white man; he has my Book; I love him very much; I have good place for him by-and-by.' The Indian is a wild man; he has no Spirit-Book. He kill one man; he have a scalp dance; Great Spirit is mad, and says, 'Bad Indian! I will put him in a bad place by-and-by.' Wabasha don't believe it."

No, the Indian is not stupid. He is keenly observant, and quick to note absurdity in an argument or inconsistency in a life. He has his opinions upon the problems of the day, and when you get at his thought you are startled at its relevancy. This statement will, I think, be verified in these glimpses of our everyday life among the Senecas, and that which the Senecas have told me about the Iroquois in general.

I have been urged to publish these reminiscences as a tribute to the rare ability and devotion of two missionaries, and also to throw a side light upon the history and character of a fast-vanishing race.

The Iroquois, long before the white man knew this country, had established his headquarters in New York State. He called it the "Long House," and Lake Erie, the "front door," was guarded by the Senecas. The Iroquois represented a powerful confederacy of six nations: the Senecas, Tuscaroras, Cayugas, Onondagas, Oneidas, and Mohawks. This last nation guarded the "rear door" of the "Long House," the Hudson River. The history of this curious confederacy told by an Indian as received from his ancestors will be read with peculiar interest.

If this simple story of everyday life among the once formidable Iroquois open the eyes of any reader to brighter and hitherto unappreciated phases of Indian character; if it incite a throb of interest in this unfortunate race; if the record of these heroic lives, willingly given for their redemption, shall inspire one young Christian to carry to the Indian the tidings of his divine inheritance, — these pages will have accomplished their purpose.

CONTENTS.

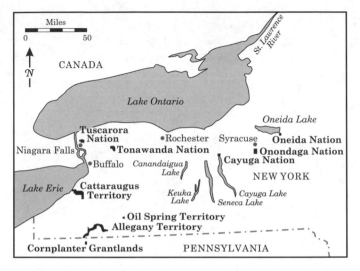

Iroquois territories in New York state, 2007. (Seneca Nation of Indians Geographic Information Services, Division of Planning.)

IF I live, this accursed system of robbery and shame in our treatment of the Indians shall be reformed.

— ABRAHAM LINCOLN.

TREAT him not as an American Indian, but as an Indian American. When the significance of this designation is practically accepted there will be a very radical revolution in Indian American affairs. — COMMISSIONER MORGAN.

EVERY human being born upon our continent, or who comes here from any quarter of the world, whether savage or civilized, can go to our courts for protection — except those who belong to the tribes who once owned this country. The cannibal from the islands of the Pacific, the worst criminal from Europe, Asia, or Africa can appeal to the law and courts for his rights of person and property — all, save our native Indians, who above all should be protected from wrong. — GOVERNOR HORATIO SEYMOUR.

Mrs. Laura M. Wright.

OUR LIFE AMONG THE IROQUOIS.

I.

THE CHILD.

IN the fine old town of St. Johnsbury, Vermont, on the morning of July 10, 1809, an event of considerable interest occurred in a certain family of wide-awake boys and girls — the grandchildren, in fact, of that well-known Vermont pioneer, Willard Stevens. For on this morning they welcomed into their circle the latest " new baby," Laura Maria Sheldon.

As the months went by this Green Mountain baby grew and thrived. She became the constant companion of her next older brother, Charles, until the arrival of baby Henry, when she divided between the two the wealth of love in her little warm heart. The strong tie of affection which united these three lives in childhood remained unbroken through seventy years of peculiar and varied experience.

When Laura was two years old the family moved to Windsor, and five years later to Barnet. It was from Laura's grandfather, the historic Willard Stevens, that the early Scotch settlers bought the land which was afterward incorporated into this lovely, picturesque town. Here resided an older sister, who, faithful to the Stevens line, had married a second cousin, bearing the name of the pioneer Willard. At the request of this sister, Mrs. Willard Stevens, Laura, at seven years of age, became an inmate of her family, and received from her the watchful care and thorough training of the old-time Puritan mother.

Soon after Laura had reached her eighth birthday, the bridge crossing the river which ran through the village was carried away by a flood. At the head of a waterfall eighty feet high a plank was thrown across the stream for the use of men who were obliged to go to their work on the other side. Here a party of Indians encamped one day upon the opposite bank, and our little Laura, filled with desire to know something about these curious people, and to see how they lived, and to become acquainted with their strange ways, gave her family a terrible fright by crossing the plank, and investigating for herself a new phase of life. Thus began with this child an absorbing interest in the Indians, which never abated.

Laura's most intimate friend at this time was Harriet Sprague Wright, now Mrs. Moore, of Barnet, Vermont, to whom we are indebted for the Indian incident, and who also furnishes the following : —

"When I was about eight years old, and Laura ten, she proposed that we girls have a prayer meeting. She and Betsey Gill and I met in a 'playhouse,' as we called it, and Laura took charge of the meeting. She opened the exercises by prayer, and called on us to follow. Betsey, who was six years old, offered a prayer, but I, like a foolish child, only laughed, for which Laura, with flashing eyes, reproved me."

One other glimpse of this child, at the age of eleven years. She sits in the "family room," by the capacious fireplace, and spends the long winter evenings in the intricate task of manufacturing the old-time "sampler." "Her eyes," says her brother Henry, "were black; so was her hair. The neighbors called her 'handsome.' She was a good student, although by nature a little stubborn, causing her teacher some trouble at times, but not for long."

Let us look over the shoulder of this dark-eyed, industrious maiden and see what the small fingers have wrought. The piece of canvas about the size of a pocket handkerchief reveals at first sight a variety of colored silks finely woven into the material. She is now deftly stitching in small stars and crosses

by way of final adornment. A closer inspection
reveals the following family record : —

SAMPLER,

WORKED BY LAURA M. SHELDON. AGED ELEVEN.

Solomon Sheldon, Born Feb. 25, 1763.
Dorothy Stevens, Born May 25, 1774.
Solomon Sheldon & Dorothy Stevens were married Feb. 3, 1792.

CHILDREN.

Royal was born, Nov. 17, 1792. Mary Oct.
1, 1794. Samuel, Nov. 7, 1796. Anna
Sept. 16, 1798. Sophia and Willard
Apr. 5, 1801. Olive, Apr. 5, 1803. Solomon
Aug. 11, 1805. Charles, Aug. 10, 1807. Laura
July 10, 1809. Lewis, Jan. 4, 1812. Henry,
Sept. 9, 1813.

The patience of the child artist must have been
sorely taxed before the last stitch was wrought into
this record of her family of fourteen !

About this time Mr. and Mrs. Willard Stevens
moved to Newbury, taking the little sister with them.
The clergymen of that vicinity, Rev. Clark Perry, of

Newbury, Rev. Silas McKeen, of Bradford, and Rev. David Sutherland, of Bath, were holding " four-days meetings " which exerted a marked influence on all that part of the state. For the first time Laura Sheldon became vitally interested in the subject of religion. Mr. McKeen and Mr. Perry felt a genuine interest in the quaint, conscientious child, and were counted among her most helpful friends.

Again the restless spirit of the early settlers impelled this family to another " move," and this time it was a return to the old home at Barnet.

II.

L AURA SHELDON," writes her early friend, Mrs. Moore, " was a pure-minded girl, naturally religious and fond of books. Her life, even as a child, was a busy one. She had little time for amusements common to most young girls. Her aim in life was to be useful, and the one thing for which she longed more than another was an opportunity to fit herself for usefulness."

In her seventeenth year this ambition was in a measure gratified. Mrs. Willard Stevens resolved to give her young charge some special educational advantages by sending her to the " Young Ladies' School," at St. Johnsbury, Vermont, taught by Miss Huldah Strobridge, " a gentlewoman," we are told, " who succeeded in making a lasting impression upon her pupils. She was a cultivated lady of marked ability." Three scraps of paper, yellow with age, have been preserved, from which more than threescore years have failed to obliterate the penciled lines carefully written in a cramped hand. Every *i* is dotted and every *t* properly crossed exactly at right angles. These papers

9

serve to illustrate the mental condition of our young friend at this time.

AT BOARDING SCHOOL, April 25, 1826.

I am attending school this season at St. Johnsbury. My studies, which are History, Philosophy, and Grammar, are very interesting —History in particular. It is the most pleasing study I ever attended to, and it is not only pleasant but useful. It opens to the mind great sources of knowledge, and describing to us what the past has been, enables us to form right conjectures of the future.

The school is very small, numbering only twelve, but not less pleasant on that account. I am projecting a map. I find it to be very difficult, but I hope that by perseverance and industry I shall be able to finish it. If we could realize the privileges we enjoy we should certainly improve them to better advantage. But it is seldom the case that we know how to prize our privileges until we are deprived of them.

April 26, 1826.

I attended school to-day and reviewed my lessons through the week past in History, Philosophy, and Defining. Read in the Testament and attended prayers in the morning; worked on my map some, and made the objects. I gave a description of Babylon in the following words: "If historians deserve credit, ancient Babylon was the noblest city ever built. It stood on a fertile and beautiful plain, watered by the river Euphrates, which passed through the midst of the city. Its walls, which were carried to the astonishing height of three hundred and sixty feet, were eighty-seven feet in thickness, enclosing an exact square whose sides were fifteen miles each. So the city was sixty miles in circuit. There were fifty streets, twenty-five running each way, on right lines parallel to each other. They were two hundred feet wide. While crossing each other at right angles they all terminated in a grand street which lay round next the wall on every side of the city. Thus the city was laid out in six hundred and seventy-six squares. These squares were lined with numerous edifices besides houses. The houses were generally three or four stories high, and within there were delightful plantations, pleasure grounds, and gardens."

It is Saturday in the afternoon. I intend working on my map and writing to sister Mary [Mrs. Willard Stevens].

ON FEMALE EDUCATION.   1826.

What can be of more importance in the present age than female education? Surely nothing. During the dark ages it was shamefully neglected, and is still in many parts of the world; but not so in America. Here, females are raised to that rank in society which as rational beings they ought to hold. Seminaries are established in all parts of our country for their improvement, in which they are taught every branch of education necessary to promote their usefulness in the world. By some these advantages are duly appreciated, by others they are not.

Since, then, the present generation of females have so many advantages, it is certainly their duty to use their endeavors in raising the degraded females of Asia to the same degree of civilization and respectability which they hold themselves. This can be done by retrenching many superfluities and sending the value of them to the missionaries who are now laboring to civilize the heathen. We have heard from good authority that they are capable of the intellectual as well as ourselves. A few shillings might purchase a little Indian girl what there would be styled a good education.

RELIGION.   1826.

Religion, what treasures untold
Reside in that heavenly word
More precious than silver or gold
Or all that this earth can afford.

The religion of Jesus Christ is not a system of speculative opinions. But it *is* a series of facts, promises, doctrines, and precepts, the belief and practice of which is eminently fitted to purify the heart, ennoble the motives, and restore fallen man to primitive dignity and beauty, and a free exercise of opinions in relation to these subjects. It is one of the greatest blessings ever bestowed upon a free and enlightened people. It is the declaration of an ancient moral philosophy that " man is a bundle of habits," and daily experience or even a slight acquaintance with human nature will convince any one of the truth of this observation.

Youth is the season for the promotion of habits, and since any vice deeply implanted at that period of life is seldom eradicated, it seems in a peculiar manner the time when the seeds of virtue and piety should be sown before the tyranny of custom gets the ascendency over our reason, or the mind becomes vitiated by indulgence.

It is said that "wisdom's ways are pleasant and all her paths are peace." And so they are to those who have spent the morning of their days and the freshness of their strength and spirits in overcoming the difficulties and asperities of the way, which serve rather to moderate than to extinguish their ambition.

A young person who boldly comes out upon the side of religion and *dares* to be decidedly pious, not fearing the scorn and contempt of fools, must be an object worthy of the admiration and imitation of others. Such a character must be viewed by all good people with approbation and delight.

> Onward, onward let us pass
> Through the path of duty;
> Virtue is true happiness,
> Excellence true beauty.

After one year of "schooling" Laura Sheldon returns to her sister-mother at Barnet, and begins to use her superior advantages for the benefit of others. She organizes a series of classes among the younger children which she calls "infant schools." Her friends in Barnet, and also in Newbury, twenty miles south, are deeply interested in these schools and furnish her with the means to carry them on in both places during the next six years of her life. She also teaches classes of older pupils, but her delight is in the children.

A small homemade record is still in existence which gives some idea of her methods. It gives the names of an "infant school" and a list of written questions and answers evidently prepared by the young teacher for her youngest pupils. After twenty-five questions and answers, beginning with "What is history? It is a story," and followed by minute inquiries concerning the size and form of the earth, its picture, the map, the cardinal points, and the dimensions of the earth's surface, the children are gradually and thoroughly brought down to America, and finally to the United States. Then come the following questions : —

What were the United States formerly? British provinces.
When were they declared independent? July 4, 1776.
How many States were united in the Declaration of Independence? Thirteen.
Was Vermont one of these? It was not.
When was Vermont admitted into the Union? March 4, 1791.

After several leading questions concerning states, counties, towns, latitude, longitude, boundary lines, etc., the children go on with another list of local questions : —

In which of the United States do you live? Vermont.
How many counties in Vermont? Thirteen.
In which do you live? Caledonia.
How many towns does it contain? Seventeen.
In what town do you live? Barnet.
What is meant by situation? The place where anything is, and the circumstances of it.
How is Barnet situated? On the Connecticut River, in the southwest part of Caledonia County.
How is Barnet bounded? How far is it east of Montpelier? Thirty-five miles.
What is the surface of Barnet? It is a land of hills and valleys.
What is the soil? Rich and fertile.
What is the growth of timber? Heavy.
Name the principal forest trees. White pine, hemlock, beech, birch, spruce, ash, and maple.
Which is the largest river in Barnet? The Passumpsic.

Where is its source? In a pond on the easterly line of West-more.

Through what towns does it pass? Newark, East Haven, Burke, Lyndon, St. Johnsbury, Waterford, and Barnet.

Where is its mouth? It falls into the Connecticut River about a mile below the foot of the 15 M. f.

Here follows a list of questions about the branches, brooks, and falls of the Passumpsic, dwelling particularly on the Stevens River, its ferry, its falls, etc., and also upon all the ponds of the place, after which we find ourselves getting at a bit of history of thrilling interest: —

Who conducted an expedition against St. François? Major Rogers.

When? On October 17, '59.

Where did he encamp on his return? In Barnet.

What did he expect to meet here? A supply of provisions.

From where? Charlestown, New Hampshire.

To be ordered by whom? General Amherst.

Was the order complied with? It was.

Who proceeded up the river with the provisions? Samuel Stevens and three others.

How did they carry them? In three canoes.

What is an island? Are there any islands in the Connecticut, opposite Barnet? Several very fertile islands.

How many islands in a cluster near the mouth of the Passumpsic? Twenty-one.

Which is the largest? The Round Island, which contains about ninety acres.

On which did Mr. Stevens and others land with the provisions? On Round Island, where they encamped for the night.

Who was near at hand? Major Rogers and one hundred and fifty men.

What did Stevens' company hear in the morning? Guns!!

What did they do? They reloaded their provisions and hastened back to Charlestown.

At what time did Rogers and his men arrive at the mouth of the Passumpsic? About noon.

What did they discover on the island? Fire!

The questions and answers then tell the story of the rafts which Rogers' company made, and upon which they passed over to the island, but only to find out to their surprise and mortification that no provisions had been left for them. The men, already reduced to a state of starvation, were so disheartened by this discovery that thirty-six of them died before morning. In order to save the survivors, an Indian was cut in pieces and divided among them. Two days from this time Rogers gave up the command and told his men to take care of themselves. Some of them were lost in the woods, but Rogers and most of his men were preserved and arrived safely at Charlestown.

The question and answer, '' When was Barnet chartered? September 16, 1763," is followed by a series of questions concerning the principal proprietors, the early settlers, the first town clerk, the first representative, first male child (who, by the way, was presented with one hundred acres of land by Enos Stevens, Esq.); also about the Scotch settlers, the religious sects and pastors of the various churches; the temperance societies and their officers and committees ; the number of villages and the number of houses and families in each ; the number of horses, cows, sheep, and oxen in town ; the number of clocks, watches, schoolhouses, dwelling houses, mills, and stores, and at how much they were appraised.

This singular list of questions closes with the following, which was certainly fifty years ahead of the times : —

What reasons can you give for not drinking ardent spirits?

1. Because they poison the blood and destroy the organs of digestion.
2. Because an enemy should be kept without the gate.
3. Because I am in health and need no medicine.
4. Because I have my senses and wish to keep them.
5. Because I have a soul to be saved or lost.

During the years 1830–32, our young and successful teacher made her home in the family of Rev. Clark Perry, of Newbury. Mr. Perry was fond of talking of his valued friend and classmate at Dartmouth College, Rev. Asher Wright, who had graduated at Andover with every prospect of a brilliant career before him, and had within three weeks of graduation buried himself in the wilderness of western New York and Pennsylvania, that he might preach the gospel to the Indians. The young girl, who had since her daring adventure with the Indians been an enthusiast in the cause, followed with keen interest the fortunes of this good man as far as they could be known through his correspondence with Mr. Perry. There was joy in the little parsonage when word came that their missionary friend had found a companion who was willing to share his life and work. The bride, Miss Martha Edgerton, — one of the original members of the Congregational Church at Randolph, Vermont, — was a frail girl of rare spirituality and beauty. After one year of hardship and exposure among the Indians, she entered into rest rejoicing that she had been counted worthy to give up her young life for Christ. The widowed missionary wrote the sad story of his bereavement to his friend Mr. Perry, and received from the Newbury parsonage many letters of hearty sympathy.

And now we reach a point in the history of our maiden where a decision must be made which was to affect her whole future. She came home from school one day to find a letter awaiting her, and a most .important letter it was — nothing less than a message from the lonely missionary among the Seneca Indians, Rev. Asher Wright, whom she had never seen, but in whose life and works she had felt so deep an interest. The blushing maiden was informed without any waste of words that his friend, Mr. Perry, had recommended her to him as the one of all others who possessed that Christlike spirit and amiable disposition which promised him in her a suitable wife and missionary co-worker. He placed the matter before her in a practical way and asked permission to correspond with her, with this result in view. Fortunately her answer has been preserved : —

NEWBURY, December 18, 1832.

Mr. Wright, — It is undoubtedly with an equal degree of embarrassment that I attempt to reply to your letter of November 27; but believing it to be my duty, I repress for once these feelings of delicacy, and, looking to Him alone for aid from whom is the preparation of the heart and the answer of the tongue, I shall endeavor to return such an answer as our peculiar circumstances seem to require.

I was much pleased with the freedom and plainness with which you have chosen to write, and suppose no apology necessary for adopting the same style myself. I think the circumstances of the case ought to exempt us both from the imputation of rashness in commencing such a correspondence without any personal acquaintance. I am sure a Christian should at all times be willing to perform whatever seems to be duty, even though it be at the expense of private feelings.

To proceed then at once to the subject. As regards the missionary enterprise I must say I have always taken a lively interest in all its concerns. I have thought of devoting myself to that object ever since I was a child, but as no opportunity has yet offered and no special providence has yet pointed plainly the path of duty, I have often almost concluded that God had nothing for me to do in heathen lands and that my sphere of usefulness was evidently elsewhere. I humbly hope I have long sincerely loved the cause of Christ, and that I have devoted my all to his service. I trust that I love the souls of the heathen, and am willing to leave the friends of my youth and encounter the toils and hardships of missionary life, if by so doing I can be useful to them.

In the present case there is apparently an opportunity for an intelligent, pious female possessing a heart devoted to the work to accomplish much good; but whether I am that female remains to be decided. I believe, however, that if I commit my cause to God and sincerely desire divine direction, he will order it all in infinite wisdom.

As to my own happiness, I know it is nothing. I certainly

ought neither to expect nor wish for more than my Saviour sees best for me to have. Nor ought I to enjoy any but that which arises from loving and serving him. It should be, if it is not, enough for me that he reigns and will take care to secure his own glory in what manner he sees fit. Indeed, if we did but reflect that our life is but a day, and that earthly joys will soon be at an end, we should not allow ourselves to suffer much from anxiety about our happiness at a future period which we may not live to see. Why should we then distrust the power and goodness of our divine Master? But let us rather pray to be prepared for adversity and trust to him to support us through the trying hour.

In regard to deciding the question which you propose, I can only say I can have no objections to commencing a correspondence with the proposed end in view, and should no objections arise on either side. . . . But still I am quite sure I can never fully supply the place of your amiable Martha. I have heard much of her ardent piety and devotion to the cause of Missions and trust I may be enabled to imitate her example whatever may be the result of the present deliberations.

I am at present boarding in Mr. Perry's family, teaching school. I think it best to avoid our correspondence being known, as much as possible, by all means, and in order to do so I propose that you direct my letters to Mr. Perry for the present. I have complied with your request in writing soon, because I supposed it desirable for you to know the result of my decision as soon as possible. If I have omitted anything which would be of importance for you to know, I beg that you will make inquiries freely, and I assure you they shall be answered with frankness. In the meantime, praying that the Master whom you serve may be your portion while you live and your reward in death, allow me to subscribe myself your friend,　　　　　　　　　　　　　　Laura M. Sheldon.

P. S. I acknowledge I have read this letter again and again. At one time I think I have written too much; at another, not enough. I think, however, it can scarcely be made better or worse, and one thing more I will mention. Provided the Board should consent to your proposal, as it would be extremely inconvenient for you to visit New England this winter, or for me to go to New York, on account of my having engaged a school three months, I will take the liberty to suggest whether it would not be expedient to defer it a few months at least. I could certainly acquire a very good knowledge of the language from you, in a short time, if you are a communicative teacher. I should not have made the above suggestion, were it not that I probably shall not have many opportunities of writing *freely,* and supposed it of consequence that we fully understand each other's circumstances.

After one year of correspondence, Mr. Wright was able to leave his Indian charge for a few weeks, and undertake the long and difficult journey from Buffalo, New York, to Barnet, Vermont. Through his friend Mr. Perry, he was presented without delay to Miss Laura Sheldon. We have no account of this interview, but the result was evidently satisfactory, for they went home to sister Mary, in Barnet, and on January 21, 1833, they were united in marriage by their mutual friend, Mr. Perry, who undoubtedly beamed upon them with the satisfaction of a successful matchmaker. After the ceremony the happy couple were put in possession of the following

CERTIFICATE OF MARRIAGE.

THIS IS TO CERTIFY that at Barnet, Caledonia County, Vermont, on Monday, the 21 day of Jan., in the year of our Lord, 1833, Rev. Asher Wright, of the Seneca Reservation, near Buffalo, Erie Co., New York, and Miss Laura Maria Sheldon, of Barnet aforesaid were duly joined in marriage by me —

CLARK PERRY,
Minister of the Gospel, Newbury, Vermont, 21 Jan., 1833.

III.

ON the following morning, January 22, 1833, tearful farewells were spoken to the friends in Barnet and to those who had come from St. Johnsbury and Newbury, and the bride went out from her home with him for whom she was forsaking father, mother, brothers, sisters, and friends, that through him she might obey the higher call to special service for her heavenly Master.

And now they were fairly started on a long midwinter journey to Buffalo, New York. Fifteen days and nights of travel without rest, in the old-time stagecoach, with so delightful a teacher at hand, was a golden opportunity, and, ignoring cold and fatigue, the young wife commenced to study the Indian language, making rapid progress in the use of both words and sentences.

On the evening of February 5, the bridal pair arrived at the door of the old Mission House. It was not an attractive building even in the more picturesque days of summer, but in the dead of winter every deformity was plainly defined. The lower part was

21

of rough-hewn logs, upon which a "frame addition" of two stories had been placed. Mr. Wright had formerly occupied a cabin which he built on the bank of Buffalo Creek, near what is now known as "the old burying ground," in Buffalo; but he and his wife were henceforth to form a part of the missionary family already established in this curious old building, consisting of Rev. Hanover Bradley and wife and a few Indian students.

The morning after their arrival many of the Indians gathered to welcome the missionary bride, and were astonished and delighted to be addressed in their own tongue in the words and phrases learned during her journey. "This gift of tongues," says one, "combined with the rare loveliness of the bride, won at once the warm affection of the Indians. Tall and straight as the traditional red lord of the soil, she was gentle and sympathetic to a remarkable degree, and was for many years the life of the settlement."

The young wife inwardly protested against the stringent rules of the mission during those first months, but whatever her thought, she was never heard to complain, but adapted herself to every privation, then and always, with cheerful Christian submission. The furniture of the house was severe in the extreme. Hard wooden chairs, with not even a "rocker" to vary the monotony, and beds to match. According to the family rules, tea, coffee, pies, cake, sugar, and asparagus were not allowed in the house. The table was furnished with food of the plainest quality, bread, pork, and potatoes being the prevailing diet. They were allowed the luxury of custards without sugar! Those who craved a warm drink were permitted to make a tea from hemlock boughs!

Soon after the arrival of Mr. and Mrs. Wright the old building began to show signs of falling to the ground. A plain frame house was erected, into which the Mission family moved, and in a few weeks the old log house lay in ruins. The frame Mission House still stands in the city of Buffalo.

BARK LONGHOUSE

THERE still live many of the descendants of the powerful Iroquois — the Six Nations — the great Indian Confederacy which once controlled a large part of the eastern section of this immense country of ours. Their hunting grounds have turned into well-cultivated farms; their wigwams into comfortable houses; their spears and arrows into the smoking bowl of peace; but many of the people themselves who remain have lost none of the bravery, firmness, and intelligence which were characteristic of the early inhabitants of America. — *The Christian Union.*

Seneca Mission Church, Buffalo Creek Reservation. Built in 1829, it is the location of Rev. Asher Wright's first preaching among the Senecas. (*Buffalo Historical Society Publications*, vol. 16 [1912]: 478.)

Mission house, Buffalo Creek Reservation. This is the first home of the Wrights as it appeared in the late nineteenth century. It was built in 1833 on what became Buffum Street, South Buffalo. (*Western New York Heritage* 8, no. 3 [Fall 2005]: 38.)

IV.

THE YOUNG MISSIONARY.

MRS. WRIGHT began her work at once. She soon gathered a class of Indian girls for daily instruction and training in useful arts. She traveled over the rough roads and through the swamps and streams on horseback, with saddlebags securely fastened to her side. In these she carried food, medicine, etc. She not only visited the Indian homes; she looked after the distant, lonely teachers — Miss Asenath Bishop, Miss Rebecca Newhall, and Miss Phebe Selden, who were teaching, and keeping house in small log schoolhouses, miles away from the mission station.

Miss Bishop, who went to the Senecas in 1823, and labored with untiring zeal during eighteen years, was noted in the tribe for her wonderful patience under manifold persecutions. To illustrate: the larger boys of her school one day devised a scheme by which they hoped to gain a victory over this unendurable calm. Arriving at her little schoolhouse one bitter cold morning, she prepared with benumbed fingers to build a fire. Upon opening the door, she found the stove packed with snow. She stood a moment in bewildered surprise, and then, realizing the situation, calmly took the stove shovel and the water pail and without a word or change of expression began to shovel out the snow. Before she had half filled the pail she heard a rustle, then a scrambling from behind the benches, and half a dozen Indian boys leaped into the air, shouting, " Miss Bishop! He *can't* mad! Miss Bishop! He *can't* mad ! "

The shovel and pail were taken from her, the stove cleaned out, and a good fire made by those young rogues, who said years afterward, " We boys gloried in her spunk ! "

The following characterization illustrates " Indian English." Miss Bishop missed Mr. Little Johnny John from church, and asked Deacon Fish Hook what had become of him : —

" Miss Bishop," said the deacon, using with pride the English at his command, " Little Johnny John he not good! Much afraid just like this : devil — you know him — he got chain round Little Johnny John's neck. Well, sometimes devil hold chain loose ; then Little Johnny John think : ' I go see ; maybe Christian good ; maybe I like it ; I go to meeting.' Well, devil say : ' I watch ; I let him go little while ; I see ! ' Little Johnny John he come to meeting. He think, ' Pretty good ' ; so he come to meeting again. He

like it good deal. He say, ' I will be Christian.'
Devil let chain out little more, little more. Little
Johnny John pretty good Christian. By-and-by devil
think : ' I don't know ; maybe guess he go too far ;
maybe lose him ! ' So devil he pull it — chain !
Pull it — chain ! and Little Johnny John he go back
— he go back. Now Little Johnny John — guess he
no good. Devil hold chain pretty tight now ; guess
Little Johnny John he can't repent now ; guess devil
— he can't willing."

Deacon Fish Hook was a true prophet. Little
Johnny John returned to paganism.

In her visits from house to house, Mrs. Wright constantly used the Indian phrases she had acquired, and
daily added others, until in an incredibly short time
she spoke the language fluently, and was able to render valuable assistance to her husband, who was also
a natural linguist. During his life he acquired seven
different languages. He not only mastered the very
difficult Seneca tongue so that he could preach in it,
but set to work to establish a system of orthography
by the aid of which the Indian tongue could be reduced
to written characters. In this he was successful, and
with the help of his young wife put his system to
practical use by translating into it a hymn book, the
Four Gospels, and portions of the Old Testament.
They likewise procured the type, and printed these

books themselves. They compiled a spelling book for the school children, and partly completed a dictionary in the Seneca tongue. Mr. Wright imparted his knowledge of medicine to his wife, and they were both widely sought by the sick and suffering, not only among the Indians, but among the surrounding whites as well. They gave medical service, without compensation, to all who applied.

Within a few months after the arrival of these missionaries, the cholera broke out and wrought sad havoc among the Senecas; but through all the dreadful weeks that followed, Mr. and Mrs. Wright were constantly at the bedside of the sick and dying, ministering to their physical and spiritual wants without thought or fear for themselves.

The first church edifice among the Senecas was a plain frame building painted white. Two services were held there every Sabbath, and it was always customary for a large part of the audience to visit the Mission House at noon, and there be made happy with the " white man's bread." This hospitality helped the Indian to travel many miles, and to reach the church before noon at least. White people sometimes passed through the Reservation, and while receiving the hospitality of the Mission House became acquainted with the interesting young missionary, and soon it came to pass that every one, whether Indian or pale face, loved her and came to her for advice and consolation. In after years her influence became all-important in counteracting the evil effects of treachery and cupidity displayed too often by the whites toward the Indians. It has been said that to her personal influence, teaching, and example was largely due the fact that so many of these Indians embraced Christianity.

After fourteen months of uninterrupted companionship with her husband, and successful work by his side and under his direction, the young missionary is left alone a few days and avails herself of this opportunity to write her first letter as a wife.

My Room, April 9, 1834.

Dear Husband, — As much as I dreaded to have you leave me, I have almost wished sometimes that I could have an opportunity to write one letter to you, and after you went away to-day I thought I would sit down and write to you. You will see that I have been arranging your desk. I hope you will be pleased with it. There were so many things which have no kind of relation to each other that I could hardly find places for them all. I fear you may discover some confusion among your papers. I look the liberty of reading a few of Martha's letters. I have prayed much that I might be like her as far as she was like Christ. I feel sensible that I am not much like her. Last night I thought I felt some as Abraham did when a horror of great darkness fell upon him. I could see no light, and it seemed as though my prayers were an empty noise. I hope I feel more comfort to-day, though I scarcely restrain the tears a moment. I hope you pray for me, my husband, though I do not wish to trust at all in your prayers. I think I desire to trust in God alone.

Perhaps you will think me childish to write a letter to you when I expect to see you so soon; but I thought it would be so pleasant to write "dear husband" and then to subscribe myself "Your affectionate wife."

Twenty months of united missionary work and **Mr.**
Wright was called to the other Seneca Reservations to
assist the resident missionaries in a " protracted meeting." And so one cold morning in December, accompanied by his guide and interpreter, Indian Robert,
he started on that difficult and dangerous journey of
thirty miles through the almost unbroken woods to
the Cattaraugus Reservation, and from there forty
miles farther on to the Allegheny Reservation. Mrs.
Wright, with a heart burdened with anxious forebodings, bade him good-by and promised to keep a
daily record of her life and work to be sent to him by
the first trusty messenger traveling in the same direction. A few sheets of this record, giving us a glimpse
of her life at that time, have been preserved.

SENECA MISSION, December, 1835.

My dear Husband, — According to my promise I must commence a letter this evening, although much fatigued, having just
returned from a visit to Mary King, whom I found in a most dis-
tressing situation. She said she had not clothes enough to keep
her warm, and at times was very hungry indeed. Her bed consisted of one blanket, spread on a couple of boards. She did not
think she could live long, for she found it extremely difficult to get
into the house to-day when she went out. Peter went with us
as interpreter. Everything to-day has gone well, only I am lonesome to-night, and can't help thinking of the Cattaraugus woods
and hoping that you are not in them.

Sunday evening. Assisted to-day in moving Mary King. After
I left her last night she coughed up a great deal of thick, bloody
matter, which indicates an ulcer, does it not? She is very comfortably situated now at Mrs. Seneca's; and I hope to visit her

often and minister to the wants of both soul and body. As for myself, I hardly know what to tell you. I still find in myself the same proneness to forget the solemn things of eternity, although I am surrounded with so much to remind me of them.

Monday evening. I have tried to do my washing to-day, and have succeeded pretty well. I learn that there is trouble again between Greenblanket and his wife. How sad to have such a reproach thrown upon the cause of Christ! When will Christians learn to live in peace? What a question! As if Christians could live in a quarrel! Alas, that we should possess so little of the spirit of our Master!

Tuesday evening. Deacon Blue Eyes came this evening, and is to spend the night with us. We expect to kill hogs to-morrow. Thermometer eight degrees below zero to-day. I took cold yesterday, and have a dreadful face, I assure you. Can scarcely see out of my left eye. My jaw is somewhat painful and I have been obliged to keep still all day. Your letter was truly welcome, and the more so as it was entirely unexpected. You were in the woods at the very time I feared. I should not have slept that night had I known that. You must not do so again! No, no! You must be willing to stop where darkness overtakes you, and not risk your life and health by traveling in the night. I am glad you have bought a cow, and I shall do my best to make a great deal of butter, but you must not form too high expectations.

Monday evening. Well, my dear husband, you see I have skipped a few days. My face was so painful Friday and Saturday that I dared not write lest I should communicate some of my pain. Sunday forenoon a large swelling between my cheek and jaw broke, and I felt almost immediate relief and have continued to mend since.

Daniel Two Guns' youngest child is quite sick and they fear it will die.

I send you your compass, that you may have a guide through the woods. But oh, keep near to the great Guide of feeble, wandering sinners! There is safety only there, and peace only there. Tell Indian Robert he will need a true compass to guide him through the wilderness of this world, where are a thousand snares into which he may fall at any moment.

I should like to join you at the missionary meeting if I could consistently do so, but I do not wish to leave one duty undone for the sake of going.

This letter having been sent by a trusty messenger, the faithful correspondent continues her record : —

SENECA MISSION, December 30, 1835.

My dearest Husband, — This evening I received your precious letter and could scarcely keep from crying when I found you had not heard from me. You must have met my messenger before this time, however, and received at his hand the letter and other things which I sent to you.

Peter's wife sent for me yesterday. I found her in great distress; respiration exceedingly difficult. She turned upon me in a most beseeching manner and begged me to relieve her. I told her no mortal power could relieve her much, but her bodily pains would soon be over. I questioned her about her soul. She has remembered all this time what you said to her when you went away. I thought she seemed almost to despair of God's willingness to save her. I tried to convince her that though she had been a great sinner, Jesus was an all-sufficient Saviour. I think her mind was very dark. I urged her to repent of her sin and cast herself upon the mercy of her Saviour. She was too much distressed to think about these things, and died, a warning to all of the danger of " breaking covenant with God," as she herself said.

I am now writing in our own little room again. It is the pleasantest place in the house for me, although it seems so lonely since my other half has deserted it. But you know there is a secret joy sometimes in indulging loneliness when it reminds us so strongly of the cause of our past happiness and present sadness.

I hope, my dear, that you are making rapid progress in the Indian tongue. Do not faint or be discouraged. Go forward, keep looking at the crowd of precious souls going down to death, and at the example and command of our divine Master, and if I may say so, " have respect to the recompense of reward." These considerations are enough to incite us to zeal and faithfulness.

V.

AFTER Mr. and Mrs. Wright assumed the charge of the Mission House in 1834, many white people and Indians were sheltered under this hospitable roof. Having no children, their hearts and home were open to the wants of many a homeless little one in need of care. Concerning some of these children we have no record, and but slight knowledge of others; but that future allusions to them may be understood, its seems best, before proceeding further, to furnish at once whatever information has been obtained concerning this group of adopted ones.

Catherine King, an interesting girl of fifteen years, was taken into the mission family soon after Mrs. Wright's arrival, and became her special charge. She gave the young girl much needed instruction, and won her to the Christian religion. Catherine repaid her faithful care by teaching her the Indian tongue and becoming her interpreter.

Two years later Mrs. Wright adopted her own

favorite niece, a girl of fifteen years, Martha Hoyt, who for many years rendered efficient service in the mission household. Miss Hoyt married Nicholson H. Parker, an educated Indian, who held the office of United States Interpreter for his people. Mr. Parker was a member of the mission family, and rendered invaluable assistance in translating the Scriptures into the Indian tongue. The children of this marriage were born at the Mission House, and were objects of tender solicitude and loving care through the life of this devoted foster mother.

One day, an Indian mother, whose soul had been stirred to desire better things for her child than she had known, brought her babe of six months to the Mission House, and laying it in the arms of the young wife said, " I give you my boy ; take him and bring him up in your faith." The sacred trust was accepted. The Indian baby was baptized Asher Wright Two Guns. He lived to be nearly three years old. His brain was unnaturally active, and he seemed to understand that Jesus was the friend to whom the loyal love of his little heart should be given, and so we find upon record these words : " We think this child gave good evidence of being a Christian."

But the sad heart of the foster mother was not

long left uncomforted. One day in February, 1836, she was called to the bedside of an Indian mother, who died in the triumphs of the Christian faith. With her latest breath she commended her children to the care of her covenant-keeping God, praying that she might meet them all in a better world. The motherless babe was taken to the Mission House to receive the same tender care which had sheltered the little Asher. This child, Louisa Maria Jones, was the daughter of the Seneca chief, William Jones. Inheriting, as they feared, the consumptive tendencies of her mother, it was with the greatest difficulty that she was carried through the period of early childhood. It pleased God, however, to raise her up, and at the age of five years her health was so confirmed that hopes began to be entertained that she might see many years and be prepared for usefulness among her people.

When little Louisa was about six years old, the occupants of the Mission House were awakened from their midnight slumbers by the piteous cry of an infant. It was November, and the plaintive moan of the little one mingled with the howling winds without. They thought that some deserted mother had come to them for relief, and hastened to open the door. Looking out into the darkness they saw nothing, but continued to hear the cry, although it grew fainter, as though the strength of the little one were failing. Further investigation revealed a small bandbox upon the doorstep! Through an opening in the top of this box they saw a little hand move, and when the cover was removed the blue eyes opened to the light; but the pale-face baby seemed stupefied by the effects of some drug, and scarcely showed signs of life for twenty-four hours. Then it awoke and looked into the faces of its new friends with a bright smile which won their hearts. Upon a paper found among the folds of the blanket were written these words: "Farewell, my little baby! Thy mother must desert thee, but may God take care of thee, and find thee friends." The words were blotted by tears.

Under the tender care of its foster parents the little foundling, who was called at his baptism Henry Morrison, became a healthy, vigorous child, and remained so until a few weeks before his death, which occurred in nine months after his strange entrance to the Mission Home. As no clew had been afforded to his real parentage, the following paragraph, written by Mrs. Wright, was published, that those to whom he belonged might know the fate of the little outcast:

Beneath the shade of a spreading black walnut, in the gateway of an ancient fort, now occupied as the burying ground at the Seneca Mission Station, is a little inclosure which contains the dead of the mission family. In that inclosure was deposited on the 22d instant the remains of a little stranger probably about nine months old, whose origin is veiled in mystery.

On the morning of the fourth of last November he was found in a bandbox on the doorstep of the Mission House, appearing to be about four or five days old. Some time in the night the inmates of an Indian house near by observed a wagon coming from the direction of Buffalo with several persons in it. They stopped opposite the path which leads to the Mission House. At this time a child, apparently very young, was heard distinctly to cry for several minutes; then all was still for several minutes longer, when the wagon moved slowly away, as if proceeding on its journey away from the city. When found, the little boy was sadly chilled, besides manifesting indications of having been drugged, and for several days his life hung in doubt. Subsequently, however, he became very healthy and vigorous, manifesting a sprightliness and a loveliness of disposition which endeared him to all who saw him, and especially to the family whose sympathies for the outcast had led them to adopt him. He died on the morning of the 21st, of cholera infantum, brought on by teething.

In digging a grave for this child a quantity of bones were disinterred at the depth of about two feet, which seemed to have belonged to a full-sized man, probably deposited there when the fort was occupied by soldiers — perhaps in the French war, or perhaps previously. As even conjecture itself is silent among the Indians as to the origin of the fortification, the bones were reinterred in the bottom of the grave; so that this little babe, one of the mildest and sweetest of that tender age, now awaits the resurrection morning, in the bosom, as it were, of a fierce old Indian warrior, or perhaps some gruff French or Highland soldier.

The gateway of that fort is now the gateway of the City of the Dead; and at its very entrance lie Red Jacket, Mary Jemison, the " White Woman," and her granddaughter, the little children in the inclosure, and underneath, in forgotten silence, the relics of fierce and sanguinary battles. Could the infinitely higher excitements of the scene portray it, with what astonishment would that incongruous group, " unknowing and unknown," survey each other when starting from their final slumber !

But the Mission House was not wholly desolate, for little Louisa was still spared to share the love and care of these warm hearts. It was their constant prayer that she might be converted to God in early childhood, but, although apparently much interested in all that was said, no special change was observed in her until she was seven years old, when, on her return from a communion service at the little mission church, she seemed much affected and asked her foster parents to pray for her. She said she wanted to be a Christian, and hoped that she might be prepared to unite in the next Communion and thus obey the command of Jesus. When alone with her mother she wept and said, " Do tell papa that I want to be a Christian, and I want to go forward at the next Communion if he thinks it would be proper." From this time a marked change was noticeable in her character. She was in the habit of secret prayer, and in the little Mission praying circle she would often take part with much earnestness. Her favorite book was the "Peep of Day." She read it through again and again, and never seemed weary of it. Her natural disposition was peevish and irritable; but she now acquired a degree of self-control which she had never before exhibited.

But the inherited seeds of disease had been doing their work. She was taken very ill with inflammation of the lungs, attended with severe attacks of suffocation. In these paroxysms she sometimes manifested great impatience, but would say afterward, " I don't want to do so, mamma, but I am so distressed I can't help it."

It seemed best at last to tell this Indian child that she might not get well. She was very quiet a few moments, and then said, " Mamma, please shut the door. I want to pray with you alone." These were her words: " O Lord, wilt thou bless me and give me a new heart before I die!" The next day she said, " Mamma, I am willing to die if God sees best; though I should like to live and do good among my people."

She talked much about heaven, and said one day, " I wish very often that God would send little Henry to take me up to heaven; I want to see how it looks before I die. I want to see Jesus, too, and know how he looks." They sang to her, "Ye angels who stand round the throne." "That is a very sweet hymn, mamma," said she. One day she threw her arms about her foster mother's neck, and exclaimed, "When you used to talk with me about Jesus, and when I saw you cry so, you don't know how badly I felt. It seemed sometimes as though I should die!"

"I feel now, Louisa," said her mother, "that I can give you up into the Saviour's hands. I hope you feel that you can give yourself up?"

"Yes; I do," was the reply.

"Do you feel sure that Jesus will be your friend if you should die, Louisa?"

"Yes; I think so," said she.

"Why do you think so?" asked her friend, longing to reach the inmost thought of this dear child.

"Because I know he loves little children who love him, and I know I love him," said she, in simple faith.

"And, mamma," she continued after a short silence, "I am not afraid to die, because I do trust Jesus."

The day before her death she appeared very happy, and often requested her adopted mother to sing to her. She read, herself, the Twenty-third Psalm and said, "That is a sweet psalm."

A few hours before her death she said many times,

" I am happy ! " Calling her mother to her she whispered, " Mamma, I feel as though I could praise and bless God; perhaps even now he will let me live to do good to my people." Her mother replied, " Perhaps, Louisa, he will see it best to take you away to-day; do you feel as if you could praise and bless him still? "

" Yes, mamma," she answered, with a sweet smile upon her countenance. A little later she exclaimed, " I feel happy; it seems as though angels were all around this room, and Jesus is in the midst. I do not know whether I am a Christian or not, but I think I do love the Lord Jesus Christ. I am not afraid to die, because he is my friend. He loves little children."

She frequently expressed a sense of her sinfulness, and her hope of forgiveness through Jesus alone. A few moments before she breathed her last she said in a faint whisper, " Mamma, bury me in the garden, won't you? "

" Would you not choose, Louisa, to be buried beside little Henry? " her mother asked.

" Yes, if you wish it," she replied; " or beside my own mother."

Looking around upon the circle gathered about her she said, " I love everybody." With perfect calmness she gave each a parting kiss, and sent messages of affection to her father and brother, evidently aware that she was on the threshold of eternity. Her spirit went to the Saviour in whom she so sweetly trusted, and her body was placed beside that of her departed mother.

In 1848 Mrs. Wright adopted another niece, Phinie Sheldon. This child, taken at the age of five years, was reared in the Mission family, and finally entered the foreign field under the American Board of Commissioners for Foreign Missions, as the wife of Rev. Willis C. Dewey, Mardin, Turkey in Asia.

VI.

1838.

AFTER nearly six years of hard work, painful exposure, and privations unspeakable, it was decided that Mrs. Wright should be permitted to visit her friends in Barnet, Vermont. It was the only time during the fifty-three years of her missionary life that she ever availed herself of this privilege.

She took passage upon a canal boat, accompanied by her beloved little Indian Louisa, and Austria Two Guns, another Indian child, who was to be received into the family of Mrs. Henry Keyes, of Newbury, Vermont.

(It may be well, in passing, to say that Austria Two Guns was brought up in this Christian family as their own, and received the usual advantages given to young girls at that time. In later years she returned to her people, married one of her own race, William Tallchief, and established a Christian home upon the Cattaraugus Reservation.)

A penciled account of this journey is one of the few records left of that far-away past: —

BOAT ANN, June 6, 1838.

Started from the Seneca Mission to-day with much anxiety and many tears, to visit my friends in Vermont. Mr. Wright accompanied me to the boat and left me. It is the first time I have left home and husband. Have felt a great degree of anxiety since I decided to come, but have at length concluded to give up all sources of solicitude into the hands of my Father in heaven, believing that he knows what is best for me, and will do all that is right. I do not know but I have mistaken the path of duty in regard to the journey, though I think I have sought direction from above. I have prayed that if I ought not to go, my way may be hedged up.

June 7. Had a wearisome night. Little Louisa cried a good deal. She is much better to-day, and I hope will not be sick.

We were stranded this forenoon on a rock, which hindered us about three hours. I have enjoyed myself much better so far than I expected. I cannot but hope that a kind Providence smiles upon me, although I am an ungrateful sinner. It is astonishing that such a sinner should be favored with such mercy.

June 8. To-day we passed Palmyra. Got on very well. Much pleasanter than yesterday. Rested better last night. The captain tells us that we shall pass the Sabbath at Syracuse. Little Louisa is much happier to-day.

June 9. Thought much of my dear husband last night. Am afraid he feels lonely. I still feel some misgivings about the course I have pursued in taking this journey. I pray God may forgive me if I have done wrong.

The Sabbath; but I should not know it by its sacred stillness. We are at Syracuse, close by the wharf. Men and boys are idling and laughing, and singing obscene songs all about us. I never spent such a Sabbath before. and hope never to again. Attended the Presbyterian church a part of the day.

Monday. Spent the day pleasantly. Made preparations to leave the boat at twelve at night to take the cars at Utica.

Tuesday. Left the boat at midnight; went into a tavern, took a bed, but thé vermin were so numerous that it was impossible to sleep. We rose at daylight and went downstairs, where we found a number of people sleeping on the floor. After taking some refreshment we hurried to the cars. Came from Utica to Albany in a trice — only six hours. I like the speed on many accounts, but cannot say that I like the motion of the cars. The weather was warm and sultry and we were tired. Took the steamboat at four o'clock and went to Troy and spent the night at a public house.

Wednesday. To-day we took a boat to Whitehall, arriving Thursday evening. The passage was as unpleasant as anything could be, almost. Spent the night at the Clinton House. Slept well. Hope I felt some gratitude for preserving mercy so far.

June 20. At Whitehall we had to wait till Friday at one o'clock before we could get a boat for Burlington; at which place we arrived just after dark, and then waited again till Saturday noon for a stage to take us to Montpelier, where we arrived late in the evening and spent the Sabbath. Attended church all day and met a good missionary sister from Dwight, Arkansas — Miss Emeline Bradshaw. We wept together, and oh, how precious was the short interview! We stopped at the Temperance House and had good fare, and very cheap.

The people found out that we were from the Indians (the children betrayed us) and treated us on that account with great kindness and attention. Both Congregational ministers called upon us in the evening, and also the editor of The Watchman, and several others.

We left Montpelier Monday morning before light and reached home about three o'clock in the afternoon. Both the children have enjoyed good health all the way, and have received much kind treatment.

BARNET, June 21, 1838.

My dear Husband, — We arrived here Monday afternoon, safe and in tolerable health, though much fatigued. Through the abounding mercy of our heavenly Father we have been preserved from every danger by night and by day. Found all my friends well except father, who is extremely feeble. His hair is white as snow. His face is pale and his gait weak and tottering. We fear he will not stay with us long. I have not yet ascertained his state of mind, but fear that he clings to the delusive hope that God is too just to condemn any one to eternal punishment. Mother also has failed, although she is still quite active. They were both much overcome at seeing me. Mother says, " I have found the word of promise sure, that they that wait on the Lord shall not want any good thing." She seems to be in a very calm, happy state of mind, perfectly resigned to God's will for her.

The old friends and neighbors flocked around me and seemed glad to see me. I think as many as twenty persons called last evening. The village is very much altered during my absence, and the people more, but the rocks and hills remain unchanged.

I expect to start for Newbury next Tuesday and take Austria Two Guns with me to her future home. She is a good girl and very happy. The little girls here almost quarrel about which shall have the first visit from her.

Little Louisa is in fine spirits. She has mother's little white kitten, with which she is perfectly delighted. Mother thinks she must have everything she wants.

Everybody here says I have grown old, and changed very much. When I tell them that I have always been contented they do not believe me. I feel very anxious to hear from you, but I try to trust you and all in the hands of God, and I think I do feel some sweet confidence that you are safe in his keeping. I think of you every night, when I lie down to sleep, and when I awake in the night, and when I awake in the morning. I pray God to make your life precious in his sight. I do not forget while I am reveling in the affection of my friends that my dear one is lonely. Do not fail to pray that I may not always be such an ungrateful creature as I have been in time past. Your absent and affectionate wife, L. M. W.

During the absence of this " light of the Mission Home," the lonely husband one day chanced to take up her album, well filled with the old-time testimonials of early friends in Barnet, Newbury, and St. Johnsbury, of which a sample or two will suffice : —

> Laura, I know thee by thine eye,
>   And by thy manner meek and mild,
> And by thy words of charity,
>   That God has made thee his own child.
>
> ANN M. GOULD.

> How honorable, safe and happy are
>   the servants of God!   C. W.

The entire hymn "There is a fountain filled with blood" had been written upon one of these pages, and signed by a converted Indian; the only time in its existence, probably, that this choice bit of pure old gospel ever found itself amid similar environments.

The observant eyes of the printer and publisher of Indian literature very soon noted a peculiarity in the curious little book, which he quietly exposed in rhyme upon the fly leaf : —

Laura, thy friends, the writers in this book,
  Have turned it wrong end upwards; was it haste?
Did they upon the back forget to look
  In want of title page? or deem it taste,
Or mode refined, to change it, end for end,
  A new-vamped, high-lived courtesy 'twixt friend and friend?

Or was it eye prophetic; a keen glance
  Far thro' the unveiled future that foretold
Thy destiny reversed? the which perchance
  Fearing to wound thee, thus, by figures bold,
Instead of open speech, they here made known?
  Or was it the sheer vagary of some old crone?

I thank them, Laura, whatsoe'er the intent;
  (Nor less because they furnish me a theme;)
The world is wrong end upwards; strangely blent —
  Weal, woe; truth, fiction; ill would it beseem
If in friends' Memory-books no type were found
  Of the queer topsy-turvy seen the world around.

"To err is human"; this, tho' no excuse,
  Should waken charity toward those who fail;
Ourselves should draw from it a better use;
  Stern watchfulness 'gainst rude or sly assail
Of error or temptation — firm in hope
  That our deeds all at last may be found right end up.

GAI WI YU (Good news, Gospel).

MARY JEMISON, THE CAPTIVE.

VII.

WHITE CAPTIVES.

IT was a happy moment for our young missionary when she stood at the Mission door, one day, to welcome her loved brother from the far-away hills of Vermont. Years of separation had only served to strengthen the strong tie of fraternal affection. This brother, Mr. Henry Sheldon, now residing at Canton, Pennsylvania, gives his recollection of that visit as follows: —

The next day after I got there, Laura took me to see some of her people who were sick. Among others we visited Old White Chief, father of Seneca White and John Seneca. He was apparently near death. After presenting a few delicacies which she had brought, she read to him from the Gospel of Luke and sang some Indian hymns. I knew almost nothing of the Indians, and they all looked alike to me; but here was a novelty. The old White Chief had an Indian face and hands, but his arms and chest were as white and soft as those of a baby. His wife was dead, but he was cared for by a daughter. He seemed comforted by the reading and singing.

I remained on the Reservation nearly two years, and I well remember how fully Laura's time was occupied in teaching classes at the Mission House, or visiting among the sick and the poor, not only among the Indians, but among whites and blacks, wherever and whenever she was needed. Each visit was marked by some little gift of clothing or provisions, or both, accompanied by good advice. In 1837 occurred the "Patriot War," and during the winter the suffering among the poor was very great. The Mission was called upon every day, and many times in the day, to care for some poor, famished creature.

Old White Chief, to whom Mr. Sheldon refers, belonged to a certain white family who left the Atlantic coast many years ago to make a home in the wilderness of the Susquehanna. Neither their name nor nationality is known. They were attacked one day by a party of Indian scouts, and the father, having offered resistance, was put to death. The mother, while attempting to save herself and child by flight, was overtaken by her merciless pursuers and speedily dispatched. The four-year-old child in her arms was taken from her and borne away, and years after we find Mrs. Wright, accompanied by her brother, at his bedside, ministering to his necessities during his last hours. He had been bedridden three years, but was always patient through pain and weakness. He was an aged man when the missionaries first came to the tribe, but he and his son readily adopted the habits of civilized life. One of his sons built the first frame house on the Reservation and painted it red; hence he was called in Indian, " The-Man-with-the-Red-House."

White Chief had formerly a fine, erect form and delicate features. He was very tall. He was naturally very white, and in youth had long brown hair, which, when the missionaries first saw him, was white as snow. The Indians testified that his whole life had been remarkably pure and upright in every respect, and that he was amiable and affectionate in his disposition.

During these last years he was sincerely attached to Mr. and Mrs. Wright, and always rejoiced to see them. One day White Chief asked Mr. Wright to sit by his bedside and write his words, which, spoken of course in the Indian tongue, were as follows : —

The last I remember of my mother, she was running, carrying me in her arms. Suddenly she fell to the ground on her face, and I was taken from her. Overwhelmed with fright, I knew nothing more until I opened my eyes to find myself in the lap of an Indian woman. Looking kindly down into my face she smiled on me, and gave me some dried deer's meat and maple sugar. From that hour I believe she loved me as a mother. I am sure I returned to her the affection of a son. She supplied my wants as far as it was in her power, and did not like to have me go out of her sight, lest some evil should befall me. She made me moccasins and leggins of deerskin, and gave me a piece of the same which she put over my shoulders, bringing it down and fastening it about my waist with a belt of the skin. I always had a warm place at the fire, and slept in her arms. I was fed with the best food the wigwam could afford. As I grew older I used to play with children of my own age, and soon learned to compete with the best of them in running, leaping, playing ball, and using the bow, which my Indian mother put into my hands telling me she would cook for me all the squirrels and birds I would shoot. I often gave her much pleasure by bringing her game and demanding the fulfillment of her promise. She never disappointed me.

As I grew older I sometimes excelled in the foot race, and I well remember that on one occasion, when I had outstripped all the other boys and received a hearty round of applause, they seemed much displeased. One of them said, " I don't care, he is nothing but a white boy! " I immediately hung my head and ran from the playground to my mother, and hiding my face in her lap, I cried bitterly and loudly. She soothed me as well as she could, asking what was the matter. After a while I was able to tell her the bitter taunt I had received. She took me in her arms and said, " Well, my son, it is true. You are a white boy. You can't help it; but if you always do right and are smart, you will be none the worse for belonging to that wicked race. Whatever you undertake, do your best, and the Good Ruler will bless you."

I had often heard the Indians speak the name of the Great Ruler before, but I never thought he had anything to do with me, and now a feeling of awe came over me, and I resolved that if there was a great and good Being who knew me and would care for me, I would be good and do all I could to please him. I was careful after this not to do anything to make the other boys feel bad when we were at play. I loved my mother more than ever, though I could not help feeling humiliated to know that I was a pale face, and must bear that reproach all my days.

The whole family by whom I was adopted treated me with uniform kindness, and regarded me, as I have reason to believe, with sincere affection. When they saw me excel in any boyish sports they manifested great pride in me. If my companions showed any disrespect or jealousy toward me they were ready to take my part. When I grew older they took me with them on their hunting excursions, taught me how to hunt and fish, and were delighted when I showed any aptitude in these pursuits.

I was never reminded by a look or a word that I was not a son and brother of the family. When I grew to manhood, I went with them on the warpath against the neighboring tribes, but never against the white settlers, lest by some unlucky accident I might be recognized and claimed by former friends. In time I married and came with the tribe who settled upon this Buffalo Creek Reservation, since which time my life has been a very quiet one. I had three sons who grew to be good men.

I was made a chief at an early age, and as my sons grew to manhood they also were made chiefs. The family who had loved me and cared for me in my early days died, but I was still treated like a near relative by the clan of my Indian mother.

After my youngest son was made chief I could see, as I thought, that some of the Indians were jealous of the distinction I enjoyed and it gave me uneasiness. This was the first time I ever entertained the thought of leaving my Indian friends. I felt sure that it was displeasing to the Indians to have three of my sons, as well as myself, promoted to the office of chief. My wife was well pleased to leave with me, and my sons said, "Father, we will go wherever you will lead us."

I then broke the subject to some of my Indian relatives, who were very much disturbed at my decision. They immediately called the chiefs and warriors together and laid the plan before them. They gravely deliberated upon the subject for some hours, and then a large majority decided that they would not consent to our leaving. They said, " We cannot give up our son and brother" (meaning myself) " nor our nephews " (meaning my children). " They have lived on our game and grown strong and powerful among us. They are good and true men. We cannot do without them. We cannot give them to the pale faces. We shall grow weak if they leave us. We will give them the best we have left. Let them choose where they will live. No one shall disturb them. We need their wisdom and their strength to help us. If they are in high places, let them be there. We know they will honor us." We yielded to their importunity and concluded to remain among our Indian friends. I have never had any reason to regret my decision.

I have never known anything about my white relatives. I do not know where they lived, nor what language they spoke. My life in the wigwam with my Indian friends has been sweet and pleasant. At this time nearly all the generation to which I belong have passed on before me to the spirit land. A great change has come over the whole people. They have exchanged the tomahawk and scalping knife for the rifle, which is of very little use, as game has now nearly disappeared from the country. Instead of garments of skin we are now clothed with warm blankets and cloth. Our people cultivate the land, raise corn and potatoes, and we live much more regularly than when in pursuit of wild game. In my opinion, notwithstanding the large territory which has been taken from us by white people, by cultivating the soil which is left to us we may obtain a more reliable and comfortable living than we ever did by hunting.

Within a few years the missionaries have come to us and brought us a knowledge of the Christian religion. When I heard this good news, the white man's way to be saved, I was impressed that this was the religion of my ancestors, and that by receiving it I might, if not in this world, still in another, find the friends from whom I had been so long separated. As I came to understand it better I realized that it brought me the Saviour I needed, and I gladly embraced it, with my whole family.

Not long after this visit, White Chief sent a messenger in haste for Mr. and Mrs. Wright, who were at his bedside as soon as possible. Looking at them earnestly, with the tears streaming down his furrowed cheeks, he said: —

"One thing gives me great uneasiness. I understand no language but the Indian. I am afraid when I go into the other world that I shall not be able to communicate with my own white friends, because I shall not understand their language."

Mr. Wright assured him that there would be no difficulty in understanding one another in heaven; there would be but one language, and that one would be understood by all. He also told the dying man that no distinction of race, color, or language would be recognized there, because they would all be the children of God. These words greatly comforted him, and he passed away peacefully with a cheerful hope of a blessed immortality.

In the papers left by Mrs. Wright is the following account of the captive, Mary Jemison: —

Soon after I came to the Seneca Mission in 1833, I was told that Mary Jemison, "the White Woman" had recently removed from the Genesee Reservation, and was now living near the mission station. As I had often heard of her remarkable history, I felt a desire to see her, and was planning to make her a visit, when our interpreter called one day to tell us that he had seen her quite recently, and that she would be glad to see a missionary. She had never taken kindly to the efforts made to give her religious instruction, and was in fact as strong a pagan in her feelings as any of the Indians. I was therefore very glad to know that she was anxious to see any of us, and went to her the next day. I did not then understand the Seneca language, and took a young Indian girl with me as interpreter. I found the captive in a miserable hut, where she lived with her daughter. There was a low bunk in the room, made by placing a few boards on logs for supports. A straw tick covered with a blanket rested upon the boards. On this bed she lay asleep. She was curled up, her head drawn forward, and did not look much larger than a child ten years old. My interpreter told her daughter what had brought us to the house, and she said her mother did want to see us very much, and she was glad we had come. She then went to the bed and tried to wake the sleeping woman. This was such a difficult matter that I feared we should not be able to talk with her at all. Her daughter shook her repeatedly and raised her up and called to her that somebody wanted to see her, and at last succeeded in rousing her so that she recognized the presence of strangers. I then went forward and shook hands with her and told her that I had come to see her. As soon as she understood the object of my visit, she said, with sobs and tears: —

"Oh, I am so glad you have come! A few nights ago I was lying awake thinking of my past life, how I had been taken away from my home, and how all my friends had been killed. Then I thought of my mother and her last words to me. It was our second night in the woods with the Indians. We had traveled all day, as fast as we could get along, for the Indians seemed to be afraid of pursuit and hurried us very much. When we stopped we were many miles from what had been our happy home only a few hours before, and we were all tired and faint for the want of food. My younger brothers and sisters soon went to sleep, and then my mother drew me to her side and putting her arm around me said, 'My dear child, you are old enough to understand what a dreadful calamity has come upon us. We may be separated to-night, and God only knows whether we shall ever meet again. I want you to remember what you have been taught by your parents and never forget to say your prayer every night as long as you live. If you are a good girl God will take care of you. Perhaps we may be killed and you may be spared. I want you to promise that you will remember what I have said.' I promised my mother that I would do what she said; and then I was led away by an Indian and I lay down on the ground and cried myself to sleep.

"That was the last time I ever saw my father and mother, or my little brothers and sisters. For many years I never forgot my mother's words, and always repeated the prayer every day; but after I had a family and was obliged to work hard to take care of my children, and had a great many troubles to think about, I began to neglect my prayer, and at last I forgot part of it, and was not sure that I remembered any of it right; and finally I stopped saying it regularly at all, although I have often thought about it. I was thinking of all this the other night, and I could not sleep. I thought I had done wrong to forget the promise I had made to my mother. I felt so badly that I began to cry and said a great many times out loud, ' O God, have mercy on me!' My daughter thought I was crazy and told me to stop crying and go to sleep, but I could not till daylight. The next day I sent word to the missionaries that I wanted to see them, and now you are come, I want you to tell me what I shall say when I pray, for I don't know what to say since I have forgotten the prayer my mother taught me."

While she was telling me this story the tears streamed down the wrinkled cheeks, as she sat on the side of her low bed bent almost double. I told her she could not have said anything more appropriate than "O God, have mercy on me!" I then repeated to her the Lord's Prayer in English. She listened with a solemn, tender expression on her face till near the close, when suddenly it was evident a chord had been touched which vibrated with the far distant past and brought back memories both sweet and painful. She immediately became convulsed with weeping, and it was some time before she could speak. At last she said, " *That is the prayer my mother taught me,* and which I have forgotten so many years!"

When she had regained her composure to some extent, I read to her from God's Word, and tried to explain the gospel plan of salvation as simply as possible. I prayed with her and then bade her good-by, commending her to Him who will not break the bruised reed. I little thought it would be my last interview with this interesting woman.

This is a remarkable instance of the permanent influence of a mother's teaching. Fully three quarters of a century had passed since she had made the promise to her mother, which it was not strange she had not kept, and yet through memory of the broken promise, conscience at last was aroused and she was led to take up the long-neglected duty; and from what we learned from her daughter and others of her subsequent state of mind, we think she died in the cheering faith of the gospel, and not in the darkness of paganism.

Reference has already been made to the old Indian burying ground, four miles from the city of Buffalo, New York. A little to the north of the principal entrance is the grave of Red Jacket, so long the steady friend and protector of his people against the encroachments of the whites, and still the watchful sentinel, as we might imagine, solemnly guarding from the desecrating touch of the pale face this little spot, where many of his chosen friends recline around him.

Nearly opposite the grave of Red Jacket, on the south of the entrance, stands a solitary white stone. This is the grave of the " old white woman," Mary Jemison. The stone is partly broken and the inscription defaced, for so strange has been the story of the ancient sleeper that strangers visiting the spot, and wishing to carry away some memento of the visit, have dared to desecrate the grave by chipping off portions of the marble.

It is a little remarkable that so many of the persons who figured on the stage with her, and took part in the eventful scenes of which she was an eyewitness, should be brought into such close proximity with her in the last scene on earth in which they were concerned. Here they lie, side by side. The stern old warrior and his feeble victim might shake hands and exchange neighborly civilities. No stone marks the spot where these primitive nobles repose; but in old times the graves of Young-King, Little Billy, Twenty-Canoes, John Snow, Captain Pollard, and others were often pointed out to the eye of the curious traveler.

In this historic burying ground was found upon a monument the following tribute to the Indian race: —

A faithful history of all the captives who have been taken by the various Indian tribes, and adopted and grown up among them, would form a very interesting volume; and if such a record could be placed by the side of the record of Indian wrongs faithfully delineated, it may be doubted whether the comparison would not be greatly in favor of the Indians, so far as humanity is concerned; notwithstanding all that has been said and written of the cruelty of savages.

Life in the woods of North America in those early times, under the most favorable circumstances, was fraught with severe suffering, and in a state of captivity, with the few comforts to be found in an Indian wigwam, dreadful indeed must have been the lot of those whom the chances of war threw into the power of an exasperated foe. But this captivity was only an incident of war, and no more cruel than the customs of civilized nations, who often burn whole cities and destroy provisions, so as to cause the greatest suffering among helpless women and children.

There were indeed instances when they deemed it necessary to take summary vengeance on individuals and make them examples, in order to intimidate their enemies; but they oftener pursued the more humane policy of adopting them into their families and extending to them the rights and privileges they themselves enjoyed. In such cases the captive was always made to feel that adoption was not a mere form. Real affection, and in fact all that the heart prizes and longs after in relationship, was bestowed upon them. After the ceremony was over and a name given, they were taught to say, " my father," " my mother," " my brother," " my sister."

It is remarkable that among those who have written on Indian character, so few have understood the subject. The masses still entertain extremely unjust views of these people. How often do we hear it asserted of them that "they never forgive an injury"! It is uniformly believed that their hate and their love are alike unending; that when in pursuit of vengeance they will stoop to almost any artifice to accomplish their ends; that they are cruel, and delight themselves in the sight of blood and suffering. True, their intercourse with civilized men and Christian men, to our shame be it spoken, has tended to bring these traits into active exercise. In the early contests between the Indians and white men, the latter possessed every advantage over the former for offensive warfare, and this inequality drove the Indians to the skillful use of what means they did possess. They were forced to meet cruelty with cruelty, cunning with cunning, and perfidy with perfidy, in order to compete successfully with the superior abilities of their foes.

Contempt of pain and suffering among the ancient Spartans was considered an evidence of true greatness of soul, and instances of their unexampled endurance are applauded and admired. The Indians embraced similar views, and it was considered a special favor to give a brave man an opportunity to exhibit his fearlessness of torture and death. To put a speedy end to his life was the refinement of cruelty, as it entirely deprived him of an opportunity to earn the most valuable name a warrior could acquire.

A truly brave man, they deemed, would never fear pain or death, however terrible might be its form. 'T was no uncommon thing for the victim at the stake to defy his tormentors to do their utmost, and again to taunt them with not being acquainted with means of producing the most exquisite suffering, and while enduring the most intense agony, he would often break forth into a triumphal war song and recite with the greatest coolness the wonderful feats he had performed, and the numbers of their people he had slain in former engagements, and then describe in tones of provoking irony the cowardly conduct of their chiefs and warriors, thus aiming to inflame their rage to the highest degree, regardless of consequences to himself. Sometimes his persecutors, becoming exasperated, would rush upon him and dispatch him at once. The memory of such an individual was always cherished with the utmost respect, and his example held up for the imitation of their youth.

Educated to these views of what constituted a truly brave man, they scorned to complain, and often preserved the greatest self-possession and coolness, when enduring the most intense mental and physical suffering. Hence, to those who are but partially acquainted with their character, they have the reputation of being morose, stern, and cold-hearted. This is a mistake, for under all this affected frigidity of manner there runs as strong a current of warm affection as ever bubbled up in the heart of a white man.

MOCCASIN.

VIII.

ONE of the most faithful friends of the missionaries in those days was Young-King, the first chief among the Senecas to see the good influence of education and the Christian religion upon his people. His influence was very great, standing as he did so high as a warrior and a chief.

Like too many, he also partook of the fire water, and for many years was a victim of intemperance. In a drunken brawl he lost an arm, and a finger from the remaining hand. After he became a Christian not one drop ever wet his lips. At one time on a journey he was thrown from his wagon and badly injured. When the physician came he was groaning upon the floor in a neighboring hut. Upon a table stood the whiskey bottle, which was an irresistible temptation to the pale-face doctor. He must drink before he could attend his patient. Young-King's eyes flashed as he asked, " What you drink there?"

The doctor answered, " Whiskey! and it will do you good ; you must take a glass."

" You — drink — whiskey?" said the chief; " then you no bleed me!" and though suffering intensely he would allow nothing to be done for him by the man who drank whiskey.

He was the first Indian who built a rod of fence on the Reservation, and often in the cold winter days he would be seen on Saturday crossing the creek in his little canoe to see if the mission church were supplied with fuel for the Sabbath; and if it were not, with his one hand he wielded the axe and chopped a little pile which he also carried to the door to be sure that it was ready for the morning service. He used to say: —

"I came so late into the Vineyard; I must work diligently to accomplish anything before I am called away."

This man could not read, yet he seemed to understand clearly the plan of redemption, the nature of the atonement, and the intricate workings of the human heart.

His fireside was characterized by old-fashioned hospitality. There the poor were welcomed, the hungry were fed, and the friendless received sympathy. Wicked white men did their utmost to tempt him to fall again into intemperance, but he always resisted firmly, and brought no dishonor in any way upon the cause of Christ. He died in 1835, and lies in the old Indian burying ground, where are also many other distinguished men and women of the Senecas who first received Christian burial.

Mrs. Wright sometimes invited the Indian mothers to what we should now call a " tea meeting." They were at liberty to bring their needlework, which consisted in ornamenting their deerskin moccasins with porcupine quills, or their broadcloth skirts and leggins with beads, or perhaps fastening a quantity of silver brooches upon their short-gowns or hats. While thus occupied she read and explained gospel truths in their own language, sang hymns with them, and frequently encouraged them to tell her some story of old times. The simple repast, which had really brought them there and held them through the afternoon, was then served, and they went away to think of the " good words" which had been spoken to them about the " new way." It was during one of these afternoon " sociables " that an Indian woman gave the following reminiscence of Chief Infant : —

He was an old man when she was a young girl. He was a very strong man. She remembered hearing that during an Indian council when there were many white people present, some of them talked a good deal, and one man in particular was very noisy and quarrelsome. He was rebuked several times but still persisted in disturbing the council by his noisy, drunken babbling. At length Chief Infant arose and demanded of him that he keep quiet or leave the council.

The cowardly fellow refused to obey and kept on swearing and threatening and boasting that he was not afraid of him or any one there. Chief Infant arose once more, went to him, and with great dignity and forbearance commanded him to go away and leave them to go on with their discussions in peace. The bully replied that he should not do either until he was ready. Chief Infant then took hold of the man's arms below the elbows and squeezed them till the blood ran through between his fingers. The man cried for mercy and was released, and Chief Infant walked calmly back to his seat in the council.

At the Treaty of "Big Tree," as it was called, Chief Infant was present. An Englishman who was a regular boxer by profession was there to see the Indians and doubtless to find a foeman worthy of his steel. When his eyes fell on Chief Infant he thought if he could fight and overcome such a magnificent looking man, he should make himself famous. So he began to feel of his opponent in rather a coaxing way at first, telling him he wanted to try the strength of the red man a little, that he did not wish to hurt him, but would like to show him how Englishmen could fight in single combat.

Chief Infant modestly declined, saying he did not wish to fight. The white man persisted in urging him, while the Indian still refused, saying it was a time of peace and he did not wish to see blood running that day. The friends of the chief began to fear the white man would think him a coward and tried to coax him to try his strength, telling him that the swift movements and cunning arts in which the boxer had been educated would stand him in bad stead when matched against his strength and coolness, and that they would see that no undue advantage was taken of him.

The white men who stood near now began to clamor for the fight, and offered money to the chief, till the sum amounted to one hundred and fifty dollars. Still the Indian seemed reluctant to fight until he saw that his friends were really ashamed of him, because they thought his conduct looked cowardly to the whites. He then arose and walked coolly toward the white man and thus addressed him : —

" Brother, I do not wish to hurt you. We have met for peaceable discussion of important matters. My blood is not hot with anger. I do not hate you ; but since you desire it so much, I will show you how we Indians fight."

The boxer immediately commenced to make his motions both offensive and defensive. But Chief Infant came down upon him like a flash of lightning, seized him by both arms, breaking the bones of each and throwing him on the ground. He left him groaning in anguish and walked back to the council as if nothing of any consequence had happened. Such a shout rent the air as was never heard before or since in that valley.

Old Fish Hook came to the Mission House one day, with a sad story of his poverty, lameness, and general decrepitude. He complained bitterly of the cruel treatment he had received from white people, and begged Mr. Wright for a " paper " which should appeal to the mercy and charity of the pale face. The good missionary immediately provided the old man with the following impromptu : —

TO WHOM IT MAY CONCERN.

Indian. — Kind friend, this paper I present
  To ask a little aid;
My wants, though seeming few, are great —
  I'm begging for my bread.
For time and sickness, grief and pain,
  And flood and fire and frost
Fell sadly on my destiny,
  And all my hopes are lost.

White Man. — Nay, come not here! though true thy tale,
  As true perchance it is,
Why should I help the Indian wild,
  With copper-colored phiz?
An idle, thriftless, heathen race!
  Go home, and beg of them!
My bread I earn by daily toil,
  Let Indians do the same.

Indian. — But thou hast strength to toil,
  While I am sickly, weak, and old;
Thy heart beats quick, thy blood is warm,
  While mine is slow and cold;

And thou may'st yet become like me,
  Ere life's brief thread is spun;
It will not be a thankless plea—
  Mercy for mercy done.

They say God portions out the lot
  Of all the sons of men;
Why then revile the darker hue
  With which he tinged my skin?
Thy Maker might have shaded deep
  Thy snow and lily face;
If white excel—compassionate
  The less exalted race.

They say God gave us all one blood,
  That brothers we might be;
That kindred love might bind us all
  In one great family.
Oh, spurn not, then, the Indian with
  His copper-colored phiz;
Three fourths of the whole family
  Have skins as dark as his;

And thou hadst been a heathen born,
  As thy forefathers were,
Had not thy Maker interposed
  With kind paternal care.
Why boast o'er me, then, whom he left,
  To follow on the road
My dark-souled ancestors supposed
  The appointed way to God?

And though, like them, my dogs I burn,
  Mock not with scornful eyes;
For mercy in the heart, thou claim'st
  Thy nobler sacrifice.
If thine the better way, and thou
  Hast hopes I ne'er may know—
Grudge not the brief enjoyment here
  Thy bounty may bestow.

Besides, they say God gives to thee
  The privilege of prayer;
That greatest, strangest mystery—
  To ask and He will hear;
While us thou callest heathen vile—
  A reprobated race—
Now might not God, if thou would'st pray,
  Give us too saving grace?

If worldly good thou canst not spare,
  At least withhold not this;
If thou art right, thou bear'st for us
  The key to heavenly bliss.
And covetous of words of prayer
  Thou wilt not, canst not be;
Wherever, then, thou bow'st the knee,
  Oh, plead for mine and me!

Else, own thou thinkest not thy hope
  To be preferred to mine;
And all thy claim to greater light,
  Or holier love, resign.
For deeds of love, thy gospel saith,
  Shall thy memorial be;
"Because thou didst it unto these,
  Thou didst it unto Me."

And what by alms or faith or prayer
  Shall be for Indians done,
May not be long delayed—the mist
  Now dims their setting sun.
Some will be changed to white men soon—
  The rest will all be gone;
None will remain to roam and beg
  In lands once all their own.

SECRETARY STANTON said to General Halleck, "If Bishop Whipple comes here to tell us that our Indian system is a sink of iniquity, tell him we all know it; tell him the United States Government never redresses a wrong *until the people demand it*. When the hearts of the people are reached the Indians will be saved."

A LETTER of inquiry was once sent to General Cass asking whether he ever knew an instance of Indian war or massacre that was not provoked by the white man's aggravation. To this letter was received the following laconic reply: —

DEAR COLONEL: —

Never! NEVER! NEVER!

Yours truly,

LEWIS CASS.

" THERE are now in the state of New York about 5,000 descendants of the Iroquois. The red man in the Empire State owns about 88,000 acres of land. This fact makes him more enemies than do all other considerations. White men want this land, and are determined to get it by fair means or foul. Hence they are interested to defame and to exterminate the Indian, thus hoping to share his goods."

IX.

A ND now we approach the "Seven Years'
Trouble," which was the darkest, most difficult, most tempestuous, and altogether the most
trying period in the missionary experience of both
Mr. and Mrs. Wright, which at its close covered more
than half a century. It is the same old story, and
the "White Man's Treaty" is at the bottom of it.

At this time (1837) the Senecas were quietly settled
upon their four Reservations, which they had thus far
held in uninterrupted possession. These were called
the Buffalo Creek Reservation, with which we have
become familiar (now a part of the city of Buffalo);
the Cattaraugus Reservation, lying upon the banks of
the Cattaraugus Creek, and washed on the west by the
waters of Lake Erie, occupying the three counties of
Cattaraugus, Chautauqua, and Erie; the Allegheny
Reservation, Pennsylvania, upon which the city of
Salamanca is situated; and the Tonawanda Reservation, near Tonawanda, New York.

When the first Mission church was organized on the
Buffalo Creek Reservation, the Indians began to get

acquainted with a better class of white people than they had known in the border settlers and soldiers, who brought them only the vices of our race. After much earnest work Christian influence began to tell upon them. Many chiefs embraced Christianity, and were leading their people in the same direction. The missionaries were joyfully reaping the fruits of years of effort, but alas! the Ogden Land Company now appeared upon the scene, and a season of fierce discussion and dissension began, which did not in the least abate until 1844.

This company wanted the rich lands of the Senecas. To achieve this end they began by gaining an influence over the Indian chiefs through the magic power of money. Each chief of influence soon discovered that he had but to ask to receive " much gold," by means of which he could supply every want, and even go through all the great country which had once belonged to his fathers, and see the wonderful life and power of the people whom these " golden pale faces " represented. The next step of the company was to organize the " Migration Party," by means of which this tribe was to be transplanted to Kansas. When these plans were well matured a general council of the Seneca chiefs was called to consider the question of selling their lands to the Ogden Land Company. Through the liberal bribery of the chiefs and the most outrageous frauds, a bargain was consummated in January, 1838, which conveyed 114,869 acres of Indian Land to the Ogden Land Company, for $202,000. The treaty was signed by President Martin Van Buren.

But the faithful missionaries of these Indians were not idle in their cause. Every moment which could be spared from their ministrations to the people was· used in collecting proof that the treaty was brought about through fraud and bribery. This collection of proofs with " protests " and " memorials " was sent to Washington, and, through the influence of the Society of Friends, received attention.

In 1842 a new treaty was prepared, which was signed by the chiefs, with the exception of the Tonawanda chiefs, who did not sign either treaty. By this treaty, which they called the " Compromise Treaty," the Senecas retained the Cattaraugus and Allegheny Reservations, and relinquished the Buffalo and Tonawanda to the Ogden Company.[1]

This transaction, which took from the Senecas all their reservations except Cattaraugus and Allegheny, was notoriously famous for the duplicity and abominable wickedness connected with it. Several of the

[1] The Tonawandas would not submit to this arrangement. They held out against this treaty for sixteen years, but the courts decided against them, and they would most surely have been obliged to go to Kansas, had it not been for a Special Act of Congress, allowing them to sell their Kansas lands to the government, and with that money buy back a part of their own Reservation. This special treaty was made in 1868.

Christian chiefs were bribed by the white man's money
to sign the treaty. This so disgusted those who had
not fully decided to accept the gospel that they returned to paganism.

" Red Jacket told us years ago," they said, " that
if we took the religion of the pale face, we should
lose our homes. His words were true."

After the treaty of 1842 had been signed by the
chiefs, the " Buffalo Indians," as they were called,
who did not go to Kansas, filled with anger toward
Christianity, began to move to the Cattaraugus Reservation. Then followed four years of bitterness and
strife. The people who were thus thrust from their
homes and driven from the graves of their fathers
were not to be comforted or pacified. They were
embittered against their chiefs, and the whole race of
the Pale Face, including even their own missionaries.
But notwithstanding the unjust accusations of these
people, so desperately wounded, the patient, devoted
missionaries, Mr. and Mrs. Wright, feeling the deepest
sympathy for their sufferings, came with them to the
Cattaraugus Reservation, and did much to alleviate
their forlorn condition. With wonderful tact and
marvelous judgment, seeking divine help through
every hour of this bitter trial, they continued to
minister to their charge, spiritually and physically.
The troubled minds were daily comforted by these

who could not, humanly speaking, see a ray of light
in the future.

As soon as possible the " Buffalo Indians " held a
mass meeting and made a solemn resolve to have
nothing to do with the gospel or the Christian Indians
or the missionaries.

" This new religion," they said in their wrath,
" must be *bad*, since those who embraced it could be
so dishonest, so unjust, so cruel."

Those who made this resolve have passed away, but
their children to some extent hold the same prejudice
against Christianity, and it has caused marked division
between the two parties from that day to this. Mr.
and Mrs. Wright, however, were always consulted with
as much confidence by the pagan leaders as by their
own Christian flock.

Nearly forty years after this stormy period, Mr.
Henry Silverheels, who well remembered those sad
days, stood over the open grave of his beloved missionary, Mr. Wright, and gave this simple, touching
testimony : —

" There was a time when we had lost every foot of
land we had in this state. Our chiefs had yielded to
temptation, and been bribed by wicked men to sell
our homes, and it was only a question of time when
we should be driven away from all that was dear to

us. Mr. Wright, fully understanding the situation, went to a prominent member of the Ogden Land Company, and induced him to use his influence with the company to consent to a compromise, by which the Allegheny and Cattaraugus Reservations were restored to us. Thus it is that we owe our present comfortable homes to Mr. Wright's love and care for us. Let us remember him with gratitude and try to live as he lived, for the honor of God and the good of our fellow men."

On a bit of yellow paper is the following in Mrs. Wright's handwriting, written during this period of trial : —

CATTARAUGUS RESERVATION, December 31, 1846.
The Lord's mercies have been infinite towards me, although I have been an unworthy sinner. I desire, this last day of the year, in reviewing all the past, to acknowledge the unceasing goodness of God towards me, and I would ask his grace to help me to consecrate myself anew to his service. " Oh, the depths !" my soul exclaims while reviewing my whole life, and oh, my ingratitude and sin ! O Lord, grant me help to serve thee better, to walk humbly before thee, and in such a manner that I may always feel the preciousness of Christ and his salvation. Leave me not to myself, lest I basely and presumptuously dishonor thy name, and ruin my own soul. Oh, may I lay myself at thy feet and quietly await the accomplishment of all thy holy will and pleasure concerning me, evermore. Amen.   LAURA M. WRIGHT.

During the two years following the removal of the Buffalo Indians to the Cattaraugus Reservation, it required divine wisdom and patience and skill to adjust the unhappy exiles to new conditions. The church work was necessarily interrupted. In 1848 the Indian nation underwent a revolution, and substituted a republican government for the government by chiefs. At a convention held at the Cattaraugus Reservation, the delegates in a very firm manner abrogated the old government and proclaimed a new order of things after the manner of the founders of our own government.

By this new arrangement the supreme judiciary is composed of three judges designated as " peacemakers." The legislative powers of the nation are vested in a council of eighteen, chosen by the universal suffrages of the nation; but nothing is binding unless ratified by three quarters of all the voters and three quarters of all the mothers in the nation.

One provision of this constitution exhibits a degree of national frugality well worthy of imitation by those gentlemen in our own Congress, who spend so much of the " dear people's " money in talking about their rights and interests. The Seneca Constitution declares that the compensation of members of the council shall be one dollar each, per day, while in session, *but no member shall receive more than twenty-six dollars during any one year!* With such a provision there will be no danger of their council becoming " dilatory."

The following are the reasons given for changing

their form of government and adopting a constitutional charter : —

We, the people of the Seneca nation of Indians, humbly invoking the blessing of God upon our efforts to improve our condition, and to secure to our nation the demonstration of equitable and wholesome laws, do hereby abolish and annul our form of government by chiefs, because it has failed to answer the purpose for which all governments should be created.

1. It affords no security in the enjoyment of property.

2. It provides no laws regulating the institution of marriage, but tolerates polygamy.

3. It contains no provision for the poor, but leaves the destitute to perish.

4. It leaves the people depending on foreign aid for the means of education.

5. It has no judiciary nor executive departments.

6. It is an irresponsible, self-created aristocracy.

7. Its officers are absolute and unlimited in signing away the people's rights, but indefinite in making regulations for their benefit or protection.

We cannot enumerate the evils growing out of a system so defective, nor calculate its overpowering weight on the progress· of improvement. But to remedy these defects we proclaim and establish a constitution, or charter, and implore the government of the United States, and the state of New York, to aid us in providing us with laws under which progress shall be possible.

INDIAN BABY FRAME.

The Indian mother has certainly invented the most convenient method of carrying and lullabying her baby. All babies are nearly of the same size, and nobody needs to be told how long or how wide a baby frame should be made. It is a straight board, sometimes with side pieces, and always with a hoop over the head

BABY FRAME.

from which to suspend a curtain for the protection of the little eyes from the sun, and to keep the child from harm should the baby frame fall. The child is enveloped in a blanket and laced to the frame, which is carried upon the back of the mother by a strap which comes over the forehead, and with much less fatigue than in her arms. The baby is kept in the frame most of the time through infancy, and it is astonishing how contented it remains in its little prison. While the mother works in the field she hangs her baby on a low limb of a tree where it is rocked by the wind. When busy in the house she suspends it on a nail, or places the frame in a corner; sometimes she hangs it where she can swing it to and fro as she passes, singing as she goes the following lullaby, which loses much in the translation:—

Swinging, swinging, lullaby,
Sleep, my little one, sleep;
It is your mother watching by;
Swinging, swinging, she will keep
Her little one, lullaby.
Swinging, little one,
Baby, baby, do not weep,
Sleep, sleep, little one,
And thy mother will be near,
Little baby, lullaby.

82

X.

THE missionary work upon the Cattaraugus Reservation was divided, Mr. and Mrs. Wright having charge of the "upper mission station," and Mr. Bliss and family the "lower mission station." This family, with whom Mr. and Mrs. Wright worked in delightful harmony several years, was succeeded by the late Father Gleason, whose works still follow him among the Choctaws, Mohegans, and Senecas. Mr. Wright and Father Gleason were both college classmates of my father, Dr. Joseph S. Clark, of Boston, Massachusetts, and thus it came to pass that while yet in my teens the call came to join these devoted workers upon the Cattaraugus Reservation, and under commission of the American Board of Commissioners of Foreign Missions, to learn how to be a missionary. Miss Mary Kent, of Grantville, Massachusetts, was commissioned at the same time. Dr. and Mrs. Treat, Dr. A. C. Thompson, and my father were our companions on the journey. We can reach California to-day in less time than it took us then to go from Boston to this Indian Reservation on

Lake Erie's shore. We arrived at the railroad station nearest to the Reservation on Friday. As the lower Mission House was near the church, the whole party was entertained there over the Sabbath.

Father Gleason and an Indian met us at the station. Mrs. Treat and myself were placed in the care of Nicholson H. Parker, the United States interpreter for these people, a tall, powerful Indian, who drove us over the nine miles through the woods to the Mission House. I remember that we were rather afraid of him, although he treated us with the utmost kindness, and was in his manners " every inch a gentleman."

I shall never forget the consecration meeting in Father Gleason's study that evening. Dr. Treat's prayer was a great comfort and inspiration to the young girl and her companion, just starting out in missionary life. The musical tones and rare expression with which Dr. Thompson repeated that entire hymn, " Oh, could I speak the matchless worth!" linger with me yet. Missionaries were present at this meeting from other Indian reservations, forty, fifty, and even sixty miles away. They had come this distance in rough lumber wagons at great inconvenience, to see these secretaries of the American Board and to welcome the new missionaries from Boston.

During the evening I became interested in the sweet, careworn face of a lady sitting a little apart from the others. I did not know that she was Mrs. Wright. With closed eyes and bowed head she seemed lost to present surroundings in absorbed communion with God. When, later in the evening, I was presented to her, she took both my hands in her own, looked at me earnestly for a moment, and said: —

"Poor child! so young and so inexperienced! You ought to be at home with your mother. How little you dream of the life which is before you!"

I had felt greatly attracted to her during the meeting, but these words chilled me, and I said, "Is there then no work here which a young Christian can do?"

She hastened to comfort me. "If you are really one of the Lord's consecrated ones, you will find work enough here. And who knows? your youth and inexperience may be used by God where our wisdom fails."

This was my introduction to Mrs. Wright, whose story we have followed as a child, maiden, and missionary wife through forty-four years. A friendship was soon established between us which steadily gathered strength and sweetness to the last.

The lower mission station was surrounded by a magnificent grove of maple, black walnut, and pine of wonderful growth. We used to call this station "the bird's nest." Sunday morning we all went to the Mission church, a plain wooden building seating about two hundred people. When we entered the church, Father Gleason was already in the pulpit with an Indian hymn book in one hand and the bell rope in the other, selecting hymns for the service, ringing the bell with all his might to call in the slow-moving Indians, and singing at the top of his voice the old hymn,—

> "The voice of free grace cries,
> 'Escape to the mountain.'"

This bell, by the way, was a present to the Christian Indians from Dr. Hawes' church, Hartford, Connecticut.

Our seats faced the two doors of entrance and we had an opportunity to watch the people as they gathered. With dignity and reverence they entered the sacred house. The men took seats on one side, and the dogs which had followed them in curled up at their feet. The women occupied the other side of the church; many of them wore blankets and carried papooses on their backs. One of these mothers thus laden took a seat beside me. She gave her blanket a peculiar hitch, and the baby came over her shoulder into her lap. I sprang to catch the child, but found my fears were groundless. Although I saw this performance repeated hundreds of times in the seventeen years that I spent with this people, no child ever met with an accident, the baby seeming to understand how to slide safely over the shoulder in response

Mission House, Lower Station.

to the mother-hitch of the blanket. And so in time the audience consisted of men and dogs, women and babies, missionaries and teachers.

Father Gleason never acquired the Seneca language. He preached and read the Scriptures through an interpreter, Mr. Henry Silverheels, a tall Indian of commanding presence, who used much more time in Indian than the missionary did in the English. A sermon of fifteen minutes' length in English occupied three quarters of an hour in delivery.

I shall never forget the singing. The weird, plaintive Indian airs were too suggestive of the sad fate of this strange race, and after the first verse of the first hymn, I could control my feelings no longer, and yielded to a burst of sobs. The Indians decided that the young missionary from the " land of the rising sun " (Boston) was homesick, and although at the time there was no indication by look or manner that this strange outburst had been observed by them, they told me afterward that their hearts went out in great sympathy to the young girl so far from her mother.

At intervals during the service, certain dogs became uneasy, and wandered about, even upon the steps of the pulpit. Then Father Gleason, giving Silverheels a long sentence to interpret, started after them with his cane and drove them out of the house, coming back to the pulpit somewhat out of breath, but in season to proceed with the next division of his discourse. The service was very long. After a while a baby began to cry; the mother made no attempt to quiet the child. Another baby followed suit, and still another, until several babies were crying at once. Then the dogs began to howl; and with the crying babies and howling dogs the good missionary was obliged to terminate his sermon and let us go home.

The day after this first Sabbath, Drs. Treat and Thompson, Mrs. Treat, my father, and other visitors, took their departure on their way to a missionary meeting farther west, and I was left alone among strangers. For a little time I was overcome by this thought, and the responsibility which I had taken of becoming a messenger of God to this people. I found a quiet corner in the Mission House and yielded to my feelings. After a time the tempest was stilled, and the message came to my heart, "Have not I commanded thee? Be strong and of a good courage. Be not afraid, neither be thou dismayed, for I am with thee, and will keep thee whithersoever thou goest;" "I will strengthen thee."

The loving devotion of Mrs. Gleason and her daughters and the overflowing spirits and good cheer of Father Gleason were a great help to me in those days.

The missionaries decided to place me in a settlement seven miles from the Mission House, upon the shore of the lake. I was placed in the family of an Indian chief to board, and my kingdom was a little schoolhouse in the woods. The house of the chief was old and loosely built. The window of my room opened upon the lake and it was not uncommon for the snows of winter to drift in upon my bed and upon the floor. The chief with whom I boarded was a man of education and culture. He had the remarkable gift of interpreting as a whole any address or sermon which might be given to the people by some orator or distinguished preacher visiting the Reservation who could not manage the ordinary interpretation sentence by sentence. He had rare power of memory, and could repeat word for word any discussion or conversation. There were certain Indian men in the family whose business it was to wait upon him. He was never known to black his boots or harness a horse or attend to the slightest detail of the house or farm, which consisted of some two hundred acres. He spent his time reading, writing, visiting among white people many miles away, and looking after the interests of his tribe. His wife, a white lady, was devotedly attached to him. Her strong affection never wavered a moment from the time she married him, at the age of fifteen, until the hour of his death. She never regretted the step she had taken, although disowned by parents and friends for taking it. It was a comfort to her, however, surrounded as she was by Indians, to have the companionship of one of her own race. She had a large family of children who attended my school in the woods.

One other inmate of this family was the aged mother of the chief, who did not speak a word of English and was never reconciled to his marriage with a white woman. It may be said that as to the white wife, this was the skeleton in the family, and many a time the missionary teacher was obliged to make peace between the two. As soon as the children could lisp the word " mamma " the old grandmother commenced to teach them the Indian language and to use all her influence to instill into their minds Indian beliefs, Indian superstitions, and the Indian religion. They were all bright children and not easily influenced in these matters. The daughters, as wives of white men, are now happily settled in life among people of their mother's race.

The first morning, when I started to go to the little schoolhouse in the woods, I was appalled by the sight of a herd of cattle outside the door. There were horses, colts, cows, calves, pigs, and dogs. I went back and said to the chief : —

" I have always lived in a city, and have not been accustomed to seeing animals loose in the streets. I am afraid to pass them alone. Will you go with me ? "

With great courtesy he accompanied me to the schoolhouse. I said : —

" Will you come for me at noon and go home with me?"

I shall never forget the expression of his face as he turned and said to me, " You have come a long way to live with us, and to teach these Indians the Jesus Way. Now I want to say something to you. If you are afraid of anything, you can never win these Indians to the Jesus Way, for they despise a coward. If you wish to have any influence over them, you must be very brave."

" But," I said, " I am not brave. I am afraid of spiders and mice and snakes and dogs and these animals on the road. What shall I do?" and I recalled with a shudder the experience of the night before, when I discovered a family of mice keeping house in my straw bed.

"The one thing for you to do," said he, " is to hide your fear. Never show it in the presence of the people. I will come for you this noon if you ask me to, but knowing that you wish to win these people to your religion I thought it wise to tell you this."

I said, " Do not come for me this noon. If I am not brave at heart, I will, at least, be brave out-wardly." He left me alone in the little schoolroom. It was a sacred moment with me, for there in the solitude of those woods I asked from One who never fails us, strength to do the work, give the message, win this people, and be delivered from physical fear. My little flock began to gather. I soon found that I was to have a company of all ages, from the child three years old to married men and women. With my ignorance of the Indian language and their ignorance of the English the situation was peculiar. It occurred to me many times during those first weeks to wonder of what use my education would be to me, shut up in a little schoolhouse in the woods on an Indian reservation. But I soon learned that I needed all the education that I had received, added to all the wit, wisdom, and common sense I could command, to master the situation. Books were of very little use. While I taught them English they taught me Indian, and I was soon able to make my own schoolbooks, which gave them the rudiments of the many things I wished them to know, and prepared them for a better understanding of the ordinary schoolbook when they should have sufficient English at their command.

I think I have never been happier than during those two years in that secluded neighborhood of Indians, whom I loved, and who loved me, and where in every home I was a welcome and favored guest. It was their joy to help carry out my wishes in every respect as far as they possibly could. Life in the woods with these children of nature, although so different from the city life to which I had been accustomed, seems even now a delightful dream.

At first they tested me in different ways as to my courage, knowledge, and ability. One night I sat in the deserted schoolhouse writing a letter home. I had heard no footstep but my attention was arrested suddenly by a hissing sound. I turned and saw an animal entirely new to me. The malicious expression of the eyes terrified me. It was an opossum. My first impulse was to leap upon the table and scream; then the thought flashed into my mind, " This is a test of your courage and you are being watched"; so I turned back and went on writing; but the letter written with shaking hand gave evidence of my fear. Then I heard a shout, and from under the windows of the little schoolhouse three men leaped up and said, " She is n't afraid! she is n't afraid!" and the opossum was carried away.

Soon after this I was asked to go through a certain lonely ravine, which some of the Indians believed to be inhabited by witches; and when I expressed my willingness to pass through this place, and I did it, though with much trembling, — not through any fear of witches, but of snakes, — they again pronounced me very brave.

One day while my school was in session, three men

came to the door and said, " We want you to come out into the woods and tell us what to do."

I immediately followed them, again trembling inwardly through fear that I should not be equal to the emergency. On the way I asked, " What is it?"

" Well," said the leader, " we have been cutting down a very large tree. We have cut off the branches, and it belongs to two of us, and we each want an equal amount of the wood to carry away; and we want to know exactly where to cut this big tree, which is very large at the bottom and very small at the top, so that he will have as much wood as I shall have."

As I followed these men to the woods, I ransacked my brain for an illustration in mathematics which might help to tell them where to strike the vital point of that tree, but without avail. Even though I knew by figures where the cut should be made, if they could not be made to understand the figures, they would never feel satisfied that it was the right place. How was I to know just where to divide this tree and to prove to them, in their ignorance of all mathematical rules, that I was right?

And here the lesson which I was learning in all these days was again emphasized. This was one of the little things, the everyday items of life, in which I might have wisdom from above if I would but ask; but while I lifted my heart in earnest petition for this wisdom, not a ray of light came to me until we reached the woods. Here was the long log. There were a couple of Indian ponies hitched to a tree ; there were ropes with which each was to drag away his own section, and close by was a fallen tree. Like an inspiration a plan came to me. I said : —

" Cut the upper branches from that fallen tree, so far (indicating the measure) ; tie a rope to the log ; let your horses draw it over the fallen tree ; stop them when it balances."

They obeyed directions, and when at last the long pine log rested and balanced upon the fallen tree, I said, " Cut it there."

They saw at once that the division must be equal if the log were perfectly balanced, and a shout rent the air : " This lady from the ' land of the rising sun,' she knows everything ! " And during that one hour an influence was gained over those young men which under ordinary circumstances might not have been gained in years.

My duties in this settlement were not confined simply to teaching, but included the duties of pastor and pastor's wife. I visited the sick, ministered to the dying, helped the friends of the dead to prepare them for burial, and occasionally conducted a burial service.

During a blessed revival of religion in my school a number of the young people were converted, among

others a frail young girl who was greatly distressed
about her father, a backslider. I missed her from
school one day, went to her home, and found her very
ill with pneumonia. Day after day during the week I
was by her bedside, and I knew that she must die.
The one thought in her mind during all those days of
suffering was the spiritual condition of her father.
One day she said to me : —

" Do you think I shall die ? "

I said, " Yes, dear ; you will soon be with Jesus."
The cold sweat was already on her brow.

" How soon do you think it will be ? "

" Well, you may live an hour, and the time may
be less."

She said, " Please call my father."

He was outside the house in great sorrow, for he
loved this child devotedly. When he went into the
room she said : —

" Father, I want you to take me out by the brook.
I want to hear it sing once more."

He took her in his arms and carried her out beside
the little brook running by their house. She beckoned
me to follow.

" Father," said she, " I am going to leave you. I
am going home to Jesus, and when I get there I want
to tell him that my father prays. I want you to pray
now, father."

"I cannot do it, my child," said he. "I have not prayed for years."

"Pray just once, father, so I can tell Jesus as soon as I see him, ' My father prays.' "

The man could not resist the pleading of the child and began to pray. His heart was melted as he poured out the story of his sins before God. He seemed to forget the child in his arms, but I had been watching her, and while this honest prayer of penitence was going forth from the heart of the returning prodigal, her spirit winged its way to tell the glad news, "My father prays!"

One day I was called to the cabin of a pagan family who had utterly resisted all efforts to win them to the Jesus Way. One of the daughters had been permitted to come to the school, but seemed thus far unaffected by Christian influences. I had missed her from her accustomed seat, but as they lived quite a distance from the schoolhouse I had not been to look her up. One day the mother came to me and said : —

"My daughter is dying. We have made her graveclothes. She has seen them all and is satisfied with them."

It was a great comfort to the Indians in their last hours to be permitted to see the clothes in which they were to be buried. "But there is one thing," she

continued, "which we cannot make. She wants a pair
of lace sleeves like those she has seen you wear."

Some flowing lace sleeves, after the fashion of the
day, had been embroidered for me by my mother, and
I had occasionally worn them, to the great delight of
the Indians, who are very fond of embroidery. The
mother said : —

"We cannot make these sleeves for her. Can you
do it?"

I said, "Yes, I can do it; and I will do it upon
one condition."

"What is it?" said she eagerly.

"That I may embroider the sleeves by the side of
your daughter's bed, and that I may be allowed to
say to her just what I please."

"Do you mean," said she, "to talk to her about
the Jesus Way?"

"Yes, that is what I mean. I want to prepare her
to meet her God."

"It cannot be," said the pagan woman; and she
turned away sorrowfully.

This was hard for me, but I believed that through
the pleading of the daughter I should in the end be
allowed to have my own way. The daughter was in
consumption, and would probably linger for some
time. I must wait. In two days the mother returned
and said : —

" My daughter gives me no peace. She wants the sleeves for her burial."

I said, " She shall have them upon my conditions."

" Is there no other way?" said she.

" No other way," I replied.

"Then it shall be as you say," said the mother.

I had already sent by mail for the necessary materials that I might be ready for this opportunity, and at once went home with the mother. From that time I spent one hour each day by the bedside of the young girl, embroidering the lace, while she watched every stitch taken with the keenest interest. During that hour the room was filled with pagan women, also watching with fascinated eyes the progress of the embroidery, and I need not add that not one moment of the hour was lost in giving to this dying girl the message of the gospel, while her pagan friends were obliged to listen to the same truths. The result was that the dear child died a triumphant death through faith in Christ, and the women commenced from that time to attend the Mission church and to hear the regular preaching of the Word. We have reason to believe that they have all joined the redeemed throng on the other side.

The young men and women in my school were addicted to the free use of tobacco, to which the young men added fire water. The floor often looked as though afflicted with the smallpox. The only clean place in the whole room was the space about my desk, which they were all careful not to pollute. As soon as they could understand me, I made a rule, and printed it in large letters upon the blackboard. It was the first rule I had made in this school : —

DO NOT SPIT UPON THE FLOOR.

"What shall we do?" said the young people. "We cannot swallow this juice; it will kill us."

Tobacco is a very sacred herb with the Indians, and they are so fond of it that I knew it was useless to fight against the habit after the usual methods; so I said : —

"I have this floor scrubbed every three days. It takes a great deal of strength to do it, and it is very hard for me to see it soiled so quickly, and that is why I make this rule. I will tell you what you can do. When you come to the door of the schoolhouse take the tobacco out of your mouths and put it away somewhere, and during recess while you are out of the room you can have it again. In this way we will keep the floor of our schoolhouse white and clean."

It was very hard for them at first, but they persevered; and finding that they sometimes forgot the quid even at recess, I said : —

" Would it not be a good plan to keep your mouth as clean as the floor? "

One of them said, " I did not think I could get along without it one hour, and now sometimes it is not in my mouth during the whole day. I am willing to give it up, and have a clean mouth."

Then I helped them draw up a pledge to give up tobacco and fire water, which was signed by all the older pupils of the school. This was the first temperance society, and the people were greatly interested in it. We held temperance meetings and had temperance addresses and discussions by the young people both in Indian and English, in which the parents took great delight.

One of these young men was induced to join a company of white men to go " rafting," as they called it, upon the Alleghany River. These raftsmen, who were addicted to the free use of liquor, finally observed that the young Indian never tasted it. They asked him the reason. He said he belonged to a temperance club and had solemnly promised never to taste it again. They laughed him to scorn, and said : —

" We will soon teach you, you miserable redskin, how much such a promise is worth ! "

But in vain they tempted him. He would not yield. They were furious, and resolved to conquer his will by heroic measures. One day they handed him a glass of whiskey, but when he declined as usual they pushed him into the river. He swam to the edge of the raft, and taking hold of it begged them to let him come on board. They said : —

" Yes, if you will take the whiskey."

He replied, " I cannot break my promise."

Then they unloosed his fingers from the edge of the raft, and pushed him away from it. He was getting exhausted and sank ; rising to the surface again he clung once more to the raft.

" Will you take the whiskey ? " said the men.

" I cannot break my promise," said the Indian.

Again they loosened his hold upon the raft, and again he sank, to rise no more. I do not think the men intended to murder him, for they were too intoxicated to realize their cruelty or to plan such a crime ; but in the sight of God, that young Indian was a martyr to the truth.

When the Indians wish to confer a very great honor upon a missionary, they adopt him into the tribe and give him an Indian name. I shall not soon forget the day when this honor was conferred upon me. A mass meeting was called and preparations made for a great feast. There were many kettles of boiling *o-nooh-gwah* — a stew of corn, beans, potatoes, turnips, carrots, onions, etc., with a plentiful supply of salt pork. I was placed upon a rude platform where every one of those piercing black eyes could watch me. An old sachem stood by my side talking in Indian, while the audience responded at intervals in an exclamatory affirmative. His speech, being interpreted, was as follows : —

"Our sister, we believe you to be our friend, and we now proceed to adopt you into our nation. We shall call you from this time forth *Go-wah-dah-dyah-seh* (She pushes us ahead).

"We give you an Indian mother and father, sisters and brothers. If they are sick, you must nurse them ; if they are in trouble, you must comfort them ; if they have good fortune, you must rejoice with them ; if they are poor, you must give them money ; and they must do the same by you."

These relatives were then separately brought forward and introduced to me. I had many opportunities in the months and years following to fulfill my obligations to them, and I am glad to testify that from them I have always received the affection and kindness which they give to one who really belongs to them.

After the speech I was invited to partake of the feast, — the *o-nooh-gwah*, — which was served in wooden bowls and eaten with large wooden spoons or ladles.

After two years of this delightful missionary service it occurred to my father and mother that they ought to see where and how their young daughter was living; and so they took a journey to the Reservation. They came to my Indian home. I had never written to them the details as to my accommodations, simply telling them about the missionary work. While the privations and inconveniences of the life seemed hardly worth noticing to the enthusiastic young girl, to my parents, fresh from city privileges, they seemed unendurable. And within an hour I was told to pack my trunk and go home with them. My mother said : —

"I shall never sleep another night, thinking of the life you are living here."

In vain I remonstrated, in vain I set before her my love for the people and their love for me. I was taken home, and kept there until dear Mrs. Wright wrote to my mother, "If you will intrust your daughter to my care, she shall become a member of my family, and live under the shelter of the Mission House."

This new arrangement took me nine miles away from my first field of labor and I found myself among new environments and more comfortably situated; but the attachment to my "first love" never waned.

The Missionary Board soon invited me to become a general missionary having the whole Reservation as my field. And so it came to pass that my days were spent with Mrs. Wright visiting from house to house, holding meetings, and carrying the glad message in all directions among these people. I was furnished with horses, wagon, saddle, and in fact whatever was needed to aid in the general missionary work; and the rest of my life on this Reservation was one of constant companionship with her who gave me the devotion of a mother, and to whom I returned the loyal affection of a daughter. In all the happy years that followed we were seldom separated, and the lessons which the young girl learned from this noble, consecrated woman have influenced all my later life.

FIREFLY, firefly, bright little thing,
Light me to bed and my song I will sing,
Give me your light as you fly o'er my head,
That I may merrily go to my bed.
Give me your light o'er the grass as you creep,
That I may joyfully go to my sleep.
Come, little firefly — come, little beast!
Come, and I'll make you to-morrow a feast.
Come, little candle that flies as I sing,
Bright little fairy bug — night's little king —
Come and I'll dance as you guide me along,
Come, and I'll pay you, my bug, with a song.

— Translation of a song by Indian children at play.

Thomas Asylum for Orphan and Destitute Indian Children, ca. 1870s. Laura Wright was instrumental in its founding in the mid-1850s. Operations were assumed by the state of New York in 1875, and the asylum was renamed as the Thomas Indian School. (William Pryor Letchworth Papers, Letchworth State Park, Castile NY.)

XI.

THE INDIAN ORPHAN ASYLUM.

SENECA MISSION, June 10, 1854.

Dear Husband, — How I wish I could see you this morning! What a blessed thing is entire confidence between husband and wife! What a comfort to know that though ever so widely separated, our hearts are the same, and we have no corroding fears of change there! You will think I am getting quite sentimental, and perhaps it will do me good to revive some such feelings. I sometimes think we have too much of real life, and need ·a little romance to quicken our sensibilities. I am thankful to subscribe myself, your loving wife,   LAURA M. WRIGHT.

IT pleased God to bring this devoted missionary, Mrs. Wright, into deeper experiences of real life and richer experiences of his grace. The summer following the short absence of Mr. Wright which furnished the wife another opportunity, as seen by the above letter, to give him a glimpse of her loyal, loving heart, was a season of extreme destitution and suffering throughout the Reservation. Mr. and Mrs. Wright, always active in seeking out and relieving the wants of the distressed, were appalled at the amount of sickness prevailing about them, and at their inability to extend adequate relief to the afflicted Indians, many of whom were actually dying of starvation. Early and late through these sad days, they labored on,

imploring pecuniary aid from such friends as they
could reach.   Before winter they painfully realized
that still greater suffering must ensue.   Then they
sent out more earnest appeals to the far and near.
The cry for help reached the ears, the heart, and
the pocket of a member of the Society of Friends,
Philip Thomas, who had previously manifested a
generous interest in the work.

Encouraged by promises of aid from this good man,
Mr. and Mrs. Wright received into their own family
ten sick and starving Indian children, thus assuming
in addition to their other labors a load of care equal
to their utmost capacity.   Is it possible for those who
live in luxury and ease, and general unresponsibility,
to comprehend such a sacrifice?   Thus began that
flourishing institution, the THOMAS ORPHAN ASYLUM,
for destitute Indian children, which is now so conspicuous an ornament upon the Cattaraugus Reservation.
This institution, an invaluable blessing to the whole
Six Nations of the Iroquois, stands to-day as one of
the many memorials of two consecrated lives.   But of
those who take such pride in the fine buildings, fitted
with all modern conveniences, the cultivated acres and
the lovely grounds, where one hundred Indian children
are comfortably sheltered and trained to be self-sup-
porting men and women, how many look back with
grateful remembrance to this self-sacrificing, noble

MISSION HOUSE, UPPER STATION.   The home of Mr. and Mrs. Wright.

man and woman, but for whose indefatigable labors, wise forethought, and judicious management there would be no refuge for the forsaken Indian child to-day!

How was it done? Philip Thomas, who represents that sect which has yet to make the first mistake in its management and treatment of the Indian, gave a generous start to this move which appealed so strongly to his judgment and charity, and which was to be under the guidance of Mr. and Mrs. Wright, in whose wise management he had unbounded confidence. Benevolent people in Buffalo and surrounding towns, through the efforts of the missionaries, were induced to follow suit. Then Mr. Wright went to Albany, and enduring much hardship there, at length obtained a small appropriation from the state. The next step was to secure a piece of land from the council of the Seneca nation, upon which a building might be erected. Through the unwearied efforts of these same missionaries, from whose vocabulary the words "rest" and "vacation" seem to have been wiped out, the building was at last erected, and great was the joy when the little Indian waifs, already gathered at the Mission House, were transplanted to the new asylum, only a few rods away, to be cared for by a motherly matron, who was to teach the girls all housewifely arts, while the boys were trained upon the farm by a practical Christian farmer.

The building accommodated one hundred children, and as the family steadily increased in numbers, a neat schoolhouse was placed upon the grounds, and under the care of Christian teachers these children received the advantages of a district school. At the age of fifteen they were placed in the families of Christian people in neighboring towns, who promised to care for them as for their own. In a multitude of cases this promise was faithfully fulfilled.

But the rapidly increasing family demands a larger appropriation, else these little waifs must return to the terrible life from which they have been rescued; and again the patient missionary assumes the (to his sensitive nature) distasteful task of appearing before the legislature at Albany to solicit an increased appropriation. While on this mission his courage is strengthened by daily letters from one who fully appreciates the difficulties of his position.

SENECA MISSION, February 24, 1859.

My dearest Husband, — You don't know how I hate to have you away so long, but I feel perfectly willing you should go, if anything can be done for the Asylum, for I am confident that it must go down soon unless something can be done. I feel that I could make almost any sacrifice to save the institution, but you must not think that I am making any sacrifice. I am not. It is you, and it is for your sake that I am troubled. Go in God's strength; believing that he who hears the young ravens when they cry will go with you and lead you in the right path and prosper your way before you. The hearts of all men are in God's hand and he can influence them as he shall see best. I hope and trust you will succeed. Be bold! Don't feel faint-hearted in this cause, because you know it is one in which any one can be bold. I want to say a great deal to help you, but you are well acquainted with the best sources of encouragement. Your loving wife,

LAURA M. WRIGHT.

In a few weeks Mr. Wright returned with the joyful intelligence that his petition had been granted, and the good work for the little ones was permitted to go on. A few incidents will suffice to show the need of such an institution and its blessed ministry to the Indian : —

Upon one of her missionary tours, Mrs. Wright was startled by the screams of a child which seemed to come from the bank of the creek. Hastening to the spot, she discovered an old Indian woman in the act of drowning a little boy. She held him under the water until life was nearly extinct. After rescuing the child from the woman and restoring him to life, Mrs. Wright asked the reason for such cruelty.

" I am his grandmother," said the old creature. "His father and mother are dead, and I am tired of him!"

Mrs. Wright wrapped the child in her shawl and drove to the asylum, where, after a warm bath and a bowl of bread and milk, he was tucked into a comfortable bed for the first time in his desolate little life. The first English words which he tried to say were

"Great many goods!" (good things) and with many a laugh he was frequently heard shouting these words, as he ran through the house or about the grounds.

An Indian mother, to whom life had brought nothing but suffering and hardship, resolved that her baby daughter should never travel the same hard road. Wrapping the babe in a small blanket, she walked to the nearest railroad, laid it upon the track, and went away. The engineer of the next train saw the bundle, and, stopping the train, picked it up, much surprised to find it alive. The baby was passed around among the passengers, until a lady, recognizing it as an Indian baby, offered to take it to the Indian Reservation. She brought it to Mrs. Wright, who gladly placed it among the orphaned babes in the asylum.

A wicked woman, whose child had been taken from her and placed in the asylum, stole it away one night. The child was wretched while traveling from place to place with her mother, who compelled her to beg. One night she escaped, and finding her way back to the asylum implored them to take her in. "And if my mother comes again, oh! hide me, I beg you, and be very stingy of me!"

One day Mrs. Wright saw a very strange-looking object before her on the road, which proved to be a small boy, dressed in the cast-off clothing of a man. Mrs. Wright spoke to him kindly and drew from him the sad fact that he had no home, no friends, but was kicked about from one place to another, and was suffering from cold and hunger. His little body proved the truth of his words, for it was well covered with black and blue spots. She placed him in the asylum, where he was clothed and fed, and slept for the first time within his memory in a warm bed. His gratitude to her was pathetic. Every time she entered the building he was sure to get near enough to take hold of her dress reverently, and say again and again in his own language, " I thank you! I thank you! I thank you!"

A pagan Indian and his wife lived happily together in a log house on a clearing which they had made in the woods. Four bright-eyed little ones were given them, to whom they were tenderly attached. One pleasant spring morning the mother rose early, and commenced pounding corn in a large wooden mortar, for the breakfast of her husband and children. These mortars may still be seen standing at the doors of the Indian homes. While pounding the corn, a little bird, attracted probably by the broken bits of corn about, hovered near her, and finally lighted upon her head. This incident struck terror to her heart, for the Indians believe it to be an omen of evil. After feeding the children she slung her basket upon her back, holding it in place by a large strap which she passed across her forehead, and started off on a journey of several miles to sell some beadwork and buy a few necessaries for her family. Toward night she returned, and before morning another little one was added to the group; but the Indian mother was very ill and knew that she must die. She said to a pagan neighbor who stood by her : —

" A few weeks ago Mrs. Wright was here. She told me about a wonderful Being who can take away our sins. I said to her that I would like him to take away my sins. Do you think that will help me, now that I must die?"

The sympathizing neighbor, as benighted as she, could only answer, " I do not know; I cannot tell you; " but she walked three miles to bring the lady who knew about this wonderful Being who could take away sin. When they arrived, the spirit of the mother had returned to God. Mrs. Wright tried to comfort the mourning husband, and offered to take the children with her to the asylum. With wild eyes he gathered them into his arms, and rudely bade her to leave the cabin. With a yearning pity she obeyed, but begged him to come to her when he needed a friend.

The poor man sustained the double office of nurse and housekeeper until the falling of the autumn leaves reminded him that through the approaching winter he could not alone provide for the wants of his children. Then, with quivering lips he came to the Mission House and begged Mrs. Wright to take his little flock. The next day the asylum team stood by the door of the cabin; Mrs. Wright found the children clinging to one another, with swollen eyes, while the father walked the floor with the youngest in his arms. The suffering face gave evidence of the struggle within. The missionary solemnly promised him that his children should be most tenderly cared for, and tried to lead his mind to that Saviour who loved the little ones. He said not one word, but taking each child separately from the house, he placed it in the wagon, and when the last had been put out of his arms, he begged them all to be good and obey their new protectors.

These children soon became much attached to their new home, and with simple faith accepted Jesus Christ as their Saviour. The father frequently visited them, and was by their little hands led into the Jesus Way.

One of the family in the asylum was a child deserted by pagan parents, because of troublesome ailments. Everything possible was done to relieve the child, but in vain.   She was a patient sufferer for a long time.   She seldom spoke to us in English, but on the night of her death, arousing from a stupor in which she had lain for hours, she pointed with her little, emaciated finger to the wall, and with her face aglow with a radiance not of earth, exclaimed : —

"See ! see ! "

"What do you see ? " was asked.

"Christ !   Christ ! " and immediately the spirit of this lamb of the spiritual fold took its flight to the arms of the heavenly Shepherd.

An Indian mother, a strong, healthy woman, who planted corn, carried heavy loads besides her baby upon her back, and supported a worthless husband, was taken suddenly ill.   Nobody knew what was the matter ; she was in great pain.   While her husband was chafing her hands she cried out, "O Ben, Ben, I am dying !   Don't let my baby starve ! " and in an instant she was quite dead.   The baby began to scream violently.   He strapped it upon his back and took the little three-year-old by the hand, and was about to start out to call the neighbors, the nearest of whom lived a quarter of a mile away.

"No," said the little girl, pulling back, "I shall stay by my mother."

The father lifted her upon the bed, and there the

child remained, keeping watch over the lifeless form until he returned.

After the funeral the little girl was placed in the asylum, and became a great pet there. But the father would not part with the baby! Through cold and wet and wind and rain that child was always strapped upon his back. Many and many a time you might have seen him with his baby in the saloons in some white settlement carousing with drunken companions, or reeling home. Such exposure proved too much for the little thing and it began to look very thin and haggard. Its large, bright eyes shone with a painful luster.

Finally, after a protracted season of intoxication, Ben brought the wasted baby to the asylum. It was almost starved to death; the sight of bread and milk made it nearly frantic. It had to be fed very carefully at first, but soon the little life, almost extinct, was brought back. The tiny creature began to put out its arms to every one who came near it with a happy smile.

Ben managed to live without his baby a few weeks and then, growing desperate, resolved to sign the pledge if we would give him back his treasure. He promised fair, but we did not dare to trust him until he should continue in the good way a while. He thought this very cruel treatment and one night he broke into the asylum, went softly upstairs, stole his baby, and departed for the Canada woods. When last heard from, Ben had reformed and was taking good care of his child.

The school connected with the asylum was taught by a faithful missionary teacher. There came a time when, in answer to earnest prayer, the Spirit of God seemed hovering over that Indian school. One morning the Bible lesson was upon the sufferings and death of Christ. Every little form was hushed into quiet, every eye was fixed in earnest inquiry upon the face of the teacher as she urged them to accept this wonderful Friend, who for love of them had given up his life.

"Poor forsaken ones!" thought the teacher. "Was there ever a flock who needed the tender care of the Shepherd more than my motherless ones?"

For they had been left friendless and homeless in the wide world, to perish by the wayside, or, worse, to become educated to every crime by surrounding influences; it had indeed been a blessed work to gather them into this Indian Orphan Asylum, where they were not only clothed and fed, but daily taught the sweet truths of the gospel.

The burden of these souls, a burden which God had

lately rolled upon her heart with new power, was becoming almost more than she could bear ; and in anguish of spirit she implored the Great Physician of souls to visit her Indian school. How her faith was strengthened when, during the exercises of the forenoon, a girl of twelve years stood before her with a glow of softened feeling upon her face !

" Teacher," said she, " I prayed to Jesus this morning."

" Did you?"

" Yes ; and Cora prayed with me."

" What did you and Cora tell Jesus?"

" We said we wanted new, clean hearts that would love him."

" And do you love him now?"

" Yes, ma'am ; " with childlike simplicity.

As each day witnessed new temptations to sin, overcome for the sake of pleasing Christ, their teacher felt that the good work had indeed commenced. She endeavored to place herself more entirely under the direction of the Holy Spirit, that she might wisely and faithfully guide these precious souls.

As the interest deepened, the exercises of the school were suspended during a part of one afternoon each week to hold a " children's meeting." It was thought not best to admit the younger classes to the first meeting of this kind, for fear they might make some disturbance. To tell the truth, the faith of this teacher was growing strong for her older pupils, but she had forgotten that her Saviour said, " Suffer the little ones"; and so they were sent away.

How she was rebuked the next day as one of these same " little ones" clasped her teacher's hand in both her own, and, looking into her face with earnest, thoughtful eyes, exclaimed in broken English, " You can't willing me to pray? I too little?"

With tears of contrition she took the child upon her lap, saying, " No, my child, you are not too little. Jesus will hear you; he has left some precious words on purpose for you."

From that time the teacher's faith was strong for the lambs. They were no longer excluded from the prayer meeting; and soon their sweet child voices were heard in petitions like these: " Dear Jesus, please give me new, clean heart." And do you suppose He who took the little ones in his arms and blessed them is deaf to such petitions as these? How delightful were the days and weeks that followed! The new love in those young hearts gave an earnest thoughtfulness to faces hitherto dull and listless. And while imparting useful knowledge to the mind, the constant prayer of the teacher was that the wants of each soul might never be neglected.

And now these Indian children have entered upon the Christian life. Is there any change in their habits? Do their lives shine? We shall see.

Stella Tallchief had naturally a quick temper. It was not an unusual thing during recitation to see her book taking wings in some unaccountable direction, because its owner had not thoroughly mastered her lesson.

One day she came to her teacher and said, " I have been giving my heart to Jesus. I want to be a Christian." Her teacher pointed out some failings which she must overcome if she would please Christ — among others, her ungovernable temper. Stella earnestly entered into the struggle against her besetting sin, and by much fervent prayer she seemed to gain strength each day to resist. But one day, not being "on guard," she fell, and for a few moments was overcome by her old enemy. After school she seemed overwhelmed with a sense of her sin, and begged her teacher to pray for her, which she did. Then Stella fell upon her face, and, when her sobs somewhat subsided, in a broken voice offered this prayer : —

" O Jesus, I 'm very wicked. Please make me good. Don't make me good little while. Please make me good all the time. O Jesus, my heart very bad. Please give me clean heart, all washed white with

Jesus' blood. Don't give me clean heart little while. I want it clean all the time. O Jesus, make me love thee. Please don't let me love thee little while. I want to love thee all the time."

One day Eva Sundown was left alone to sweep the schoolhouse. Having occasion to return, the teacher found the broom lying upon the floor and Eva sobbing violently.

" Why, my dear child, what is the matter?" exclaimed the teacher anxiously.

" Oh," sobbed the child, " I don't love Jesus enough! I'm a very wicked girl."

" What have you been doing, Eva?" asked the teacher gently.

" I got mad at some girls in school to-day."

" Did you strike them?"

" Oh, no, no!"

" Why, Eva, what did you do?"

" *I looked mad at them!*" said the child with a fresh burst of sobs.

" Was that all?" asked the teacher, much relieved.

" All?" cried Eva, looking straight into the teacher's eyes; " didn't you tell me that Jesus looks in my heart, to see if I really love him? Well, I was very mad in my heart. That's what made me look mad."

There, in the schoolhouse, the teacher knelt with the penitent child, and asked Jesus to forgive the sin and cleanse the little heart from everything which could grieve him. A little while after, happy Eva was busily plying the broom, and singing : —

"Jesus loves me, this I know,
For the Bible tells me so."

That God's Spirit was working upon their hearts is manifest from the following letters from some of these Indian orphan children.

The first one was written to a brother in the army : —

I will write to you few lines. Dear boy, you must try to do right always. You must pray to God to keep you from sin. God will hear you when you pray to him with a right heart. Don't be ashamed to do right. Go, doing good. God will help you if you ask him. I want you to be Christian, and go to meet me in heaven, when you die. Try to please him little things. Brother, get ready to die, and God will take you to heaven to meet your sisters and mother. And now, brother, good-by. Do all you can to please Jesus.

With a heart filled with gratitude for what Jesus had done for her own soul, this dear child could not rest until others were enjoying the same rich blessing. Her anxiety for a young friend who seemed not quite decided to give up all for Christ led her to write the following note one day, during school hours : —

Do you think that you love Jesus? I hope you do. I think that I love Jesus, but I want to love him better.

Won't you be a child of God? I want you to be a good girl. Maybe God will let us die to-night. Are you ready? I am ready, for he has cleansed me.

Now, won't you be a Christian? I am glad if you are trying to be Christ's lamb. I pray for you; will you remember me?

Here are other notes and letters which are self-explanatory : —

I pray in earnest. I want to be Jesus' lamb and follow him all the way to heaven. I pray very much for my brother who is not a Christian. I pray that I may not sin. I don't left out any days in my praying. I pray in the morning and afternoon and at night every day. I love my pray meeting. It comes every week on Monday. I am happy — I cannot help it — I sing because I am happy. I shall meet my mother and sister in heaven.

I did n't want to love Jesus once, but my sister — she ask Jesus to *make* me want to love him — and so he did. I don't want to be bad now, but sometimes Satan he tempt me to do wrong — and sometimes — I mind Satan. I feel bad then, but when I tell Jesus he forgives me, and I am happy in my heart again.

I am thinking about my *sins* this week. They trouble me. I do not sleep. To-day I thought, " Why, Jesus *did* forgive me sure! " I want to do right in every *little* thing. I shall be a very wicked child if Jesus does not help me.

You said you wanted us to tell the *littlest* child about Jesus. I have been telling little Helen Yellow Blanket. I feel so happy to do something for Jesus. Is n't he good to take us just as we are! I thought once — I don't know enough to love Jesus. He does n't care for *that !*

The following is from an Indian orphan girl to the missionary pastor : —

My dear Mr. Curtis, — I am feeling pretty bad to-night. I can never be happy again until I ask your forgiveness. I did play and whisper in meeting to-day. I am very sorry. I hope I shall never do such a wicked thing again. Will you forgive me? Will you pray that I may do right? I find it hard. When I think, Now I will surely do right, there are more temptations before me. I am trying to-night to seek the Saviour with all my heart. Oh, I wish I was as good as you! I could be happy if I was half as good.

Mr. Curtis, if you ever see me whispering in meeting again I want you to call my name right out in church. This will break me of it, I am sure. Will you try and forgive me? From your sorrowful little girl.

Oh, the friends of blessed memory who led these pagan children to Christ! Mr. and Mrs. Wright, Mr. and Mrs. Hall, Mr. and Mrs. N. H. Pierce; and those faithful missionary teachers, Misses Mary Kent, Cornelia Eddy, Katie Dole, Clara Dole, Sylvia Joslin, Mary Brown, and many others still held in grateful remembrance by those who were once sheltered in that happy Orphans' Home.

One day I visited the Indian Orphan School for the purpose of holding a prayer meeting with the boys. As we were about to open the meeting Blue Sky suddenly left his seat and, seizing his bow and arrows, was leaving the room. I called, "Blue Sky, wait a moment. Where are you going?"

"Going away," he replied, with Indian brevity.

"But why do you leave the meeting?"

"Can't be Christian no more—Satan—he tempt me—too much. Give it up!"

"O Blue Sky," I exclaimed, "come back! Go into the little room, and while we pray, you think about this question, and give me the answer when I come to you : Shall I give up Jesus and mind Satan? or shall I give up Satan and mind Jesus?"

The boys prayed that Blue Sky might decide for Jesus. When I opened the door of the little room, he exclaimed, "Me — can't give up Jesus — and mind Satan!"

We sent this boy away to school, and in course of time received the following letter : —

Dear Friends, — I like this place very well. I was homesick at first, but now I am happy. I have company now in my room — another boy. I read the Bible every day, night and morning, and when I get through with one chapter, then I kneel down and pray to our heavenly Father who takes care of me and keeps me from sin. It helps me — great deal.

But when that boy came here and when we got into our room, I had a great trouble in my mind. I did not know what to do. I was afraid to read my Bible and pray before that boy. This thought was in my mind about fifteen minutes. At last I said to the boy, "Do you ever pray?"

He said, "No!"

I had never seen him before; he is older than I am. When he said "No!" I felt more afraid. I was a coward before God for fifteen minutes.

Then God helped me. I made up my mind to keep right on just as I did before that boy came. I thought, "This is my duty. I must show that I am on the Lord's side, anyway!" Then it came to me what we used to sing at the Orphan Asylum : —

> Never be afraid to speak for Jesus,
> Think how much a word can do.
> Never be afraid to own your Saviour,
> He who loves and cares for you.

I thought about these words, and then I got the Bible off from the table and read a chapter in it. I said to the boy : —

"This is my way. I shall always do so. I shall read the Book and pray before we go to bed."

And so, when I got through reading, then I knelt down by the bed and I pray to our Father. And now I and that boy read the Bible every day—I pray. I feel happy now; but I came very near giving up to Satan.

Wi-yu's father and mother were pagans. She never heard a word about Jesus Christ until she came to the asylum. We were glad to take the children of pagans, even while both parents were living. One day Wi-yu (pronounced We-you) walked up to me and said: " I want to give myself away to you." I was much surprised, but looked into the little girl's black eyes, and said: " Why does Wi-yu wish to give herself to me?" "Because," said she simply, " I love you." After this, they all called Wi-yu my little girl.

One day while Wi-yu sat by my side learning how to hem a pocket handkerchief neatly, I asked her if she loved Jesus, of whom I had been talking to her. " No," she said, " I do not; but I want to. I want to be a Christian, but I'm too little."

" But Jesus says, ' Suffer the *little* children to come unto me.' "

" I don't know how to go to him: I don't know what to do," said she.

" Wi-yu," said I, " you must give yourself away to him." She looked at me in surprise.

" How can I do that?" she exclaimed.

" How did you give yourself away to *me?*"

"I came to you, and asked you to take me, because I love you."

"Why do you love me, dear?" She hesitated a moment, and then answered: "I think it must be because you love me."

"Yes, Wi-yu; that's just the reason. Now, Jesus has been loving you all this time, while you have not been caring in the least for him."

She stopped sewing and sat very still a while, thinking. I did not say a word, because I knew the Holy Spirit was teaching her. At last she said: —

"Would Jesus be willing for me to give myself away to him just as I did to you?"

"Certainly, my dear child; that is exactly what he wants you to do. He wants *all* of you, too. He wants your little feet to run for him, your lips and tongue to speak for him, and your whole heart to love him."

After some more quiet thinking, Wi-yu knelt by my side and said: "My dear Jesus, I give myself away to you. I give you my hands, my feet, my mouth, my tongue, and my heart; I give you all of myself. Please take me, dear Jesus." She arose and said: —

"Do you think he heard me?"

"I am sure of it," said I; "and you will find his answer in your little Testament." Together we found these precious words in her Indian Testament: "Any

one that cometh unto me, I will not thrust aside."
Believing that Jesus meant just what he said, she
from this moment knew that she was his own dear,
saved child.

A few days after this, I said to her : " Wi-yu, after
you had given yourself to me, did you try any harder
to please me ? "

" Oh, yes ! " said she, with a bright face, " I tried
to please you in everything — even in the very *little*
things."

" Are you willing to do anything that will please
Jesus ? "

" I think I am," she answered.

" Will you tell the other girls that you are now
trying to live a Christian life ? "

She hung her head and blushed. " I am ashamed
to tell them," said she.

" Were you ashamed to tell them that you had
given yourself to me ? "

" Oh, no, indeed ! "

" And yet, my Wi-yu, you are ashamed of Jesus,
your most precious Friend, your wonderful Friend,
who loves you so much, and who saves you from
your sins ! O Wi-yu ! Wi-yu ! Let us ask him now to
forgive you and to help you please him, even in this."

We knelt, and Wi-yu said, with a voice choking
with sobs : " My own dear Jesus, please forgive me

for being ashamed and afraid, and help me to tell them all that I have given myself away to you." When we arose, she said, " I can tell them now! I will tell everybody."

On her way to find her schoolmates, she met a minister who was visiting the Indians, and of whom she was very much afraid, because he was a stranger; but, mustering up all her courage, she looked up to him, and said : " I have given myself away to Jesus."

He was much surprised and touched as he thought of his own daughter at home, who knew so much more about Jesus than this Indian girl, and who had not yet begun to love him. He put his arm about our little timid Wi-yu, and said some very kind and helpful things to her. After this, she found it easier to tell them all, and even gained courage to write to her stern, pagan father, although she was quite sure he would be very angry with her. Here is a copy of the letter : —

My dear Father, — I have given myself away to Jesus, and I am not afraid nor ashamed to tell you of it. Your little Wi-yu.

Her father was alone when this message reached him, and nobody knows what he thought; but the very next Sabbath he walked several miles to the Mission church, and heard the missionary preach about this same Jesus to whom his little daughter had given herself ; and after that he kept coming, until he too became a Christian man, to the great joy of our Wi-yu.

Thus this Indian girl learned the most precious lesson that can ever be learned : how to give herself away to Jesus, how to trust him wholly, and how to obey him cheerfully and lovingly, no matter what he wishes her to do.

XII.

THE arrival of the mail was an event of intense
interest at the mission, but a letter from David
G. Eldridge, of Yarmouth, Massachusetts, telling us
that the gift of an old-fashioned chaise was on the
way, by canal, to the Reservation, caused great excitement. "Is it possible," said Mrs. Wright, "that at
last my poor head is to be protected from sun and
wind and rain and snow during our long drives!"
Mr. Wright dampened our ardor somewhat by a suggestion that the new vehicle might not take kindly to
the mud holes of the Indian roads.

When the chaise reached Buffalo some one had to
go after it with a horse, as the last thirty miles of its
journey were to be taken by land. Several Indians
volunteered to do this, so curious were they to see "a
wagon with two wheels and a cover."

The successful candidate returned with the chaise
in due time, and solemnly admonished all within the
sound of his voice to have nothing to do with this
"evil invention of the white man." The mode of harnessing a horse to the chaise differing from ordinary

harnessing, the bewildered charioteer found himself "looking into the sky" several times on the way home.

When Mrs. Wright and I were about to take our first chaise ride, we were particular to have the straps securely adjusted, lest we too should find ourselves suddenly "looking into the sky." At the start we were followed by an admiring crowd, but after a while in the solitude of the woods we were free to exult in the happy exchange of the hard, springless seat of the rickety, open wagon for the soft cushions and protecting cover of our New England chaise.

Alas! our exultation was short-lived. With the customary plunge into a mud hole stretching entirely across the road, Ruhama made safe passage to the other side; but the unlucky chaise remained in the center of that black sea, stuck fast, its thills thrown upward like imploring arms, its occupants "looking into the sky!" Ruhama stopped and, regarding us a moment in dignified surprise, began to nibble the surrounding bushes. After a somewhat prolonged discussion of "the way out" we were forced to submit to the inevitable, and, descending into the black sea, with some difficulty we brought the uplifted thills to a horizontal position, drew out the heavy chaise, attached it to the patient beast, and turned our faces homeward, passing through other holes with becoming caution. Arriving at the Mission House, we were glad to exchange our mud-soaked garments for something more respectable and comfortable.

Peter Twenty-Canoes was the great-grandson of a man who owned "many canoes"; yet this descendant was shiftless in the extreme. His love for fire water was his greatest affliction. King Alcohol led the man into a multitude of scrapes, and left him to find his way out as best he could.

One day, being overcome by an unusual spasm of industry, Mr. Twenty-Canoes borrowed a scythe, and resolved to work out a while. Alas! he could n't begin without his dram, which resulted in a fall upon the scythe, cutting open one side of his face, and entirely taking off his nose! It was a blessed accident to him, however, for it led to his reformation.

The ingenuity of our Indian was now taxed to its utmost to supply the very important feature which he had lost. While visiting at the Mission House one day, he observed some adhesive plaster with which Mrs. Wright was dressing a wound.

"That's the thing for me!" said Mr. Twenty-Canoes, with considerable energy. We gave him a small piece, which he immediately formed into a respectable nose, and fastened upon his face. The man was jubilant, and no longer walked among his fellow creatures noseless. This manufactured article was at times in quite a dilapidated condition, but on gala days it was fresh and new. Mr. Twenty-Canoes was fond of variety ; consequently, no two noses were of the same shape and size, which gave a refreshing diversity to the expression of his countenance.

This Indian was fond of exhibiting his little stock of English upon every available occasion. He scented a polysyllable a long way off, and brought it to bear upon his conversation in a way quite remarkable. He wrote me a note one day, in which he endeavored to express his appreciation of my worth to his people : —

Miss C.: Respected Sir, — I ask to know how long commence school again on our district. I ought not to been so negligence with my boy, and I had been recommend it, that you are mostly confidence missionary as than any others among Indians, that is to your capacity to instruct the Indians in the way to the morality, life, and perseverance for human intelligence. I know you will not afail and omission too much inform me the set time to commence school on our neighborhood.

Your respectable friend,
TWENTY-CANOES.

Mr. Twenty-Canoes kindly volunteered at one time to write a " begging paper " for an old woman to take to white people, and thereby obtain the necessaries of life. As the poor creature made her first effort with the missionaries, I had an opportunity to copy the manuscript verbatim.

BEGGING PAPER.

To all whom it may concern the bearer of Sally Silverheels which she is very old of age unable her to care of herself had no family to see her supported whosoever to do this thing to rendered unto or attribute towards the needy and indeficient the god will bless you for your great bounty of charity such thing as provision and she will be very thankfully to you give to her that article little money or clothing or anything.   TWENTY-CANOES.

Twenty-Canoes was once asked to assist in drawing up a Temperance Constitution. Of the ten articles, I have space for only three : —

1. This society shall always be open in prayer by some benevolent religious person.
2. If any member shall become intoxication, and accident occur, or death attack him in spirit condition, the society shall not be responsible for such person.
3. We shall assistance the sick, and furnish Doctor, and in case any member become mortality, furnish all necessary purposes for the funeral.

I had a Bible class of thirty young men. One of these had received a good education, and possessed an unusual degree of mental culture. He went into business in Buffalo and fell into bad company. From Buffalo he went to Chicago, only to pursue the same downward course. All this while the prayers of his mother and the missionaries followed him until the Lord directed his steps home to the Reservation for a vacation. He was very hard and even bitter toward all Christians. He was impelled to come into the old Bible class every Sabbath, where he would combat every religious truth uttered, in order to destroy its force upon the minds of others. He spoke freely of his own disbelief in the Bible and everything of the kind, quoting from infidel authors. A position was offered him in New York. He came to the Mission House and told me this.

"It will be your ruin," said I.

"Why?" he asked indignantly.

"My boy, you are like a poor boat out on the restless ocean with no compass or rudder. You will be drifted about just as your master, the devil, shall choose."

He started to his feet, his eyes flashing. "You want me to be a Christian," said he. "How can I be a Christian when I believe nothing of your religion? I will not deceive you. I have not a particle of feeling. I could die calmly this moment. It would be mockery to accept a Saviour of whom I feel no need — in whom I do not believe even intellectually."

My heart went out in great pity as I looked at him, but it was time for our weekly missionary meeting, held in the Mission Home. Mrs. Wright was calling me even then. As I turned to leave him I said: —

"You are going away. I shall not have another opportunity to ask a favor of you. Grant me this one to-night. Go into the prayer meeting with me."

He laughed and exclaimed, "What a ridiculous idea!"

"Never mind," said I; "go with me to-night."

"Well, just to please you, I will do it," said he.

Great was the surprise of the missionary band to see the young infidel in that sacred spot. He took a chair, tipped it back against the wall, and prepared to be an amused spectator. I was so overwhelmed with the sense of his condition that I knelt immediately and prayed for a young friend who boasted of his want of feeling, and I entreated the Lord to strike conviction to that heart even then. Others followed in the same strain until the poor young man could hold up his head no longer, but buried his face in his hands.

As soon as the meeting was over he vanished. I saw no more of him for several days, and supposed he had gone to New York. One afternoon he appeared at the Mission House and said, "I want to see you alone."

His face was haggard, his eyes wild, as though sleep had been a stranger to them. He walked back and forth a few times, trying to control his voice, and finally said : —

"I have had no peace in my mind since the night of the prayer meeting; no peace night or day. I cannot sleep. Tell me how you found the Saviour, for I must find him or lose my reason."

Oh, the mighty power of the Holy Spirit to convict a stony heart! I pointed him to Jesus as well as I could.

" Oh, yes," he said, as I told the story of my own conversion ; " it was easy for you to come to Jesus ; but you never knew sin as I have."

" But, my boy, he saves the chief of sinners." I then read the passage proving that although his sins were as scarlet they could be white like snow.

" But you don't know," said he, " to what depths of sin I went in Buffalo and Chicago. I drank and I gambled. Oh, I have been a terrible sinner ! "

" Yet there is mercy for you," I said, as I continued giving him messages from God's own Word, knowing well that this was too solemn an occasion to use words of my own. At last he knelt with me and surrendered all to Christ. " My heart, my hands, my feet, my all, just as I am," he cried, and found peace in believing. Great joy came to him then. The great love of Christ seemed wonderful to him.

" Why have I waited so long," he exclaimed, " so long, and wasted all these years, when they might have been given to Jesus ? " He was only twenty-one years of age.

That night when he went home his mother had retired and was asleep. He burst into her room and roused her with these words : —

"O mother, mother, I have found the Saviour!"

What sweeter sound could have greeted the ears of the praying mother? He knelt by her bed, she threw her arms about him, and together they talked and prayed until the day dawned. When he told me of this afterward he said: —

"I saw a look in my dear mother's tired eyes the next morning that I never saw there before."

The next Monday evening he attended our prayer meeting at the Mission, and here in broken accents confessed that conviction entered his soul even while we were in prayer.

It occurred to the missionaries that it might promote good fellowship between the Indian and white man to hold a social picnic together. Invitations were sent to prominent people in Buffalo and other cities to become the guests of the Indians upon this occasion. The president of the day was Henry Two-Guns, a stepson of Red Jacket; the vice-president, Dr. Peter Wilson; the marshal, Nicholson H. Parker, brother of General Ely Parker. The brass bands were entirely composed of Indians.

Nathaniel Thayer Strong, known to the Indians as "Chief Honondeuh," was elected orator. As he had a fine command of English he was asked to speak in that language. Words are inadequate to describe the condition of mind with which we listened to the following outburst addressed to our guests : —

Ladies and gentlemen : In some respects the present occasion is extraordinary.　Never before did the white man with his women and children meet the red man with his women and children in a social picnic. It is an occasion to make our hearts glad, and I would like for a moment to present the past condition and relationships of the two nations in contrast with the present.

As we all know, the red men were the first occupants of this soil.　In 1647 the Confederacy of the Six Nations of the Long House was able to raise thirty thousand warriors.　War and the sports of the chase were the pursuits of the red man.　Their clothing was made of the skins of the animals they killed in the chase ; their food was the flesh of wild animals ; the corn and beans and squashes were raised by the women, and the labor of the lodge was all performed by them.　The possessions of the Iroquois had extended far to the south and west, and their name was a terror among all the surrounding nations.　They roamed from river to river and from valley to plain in pursuit of the buffalo, the bear, and the elk ; they darted across our lakes and rivers in their light canoes to find the beaver and the otter and to take their furs.

At appointed seasons they returned to the council fires of the Six Nations for the transaction of public business, and to keep the annual feasts. More than a hundred years afterward (in 1776) we find them greatly reduced in numbers, only about twelve thousand, though their customs are the same.

Ladies and gentlemen, let us look at the white man in the same periods. In 1647 they had only three hundred all told who were capable of bearing arms. They had a system of government and written laws. Their religion was founded upon the Bible; they knew the value and use of money; they knew that land was better than money, and they made every effort to obtain it. The white man bought it of his red brother and paid him little or nothing. He bought our furs too at his own price.

In 1776 the white man numbers two hundred thousand. Forests have fallen before the woodsmen; the game has retreated until both have nearly disappeared. The land of the red man became cultivated. The white man built cities, towns, villages; he built churches, colleges, academies, and common schools.

You have made canals and railroads, and your electric telegraph sends the news with the speed of thought. This is wonderful. The red man cannot comprehend it. Your commerce extends over the world. Your ships are on every sea; your steamers are on every river. In two hundred years your population has increased from six thousand to three millions.

Allow me to ask what price did the red man receive for all this broad domain? Allow me to read you a public document : —

" By these presents we do for ourselves and our successors, ratify, confirm, grant, and submit unto our most sovereign lord, King George, by the grace of God King of Great Britain, defender of the faith, all the land lying between " — here follows a description of the premises, including lakes, rivers, etc., of our land — *never paying a cent for it !*

Ladies and gentlemen, you see from this that your forefathers wronged the red man, and took advantage of his ignorance. The red man has a long history of wrongs and grievances ; though unrecorded by the hand of man they are written in the great Book of Remembrance kept by the Great Spirit, and he will inquire into this at your hands by-and-by, and he will do justice to his red children.

Ladies and gentlemen, I appeal to you whether we are not entitled to your sympathy, whether we have not claims upon your assistance, while we try to raise ourselves from the condition in which ignorance and prejudice have sunk our nation. The red man is aware of his condition — he feels it deeply — he feels an alien from the Commonwealth. There are no monuments to commemorate the deeds of our fore-fathers, but there are the mighty rivers and the eternal hills which we have named.

Ladies and gentlemen, the Six Nations of the Iroquois are now represented before you. The president of the day is a Seneca, the vice-president on his right is a Cayuga, and on the left you see an Onondaga. In this audience are representatives of the Mohawk and the Oneida. One of your own poets has said that music hath charms to soothe the savage breast. Here is a band of musicians delighting us with their sweet strains, composed entirely of the descendants of Senecas and Tuscaroras; and I doubt not they have gratified even civilized ears.

Ladies and gentlemen, you perceive we are changed. We have schools and books and churches, and are fast adopting the customs of white men. For these improvements we are indebted to Mr. and Mrs. Wright and other missionaries of the American Board. Great is our debt of gratitude to these persevering and devoted men and women. If you will but extend to us the right hand of fellowship, we shall abundantly reward your efforts, and you will at least see among us a state of cultivation and refinement. The missionaries have not made a great noise by blowing of the trumpet, but quietly and peaceably they have gone about among us doing good, and may they live to see fulfilled their most cherished hopes, and answered their fervent prayers!

SENECA INDIAN NAMES.

HALFTOWN.	TWENTY-CANOES.	SILVERHEELS.
WHEELBARROW.	CORNPLANTER.	LONGFINGER.
BLUE SKY.	BLACK SNAKE.	SUNDOWN.
DESTROYTOWN.	TALLCHIEF.	BIG KETTLE.
RED JACKET.	PORCUPINE.	CORNFIELD.
GREYBEARD.	YELLOW BLANKET.	GREEN BLANKET.
STEEP ROCK.	FISH HOOK.	DEER FOOT.
CASTILE SOAP.	BIG TREE.	GHASTLY DARKNESS.

IT must be acknowleged that much of the romance of the ancient Indian character has passed away. The wigwam of so much historic interest has vanished, and the Indian has become reconciled to a sheltering roof. They used to say : —

"It is a shame to cover the top of our wigwam so that the Good Ruler cannot look down upon his children in their home life."

For the same reason the top of the head was never covered. "It is a shame," said they, "to conceal the thoughts passing through the brain from the Good Ruler who is our Great Father."

The time-renowned skins and fur are replaced by broadcloth and calico. Venison is supplanted by beef and pork. Formerly a hoe in the hand of an Indian brave was a terrible disgrace; now a hoe in the hand of an Indian woman is quite unfashionable.

XIII.

AMONG THE PAGANS.

THUS far we have followed Mrs. Wright in her everyday life among the Christian Indians. Not all, however, who belonged to the "Christian party" were believers in Christ. Many who called themselves Christians had simply ceased to believe in paganism through having lost faith in Handsome Lake, the pagan prophet.

About one third of this Indian nation, however, still held to the old pagan belief. These lived in settlements by themselves apart from the missionaries and Christian Indians, and faithfully observed the old rites, including all the feasts and dances. Many of these rites are observed there to this day. The dance house was located at New-town, the stronghold of paganism. The people of this settlement were so prejudiced against Christianity that they resisted every effort to win them to the Jesus Way. The pagan leaders declared that the Name should never be spoken there. Two men were required to locate their cabins on each side of the entrance to this settlement, and turn

back any one who came to bring the white man's
religion.

Mrs. Wright's heart yearned with unspeakable
anxiety over these souls who thus condemned themselves to the darkness of ignorance and pagan superstition. They must be reached. But how? Many
plans were discussed, and much earnest prayer offered
that a way might be opened — and it *was* opened,
quite unexpectedly, and not in the least according to
our planning.

While on a trip home to Boston I attended the
Sunday-school in West Newton, then under the care of
Mr. B. F. Whittemore. The children had decided to
purchase a new organ, and were about to consign a
small melodeon to the cellar of the church. I asked
for it to use among the Indians. The request was
cheerfully granted, and soon after I returned to the
Reservation with my prize.

One Sabbath afternoon Mrs. Wright and I started
with the old Mission horse and wagon for Newtown,
the stronghold of paganism. In the back of the
wagon was the little melodeon given by the Sunday-
school children. We drove three miles and ascended
the long steep hill to the pagan settlement. The men
at the top came out and said : —

" You cannot come here. We do not wish to hear
anything about your Jesus Way."

Do'syową Ganǫk'dayąh, Oh noot'ah 22, 1843.

Degaisdóãgǫh 7.

"Neh nonąh dąhsat'haak neh ąsa'gwih'sek neh nonąh ąh-sąndah ąsa'yahda'nonąk : neh nonąh ąhseh ąsáwą nąh'sek.

"Nesąhąh ne gai'wihsáhǫh, yontchisdodah'gwah ; nehkuh ne gaya'neshąh, deyiúhhatheh; nehkuh nonda'detgẹhąhdanih na'yagúhnigǫh'dahet nehhuh heyuthai'nehsǫh ne yǫhhehǫweh.

Oyadǫhshádǫgãhdihgeh tgáwąnągwãh nehhǫǫweh, ne Proverbs 6: 22, 23.

THE MENTAL ELEVATOR.

Buffalo-Creek Reservation, April 22, 1843.

Number 7.

"When thou goest, it shall lead thee ; when thou sleepest, it shall keep thee ; and when thou awakest, it shall talk with thee.

"For the commandment is a lamp ; and the law is light; and reproofs of instruction are the way of life."—Proverbs vi : 22, 23.

(Printed at the Seneca Mission-House.)

Mental Elevator, no. 7 (1846). Nineteen issues of the *Mental Elevator* were published in Seneca, and sometimes English, between 1841 and 1850 at Buffalo Creek and Cattaraugus. Its primary purpose was to print Seneca translations of the Bible, which were prepared by Rev. Wright and his Native helpers. (Private collection.)

As we turned to go down the hill, the men noticed the box in the back of our wagon and their curiosity was excited. This was what we had anticipated, for although he holds himself under such perfect control, the Indian has as much curiosity as the white man.

" What is in that box? " said one of them.

" That is a most wonderful box," I replied. " You never saw so wonderful a box."

" Open it," said he, " and let us look into it."

I said, " I will if you will let us pass by and go to the dance house."

" We cannot let you do that," said he with a dark look.

" Then we must go home," I said.

" But you will open the box first."

" No," said I, " I cannot open the box here. I will open the box only at the dance house."

" Wait ! " he said, and ran to the dance house and consulted the pagan leaders.

" They have," said he, " in their wagon a wonderful box which they will not open unless permitted to pass in and come to the dance house."

After long consultation the pagan chiefs decided to let us come, that the wonderful box might be opened before all the people there assembled. And so the offering of the Sunday-school children opened the way for us to reach these pagans. We immediately took the instrument from the wagon and set it up on the ground. I had brought a stool with me and sat down and began to play. They had never heard such sounds before. Indians are naturally fond of music and they were captivated by the sweet tones of this little instrument. Mrs. Wright and I, hoping by means of the musical missionary to reach them, had prepared some Indian hymns which contained the simple truths of the gospel. We sang one of these hymns. They listened in breathless silence, and shouted, "The wonderful box speaks! It speaks! Let it speak again!" We sang another hymn. They cried, "*Ahsoh! ah-soh!*" (Another! another!) After a while we closed the melodeon, put it into the wagon, and started for home. They followed us in crowds, crying, —

"Will you come again, and bring the wonderful box, and sing to us?"

We said, "Yes; we will come next Sunday."

What were these pagans doing when we passed the guard and came to the dance house? Perhaps I should say here that the pagan dance house is a building about forty feet long by thirty feet wide. There is an immense fireplace at each end. Seats are arranged around the sides, one tier above another. The house will accommodate about four hundred people. The only furniture upon the floor of the house is a long low bench. When about to have a dance the people arrange themselves upon these tiers of seats. When the house is full a man comes in with an Indian drum, seats himself upon the low bench in the center of the hall, and begins to beat the drum. Soon another man comes in, with a turtle-shell rattle. The turtle is a sacred animal with these Indians, and always used in their religious festivities. The animal is killed, the legs cut off, the inside removed, and the shell filled with pebbles; the neck is drawn out and tightly wound with catgut, furnishing the handle of the instrument. While the first man beats the drum, the second man shakes the turtle-shell rattle, and a third man joins them with a squash rattle. Three men now take their places beside these, who commence to sing the weird Indian songs. This Indian orchestra now being complete, the Indian maidens come from the sides and form a line around them and commence to dance to the measured and monotonous beat of the Indian drum, the shaking of the rattles, and the sudden shrieks of the singers. It is difficult to describe the step of this dance. They do not lift their feet from the floor, but shove them with a certain peculiar movement in perfect time to the music. When this circle is complete the mothers descend from the seats at the side and form a second ring, dancing around the first with the same peculiar movement. When that line is complete the fathers form a third circle with the same movement. The fourth circle is now formed by the young warriors, who, with wild shrieks, and tomahawks brandished in the air, leap around the other three circles. At this time it becomes very exciting and those who are left upon the benches shout with delight. The performers are dressed in gala attire, plentifully ornamented with beads, brooches, and feathers. The young warriors have painted their faces. The scene is exciting and frightful to a stranger. Outside upon the ground there are various games in progress, and here and there the Indian kettle in which their favorite soup is being prepared for the feast hangs over the fire.

The next Sabbath we went again to this pagan settlement, and received a warm welcome, with eager requests to open the wonderful box and sing. This we did for several Sabbaths, always singing the simple truths of the gospel. Had we spoken one word about the " Jesus Way," we should have been obliged to leave at once. But we were only too happy to be permitted to *sing* the glad tidings to this people.

The Missionary Board had built a schoolhouse near this settlement with the hope that the people would allow their children to go to school, but so far its very existence had been ignored.

One Sabbath, after singing several hymns, we said : " Next time we shall go to the schoolhouse over there in the woods."

They were very indignant, and with angry faces declared that we must not go, because they could not follow us there.

We said, " We shall go there next Sabbath with the wonderful box, and you can do as you please about following us."

So on the next Sabbath, when they ran to greet us as we ascended the hill, we kept on our way toward the schoolhouse. They shouted to us to stop there by the dance house, but we shook our heads and passed on. This was more than they could bear, and they followed us in crowds to the schoolhouse, packed it full, and stood upon the outside peering in at the low windows. Again we sang the hymns. Mrs. Wright said : —

" It is now time to hold meetings with these people, and I will open this one with prayer."

I said, " You do not know what will happen if you do this."

She answered quietly, " God will take care of us."

She knelt in prayer. When these people saw that woman on her knees, there was a strange hush for a moment, and then in a body they started for the door; those who could not get out by the door quickly leaped through the windows, and when she arose from her knees we were alone. There was no one to be seen in any direction. I put my fingers upon the keys of the little instrument, and as soon as the sounds floated out upon the air they rushed in, and again filled the house. It was a moving audience that we had for several Sabbaths. If we did anything but sing they left us, but the wonderful little box could always bring them back again.

At last one Sabbath Mrs. Wright said, " Would you like to hear the story of how this earth was made?"

" Yes, yes!" they shouted.

Then she told them the story as given in Genesis. She spoke of the earth as being round. Mr. Cornplanter arose, and said in Indian: —

" Stop! You have made a great mistake. This earth is flat and rests upon the back of the great sacred Turtle. How could he hold it if it was round? It would certainly roll off. I should suppose," he continued, " that one need only look from these windows to know that this earth is flat."

She did not contradict him but went on with the story. She spoke of the great and good God as creating all things. Mr. Longfinger arose and said:

" Stop! stop!"

" What is it, brother ? " said she.

" You have insulted Ha-wen-ni-yu, the Good Ruler."

" How have I insulted him ? " asked she calmly.

" You say he made all things. He never made anything evil that would hurt his children. He never made bad people, or the cruel animals that would destroy us, or the poisonous herbs that would kill us. Ha-wen-ni-yu made only good people, the beautiful trees and flowers, and the herbs that we use when we are sick, and the animals that are useful to us."

" Well, Longfinger," said Mrs. Wright, " who did make all these things that we do not like ? "

" The Evil-Minded, his brother, made them," said the man.

The next Sunday, when we came to the school-house, after the usual songs the people asked for another story. Mrs. Wright resolved then and there to tell them the story of Christ. But knowing the consequences if they realized this, she used no names at the beginning. She told the story of a beautiful babe, who was born in an Oriental country. She described the surroundings. She told them about the wicked king, the shepherds, the wise men, and the wonderful star. She told them about the childhood of Christ; his three years of loving service for the people ; how he healed the sick, made the blind to see, the lame to walk, the deaf to hear, and at last she told

of his cruel death and that he was the Son of God.
They listened intently.   After she sat down old Silverheels arose and´said : —

" That is a story of great interest, but it is a shame
that the white man should have murdered a son of the
Good Ruler, Ha-wen-ni-yu.   It is a dreadful thing.
I am glad that we Indians had nothing to do with it.
It is none of our affair.   We would not have killed
him ; we would have treated him well.   The white
men who killed the son of Ha-wen-ni-yu ought to be
terribly punished.   The Great Ruler will punish them.
He will be revenged on them.   You must make amends
for this great crime yourselves."

Then she told them that this was the Christ of
the Indians too, of whom we had sung to them these
many Sabbaths.   The leaders were very angry, and
said : —

" You shall never come here again."

The young people, who had been growing more
and more attached to us, said, " They shall come
here again.   We want to hear more about this Jesus
Way."

The leaders said, " If they come here again, we will
throw them from the top of the cliff upon the rocks in
the river below."

The young people said, "You shall not harm them,
for we will protect them."

This discussion grew more and more exciting, re-sulting in long speeches on both sides, which kept us in that house until two o'clock in the morning. Neither of us said one word through the whole of it. I sat at the melodeon and Mrs. Wright by my side. Although we realized our danger, we were enabled to maintain a calm exterior.

When at last the meeting broke up the young men went out with us, and stood about our wagon until we were ready to start. We began to dread the long, dark, dangerous way home through the woods, through mud holes, over broken bridges, through streams which we had to ford. We need not have trembled, for the angel of the Lord was even then encamped round about us to protect us from evil. Twelve of these young Indian pagans had secured pitch-pine torches and were making preparations tò go with us.

A picture for an artist! Two lone women, the old Mission horses and wagon, the dense forest on either side, the young Indians in a variety of indescribable costumes, with their long hair streaming in the wind, running before, behind, and on either side, holding high the torches and singing the Christian songs taught them by us. They placed themselves about us as we started and followed us all the way home, giving us their protection and the light of the torches.

From that time until there was no more danger this bodyguard with their pine torches always ran beside us on our way home, when we had held an evening meeting in the pagan settlement.

At Christmas time we had the audacity and faith to ask for the use of the *pagan dance house* in which to hold a Christmas festival. This produced the most profound excitement. The leaders declared that those sacred walls should never be so disgraced. The young men said we should be admitted. The old men would not give up the key to the house. The young men took it by force, and, following our directions, secured two large hemlock trees and placed them in each end of the house, and invited us to fill them and defended us while doing it.

Boston friends sent me at that time two hundred dollars in money, and several boxes of valuable articles for this occasion. Every pagan of the settlement was remembered with some useful present. With a part of the money we bought provisions and gave them a great dinner. We noticed that as soon as the doors of the dance house were thrown open to the people, the angry leaders were ready to enter with the rest and to accept the valuable gifts which we had prepared for them. There only one moment of friction during the day, and that was when a young clergyman whom we had invited to come insisted upon offering prayer. We knew well how hard it would be for these pagan leaders to endure this, and so we interfered and begged the good man to allow us to *sing* a prayer, which was perfectly satisfactory to all parties.

Of course the little melodeon, which had been the means of opening the door to this great opportunity, was placed in the center of the hall, and by the grateful young people, who loved it as a human being, was gorgeously decorated with hemlock boughs and a profusion of red berries.

This festival gave us great power in that community, and although the leaders declined to enter the Jesus Way, their bitter opposition to us was much modified.

Through the blessed offering of the Sunday-school children, the little melodeon, we were able to enter another pagan neighborhood called, because of a dilapidated plank road, the Plank Road neighborhood. Here we ventured to take possession of an empty log house, where we invited the people to meet us every Thursday evening and hear about the " Shining Jesus Way." Of course they came at first simply to see the wonderful box and to hear the music ; but we asked that through this means they might receive light.

One Thursday evening the weather was intensely cold and the snow so deep that our courage nearly failed us ; but the thought of those poor, benighted ones impelled us to go forward in the work ; and so the two steady missionary horses, Roxana and Ruhama, — named for two of Mrs. Stowe's characters who went about doing good, — were attached to the sleigh and brought to the door. The missionary sleigh was simply a long box upon runners. This box was well filled with straw, upon which we sat, because less exposed to the cold than upon boards laid across the top. The melodeon was first placed carefully in the sleigh ; then came our missionary bag, our companion on all excursions. This bag contained straps, bits of rope, twine, hammer and nails, a gimlet, a buggy wrench, bread, chalk, medicine, a teaspoon, Indian hymn books and Indian Testaments, matches and candles, lint and linen bandages, adhesive plaster, bright picture papers, a tin horn, cookies and sugar-plums to keep the babies quiet while we talked with the mothers. This seems a strange medley, but in many places, far from human habitations, our bag was invaluable.

Upon this particular Thursday evening, being fully equipped as I have described, we started for our log house in the woods. It was a terrible night for the horses on account of the icy roads. We were really suffering from the cold when we drove up to the house.

" No light ! " said I.

" Perhaps," said Mrs. Wright, " Castile has no oil. I have brought a small can with me and we will fill the lamp."

Castile Soap was the name of the Indian who pretended to take care of our house and have it lighted and warm for us every Thursday. I use the word *pretended* significantly for, alas ! Castile had failed us this time, as many a time before. After securing our horses we were obliged to climb a rail fence and jump into the snow upon the other side, which was not pleasant. We reached the door, shivering uncomfortably ; it was fastened. Our missionary bag yielded a key. Once within the house you might suppose our troubles at an end. Far from it. There was not a dry chip upon the premises with which to kindle a fire. Outside under the snow we found a few sticks of green wood. These we placed in the stove and by pouring oil over them succeeded in forcing a blaze — an example not to be followed under ordinary circumstances. Having no bell, we resorted, as usual, to our powerful tin horn, which made the woods resound with its shrill note, and from various directions our pagan friends assembled. To our great surprise Logan came with them. Now Logan was a powerful chief

among the pagans, and had been decidedly opposed
to us. The fierce scowl and flash of his eye boded
no good. Mrs. Wright and I inwardly asked for
heavenly guidance and proceeded with the meeting.
We sang and prayed and talked. Finally Chief
Logan arose. I wish I could describe this man, but
such a face as his beggars description. You might
imagine him, scalping knife in hand, looking upon
his victim as he looked upon us that night.

"You white women!" said he, "you who come
here and disturb us in the religion of our fathers, I
wish you would let us alone." This was said with
great emphasis. "I suppose you are good enough in
your way. You visit the sick and you take care of
the poor. All that is well enough. But you break up
our dances. I wish you would let us alone! We like
your singing, but we don't want your meetings. We
do not like your praying and talking. Now I am
resolved what to do. You want these children to go
to school. If you do not stop your meetings, these
children shall never go to school. Now, there is a
bargain. Stop your meetings, and we will let these
children go to school; go on with your meetings and
these children will never know anything and you will
be to blame."

This logic caused a smile to quiver upon my lips,
but, noting an additional touch of fierceness in his

manner, and a quick flash of the eye, I subsided into an attitude of grave attention.

" Now," continued Logan, " I have resolved that if you keep on coming here with your meetings " (always alluding to our meetings as to some commodity taken with us or left, at pleasure), " I will turn your horses' heads home the very next time you come to the top of that hill out there. *I shall do it!* " (Great emphasis.) Do you hear?" he shouted.

" Yes, brother," we said calmly. We sang a hymn as though nothing had happened, appointed another meeting there, and passed out without a word.

The next Thursday evening, as we were slowly climbing that same steep hill, whom should we find standing at the top but Logan.

" Where are you going?" said he.

" To hold our usual meeting, Logan."

He took our horses by the bridles; we were quite helpless as to human aid, but we had learned that we could depend upon the Master whom we served for protection. The face of our deluded opponent was very dark, and he seemed possessed by a demon. The road where he stopped us was very narrow. Had he attempted to turn us there the consequences would have been serious. Suddenly Logan let go the bridles, and plunging down the embankment at our side, disappeared. Why had he left us? Was it to

bring others to assist him in his wicked designs?
"O ye of little faith, wherefore will ye doubt?"
We held the meeting with nothing to molest us. Late
in the evening we drove home, passing the place of
our encounter with some dread lest evil awaited us
there, for we were alone, two defenseless women.
We sang hymns of praise on our way, and late at night
arrived safe at home. But we never knew why there
came such a sudden change into the mind of our enemy
at that moment. Again we said, as we had said many
a time before, "The angel of the Lord encampeth
round about them that fear him, and delivereth them."

Chief Logan had a cousin bearing the illustrious
name of George Washington. This man quarreled
with his wife about some trifle, and without further
ceremony drove her from the home where for so many
years she had boiled his corn and cooked his venison.
An angry pagan prides himself upon a stony heart.
Appeals fail to move him. She went forth sadly and
feebly. She did not know that she was looking upon
her home for the last time. She did not know that
through this great sorrow the Saviour whom she had
rejected so many years was bringing her to himself.
She went to the house of Logan, and with a great
pain in her heart longed for death. Little did this
stricken woman expect to meet her Lord in the house
of this gospel hater.

One day, not long after our unpleasant encounter with Logan in the woods, we heard a feeble knock at the Mission door. Upon opening, these words greeted us in a trembling voice : —

"Pity me! Do not thrust me aside. Let me lean upon you for I am in trouble."

The face of the young girl was very sad as she stood at the Mission door. She was the only daughter of George Washington, who had driven his sick wife from her home. The trembling voice and haggard face of the girl contrasted strangely with her picturesque dancing costume, heavily ornamented with silver brooches and beads. The poor child had been dancing at a feast all night.

"I am afraid," she said, "that my mother is dying. My father will not see her. She wants you."

The sick woman was miles away, the roads in a wretched condition, but as soon as possible we were at her side.

"My mind is in great agony," said the poor creature with difficulty. "Can you help me? I have always been a pagan, but sometimes I have secretly attended your meetings. I have heard you sing and pray and tell about that wonderful Being who came to take away sin. The last time I was there you taught us how to say these words in our own language, *'Christ died for all.'* *'The blood of Jesus Christ cleanseth us from all sin.'* '*God so loved the world that he gave his only begotten Son, that whosoever believeth in him should not perish, but have everlasting life.'*

"Now in my trouble," she continued, "these words are ever before me, but I am afraid of God. I want to hide. I am in danger. My mind is very dark. Will you tell me more?"

We told her the story of Jesus in her own language, as to a little child. When we finished there was a new light in those troubled eyes and she said: —

"I believe; I need him; I take him! I need him more than any other sinner in the whole world."

She closed her eyes and seemed to be taking into her soul the message of forgiveness and release from the burden of sin. There was silence in the little room as we lifted our hearts to God that this benighted mind might at the eleventh hour receive the illumination of the Holy Spirit. At last she opened her eyes, from which shone a new light, the light of peace.

"I shall die soon," she said. "I beseech you, promise me that you will take my body away from this place, and give it a Christian burial. I do not wish any pagan ceremonies over me." She asked us to sing a hymn, which translated reads thus: —

Jesus, I come to thee, pity me! pity me!
I am a poor sinner, oh, pity me!
As thou art merciful,
Thrust not aside my soul;
Pity me, for I am a poor sinner.

Only thy precious blood
Is able to give me relief.
According to thy mercy,
According to thy lovingkindness
Wash me in thy blood.
I am a poor sinner,
But thou art able to save me.

About half an hour after we left the house Logan came in. He was told of our visit, of the singing, talking, and praying. He was told of Mrs. Washington's request as to a Christian burial. The man was furious. He cursed us again and again. He walked back and forth, threatening vengeance. He called upon the Evil-Minded to bring upon our heads every curse that the "House of Torment" could furnish.

"What!" said he, "praying in my house? These walls have never known a stain like that before." He cursed his pretty wife, who shrank from him in fear. He cursed even the sick woman.

"If it had not been for you," he said, "this would not have happened. A Christian burial indeed! You will be buried as I say. If they lay a finger on your dead body, they will arouse an Indian tempest such as they never dreamed of."

The sick one was too much terrified to speak. A pagan woman came to the bedside.

"What are you thinking of?" said she. "Don't you know your father and your mother and all your forefathers had a pagan burial? Are you so heartless as to disgrace their dust in this way? Don't you want to go to the 'Happy Home beyond the Setting Sun,' where they are? Oh, how lonesome you will be among the white folks, and your own relations away off where you cannot reach them!"

The dancing girl threw herself beside her mother and begged her not to leave her all alone in this world and the next too. The persecuted one tried to speak, but in the exhaustion caused by these trying scenes she could only murmur the words of the hymn, "Jesus, I come to thee, pity me!"

The next morning we went again to the house of Logan, quite unconscious of the storm we had caused the day before. A frightened look upon the face of the young wife enlightened us. Chief Logan was there, but simply ignored our presence. His wife dared not ask us to sit down. We quietly ministered to the wants of the sick one. She whispered: —

"Be cautious; the man who hates you and your religion is here."

Logan was suddenly called from the room. Then the women told us all.

" Will Jesus indeed receive my soul if I am buried with pagan ceremonies?" asked the dying woman.

" Do you cast yourself entirely upon him?"

" Yes, yes!" she exclaimed. " I believe I do."

" Then he accepts you. He knows your desire; you may tell him all about it. You may talk with him all the time in your mind and he hears you. These pagans refuse to answer your prayer about your body. Jesus hears and answers your prayer about your soul, and that is safe."

She was quite satisfied. Again we sang and prayed with her and repeated the sweet promises of Jesus. We told her about heaven, expecting every moment to be confronted by Logan; but the Lord in mercy held him back that this trembling disciple might be comforted. And very soon her spirit took its flight to that land where there shall be no more night, for the glory of God and of the Lamb is the light thereof. We were powerless to carry out her wishes, and she received a pagan burial.

Several months later some mysterious impulse moved Chief Logan to appear at the Mission breakfast table one morning and utter these words : —

" I have got through fighting you. You may go on with your meetings if you will. I shall never oppose you again."

Overcome by surprise we hardly answered him; but he kept his word. He did not attend the meetings himself, but he permitted others to do so without persecution.

One lovely spring morning a messenger came for us to go as quickly as possible to Logan. He was near death and greatly desired to see us. Although we went with all possible haste, death entered this dwelling before us. Those who were with him told us that he watched for us with great anxiety to the last. He wanted to hear more of the " Shining Jesus Way." The words of Christ which he heard during that one evening when he came to silence us had followed him from that day until the day of his death.

John Hudson, a leader among the pagans, was awakened to search after the real truth. He was a man of great natural ability; like Paul he was very zealous in preaching and teaching his false doctrine. He was one of our bitter opposers, but at one time was induced to listen to us as we talked most earnestly to him of Christ, his life, his sufferings, his death on the cross. With great emphasis he replied: —

" I do believe in Ha-wen-ni-yu — the Great Ruler; I pray to him every day; but it has never been revealed to me that Ha-wen-ni-yu has a son, and I can never, never pray to him or believe in him whom you call his Son, Jesus Christ."

But the Spirit of God was at work upon this man's heart, and gradually light broke in upon his darkened mind. Finally he came into one of our meetings among the pagans and told his feelings; but that which we longed to hear most from his lips, his faith in Christ as his Saviour, we heard not. With a proud, defiant manner he stood there and declared that he was ready now to defend the Christian party and embrace the Christian religion.

Nothing is impossible with God, and at last in answer to much earnest prayer among the missionaries and Indian brethren of the church, the truth in all its radiance shone clearly into the benighted mind of John Hudson, and he came forth trusting only and trusting wholly in Christ's righteousness for his salvation. He came daily to the Mission House for conversation upon the new religion, and many a night was spent by Mr. and Mrs. Wright in earnest conversation with this man upon the subject now so dear to his heart. He would sit with the Indian Testament in his hand asking questions until two and three and sometimes four o'clock in the morning.

His wife continued in strong opposition to the Christian religion. After having remained a whole week with us in the beginning of his new life, he started for his home several miles away. He was somewhat troubled with forebodings as to what kind of a reception he should meet from his family, with whom his path in life for the future must lie in a separate direction unless they should follow him.

While walking through the woods it occurred to John that he would tell his new friend, Jesus, of his difficulties, and ask for strength to endure the trial before him. With the simplicity of a little child pleading with an earthly parent, he knelt down and asked that his family might receive him kindly and that there might be no collision between them on account of the great change in him, but that they might be induced also to enter the Shining Jesus Way.

Strengthened and refreshed, he went home. His wife and family received him in a very different spirit from what he had anticipated. He told them the history of the change in his views and feelings, and to his grateful surprise met with no opposition. But the faith of John Hudson was soon to be sorely tested. The other pagan leaders, his friends, used every argument to draw him back to his former faith, but he remained firm, and in reply to all their entreaties that he would not leave his children, the pagans, he said : —

" If you are my children, you must follow your father."

This exasperated them, and they withdrew from him in indignation, and began to devise ways and means to torture their former beloved father. The first step was to erect a new dance house directly in his neighborhood. John expressed his feelings upon this matter to his family, and earnestly entreated them to have nothing to do with this dance house ; but there is a custom among the Indians that the uncles and aunts shall have as much authority over the children as the fathers and mothers. John Hudson had one son who was his pride and delight, whom he was gradually winning to look upon his new faith with favor. The son listened to the counsels of his father, and determined to abide by them and give up the pagan dances. During the absence of his father from home at one time, his aunt used all the inducements in her power to bring the young man back to the dances. He yielded to her authority, and by her command assisted in the work of the house with his father's oxen. While drawing a very heavy stick of timber one of the oxen fell down and died instantly. When the father came home and learned that his son had been won back to the dances, and that one of his valuable oxen had died in the work of building the dance house, he was not in an enviable frame of

mind. He had not yet commenced his spring work.
How was he to prepare the ground for his crops?
His Indian temper was well roused, and he was determined to give vent to his feelings as soon as he
could reach these relatives.

But suddenly this thought came into his mind: "Is
not this a temptation of the Evil One that he may stir
me up and get the victory over me if he can?"

He went into the deep woods and prayed that God
would strengthen him to endure this trial in a Christian spirit and enable him to trust Him for his daily
bread. He also prayed that this new dance house in
his neighborhood might never be completed. There,
in the depths of the forest, upon his knees, this converted pagan made a resolution that no word or look
should escape him when he met the people who had
brought this trouble upon him, which should indicate
that he had cherished any unpleasant feelings about
his misfortune.

God heard John Hudson's prayer. That dance
house was never completed. The timbers yet lie upon
the ground, gradually becoming a part of the surrounding soil.

One day we met John Logan [1] on the hill at the
pagan settlement. He said in English: "You know
my wife blind. I leave her. Last night had a dream.

[1] Not Chief Logan.

Dreamed a man came to my house — took my wife away; felt anxious — followed on to see her fate; took her long distance — could not find her sometime. After a while I found her; she was hid in a cave — very little sun, very little light — could not see sùn — could not see moon nor stars; she sat there lonely. Others sat there too — very sad, very gloomy. Man came to my wife and said 'Where's your husband?' She said, 'Don't know — gone away — left me because I'm blind.' I felt very bad to find her in such a place. I waked up. I think about my dream: no sun — that means evil; afraid I have done wrong — afraid great trouble coming to me and to my wife — afraid I ought to take your religion and go back to my wife."

We asked him to come to the Mission House and talk with us about the new religion. The next day he came, and asked permission to put to us a few questions for instruction. These were given in his own language : —

1. When we die do our souls lie in the ground all the time until our bodies are raised up? 2. What tribe does God belong to? 3. What language does God speak? 4. What road shall we take to go to heaven?

At last he was persuaded to stop asking questions, and give himself to the Lord Jesus Christ. We urged

him to come to one of our meetings among the
pagans, to commit himself there, and show which side
he was on. When the opportunity was given him he
sprang to his feet and owned that he had been too
proud to accept Christ or to pray to him.

"Now," said he in his own language, "I am going
to pray before you all." His embarrassment was so
great that when he knelt he seemed to fall upon the
floor all in a heap. He cried out: —

"O God, you know what a poor sinful creature I
am. I don't know how to pray. Nobody ever heard
me pray, but I'm going to try now, and I hope you
will teach me how, so it will please you to hear and
answer me. O God! forgive my sins and help me
now truly to believe on Jesus Christ."

In the course of the meeting he arose again and
said, "Now you shall hear my voice. You all know I
am a great sinner. God knows it. But I have determined to repent. A little while ago I did not know
anything about the gospel, but the more I heard the
more I believed there was something in it that we
have not got, that we pagans did not know anything
about; and now at this time I want you to hear me say
I do believe this gospel, I believe that Jesus Christ
is the Saviour of sinners. I have repented of my sins
and now I want to give them up. I here resolve I
will never drink another drop of whiskey in all my

life; I repent of that. I repent too of my disobedience to my mother; I will never disobey her again. When she reproves me I will never answer back. I want to become like Christ. I have been in the habit of going to the dances every Sabbath day. I never got any good there but a great deal of harm. When I come to these meetings I hear something that makes me better."

A woman arose: "I have never been to one of your meetings before. My child has been in your Sunday-school. He said to me, 'Mother, why don't you go to the meeting? I wish you would go, mother.' I said, 'My child, I am a pagan.' 'But, mother,' said he, 'will you go once to please me?' When my child said that it went like a knife to my heart; it made me weep and tremble. I could not get over it. Something kept saying to me, 'You must go! you must go!' I resolved to come and tell you my feelings, and confess my sins, and ask you to lead me into the Shining Jesus Way."

A LITERAL TRANSLATION OF A SENECA INDIAN HYMN.

> Ye people! Ye miserable ones!
> Receive
> The mercy of Jesus.
> Come! Receive it!
> Why will you die?
> Life is free to you,
> Receive it! receive it!

A long time ago—he has waited for you,
  Come! Receive
That which is so much to be coveted,
  Which he brings you,
Come! Receive it!
  He is ready to heal you
Of the sin that is killing you.
  Receive him!
Come! Receive him!

In our missionary rounds one day, Mrs. Wright and I found one of the most extreme cases of suffering I ever witnessed among the Indians. We entered a log house about ten feet square. The one room of the house contained three beds and the family, of about a dozen people, none of whom were especially neat in their habits. When we entered they were holding a consultation upon some matter which perplexed them. Our eyes followed dark glances directed to a certain corner of the room, and rested upon a helpless man lying upon the straw. I can never forget the look of wistful entreaty with which he regarded us. This man was unable to move a hand or an arm or to sit up a moment. He had lain in the corner of this wretched log hut for three months, not even a blanket between that bruised and aching body and the little straw upon the floor. One hand was decaying and dropping off; mortification had reached the second joint of one of the fingers. The least jar of the arm was painful to him. The hand and arm were so swollen that you could hardly have told what they were, and as black as the stove. The other hand and arm, in sympathy with this one, were paralyzed. Upon questioning him he told us that when he was taken sick he had a wife, who had forsaken him; all his friends had forsaken him. They were afraid of his disease. He was famishing for want of food. Three months before his friends brought him to this hut, laid him in the corner on the floor, and left him. Ever since, these people had been trying to get rid of him. Sometimes, when he begged hard enough, they put a piece of bread in his mouth, and sometimes when he wept and prayed they gave him a little water. They were now consulting together because one had proposed to put him out in the woods and let him die there.

"I have begged these people," said he, "to go to the missionaries and tell them my condition; but we are pagans and they would not go to you. All these days I have lain here and listened for your footsteps, and hoped that you would come to this house. This morning I said, I shall be dead when they come here. This afternoon they are resolving to put me in the woods."

We promised these cruel people that if they would let him remain there until we could find a place we would move him away and take care of him. This was easier said than done. We were several miles from home, but we canvassed that neighborhood until dark trying to rent a shanty where we could lay our patient. They said : —

"He is poison ; we dare not let him in." These choice shanties which we could not rent for love nor money were simply rough boards or logs carelessly put together. Finally one man relented, and for a liberal consideration consented to let us have a shed attached to his house ; but it was too late to move the poor man that night.

The next morning the old Mission horse started for the pagan settlement with a mixed load ; a mattress, bedquilts, sheets and pillowcases, a cook stove, a bag of meal, some pork, a bag of potatoes, a tin dish or two, some boards to nail over the top of the shed to keep the patient from being deluged with rain. While looking up bedding Mrs. Wright's face wore rather a perplexed expression for one moment.

"How can I spare these bedclothes!" she exclaimed. "I never was so short of bedding since I came to the Mission. I actually cannot supply the beds for my family comfortably now."

"Never mind, auntie dear! The Lord will provide."

"Of course he will!" she exclaimed. "Why did I doubt for a moment?"

It was not strange that she should feel perplexed,

for this was not the first time, nor the second, nor even the third, within two weeks, that we had been obliged to share the clothing upon our beds with the suffering.

Oh, what a happy, expressive face, what shining, grateful eyes, greeted us from the miserable corner as we told the poor man we had come to take him away! It was Sabbath morning, but this was surely Sabbath day work. There were several men standing about watching us curiously; we asked them to make a litter and carry him to the shed which we had prepared for him. They said: —

" We cannot touch him; we cannot carry him. We shall be poisoned."

My soul was so filled with indignation at that moment that I felt like shaking the dust from my feet and leaving them forever. Here was a dilemma. We began to think that we should have to carry the man ourselves, when — oh, what joy! — we saw a wagon passing by containing four of our dear Indian brethren of the church. How good their faces looked to us at that moment! How quickly they understood our trouble! How promptly they leaped from the wagon, prepared the litter, and under our instructions drew a blanket gently under the afflicted one and lifted him slowly and carefully upon the mattress, which was arranged upon the litter, and gently carried him to the shed which we had hired! With all their care the poor creature groaned with pain at every step. Was it possible that these dear Christian brethren had only a few years before been sunk in the same darkness, superstition, and hardness of heart in which we found these cruel pagans?

A week later and our patient lying in a shed, seven feet by nine, upon a bedstead covered by a comfortable mattress, was much better and very happy. His hand was properly dressed, his system strengthened by nourishing food, and his sister had consented to become his nurse. This kind of treatment he had never received from his pagan friends. It won him to believe that there must be something in the blessed religion of Jesus, and he delighted to have one of us sit in a chair by the bed and tell him of this wonderful Friend, and sing our hymns, and always offer a prayer by his bedside.

When we attempted to set up our stove in this little shed we discovered that there was no chimney; so we made a hole in the side of the house and put the pipe through. It rained, and the rain came pouring through the roof. We induced a man to lay slabs upon the roof. The wind blew through cracks in the sides of the room, upon which we tacked pieces of old oilcloth. Upon the side opposite the bed I saw a long shelf covered with straw.

" This," thought I, " will make a nice place for the dishes and medicines." I commenced pulling down the straw, but my hand was arrested by three indignant, motherly hens, each of which anticipated a fine brood of chickens very soon.

" Let them stay," said the sick man ; " they will be company for me."

Well, we took care of Moses Crow in that shed one month. That is to say, we went to see him every day, carrying nourishing food to eat, and washing and dressing that terrible hand. This superstitious, ignorant pagan entered the " Shining Jesus Way," and found the great love broad enough and deep enough even for him. Almost the first words we heard every day were, " Tell me more about my wonderful Friend." At last the owner of the shed declined to let us have it any longer, and we were obliged to look up another house two miles away, where he was moved with less agony than at the first.

One day Moses said to me, " My friend, do you think I could learn to read?"

" I think you could," I said.

" But how? I have no hands with which to hold the book."

" I will make a book," said I, " that you can read without hands."

During that week I printed the English alphabet in large letters upon a big sheet of paper which we used in publishing the Bible and hymn books. This was tacked on the side of the room at the foot of his bed. One chart succeeded another as Moses advanced in the art of learning to read both in English and in his own language. I used to wish that the boys and girls who did not care for school, or books, could see the wistful eagerness with which this poor creature studied his lesson each day. What would he not have given for one small privilege of the schoolboy!

One day Moses Crow asked us to invite some of the Indian brethren of the church to his bedside. He had something to tell them. When we were gathered there he said:—

" Brothers, I want to tell you that I believe in Jesus Christ as my Saviour."

How this public confession touched our hearts! One brother said:—

" Moses, do you give up paganism?"

" Wholly," said he.

" How did you come to give it up?"

" Well," said Moses, " this was it. These kind friends who have taken care of me told me of Jesus and their religion. As I lay here all alone so many hours I began to compare it with my pagan religion. I remembered how cruel my pagan friends had treated me in my great trouble. I thought, What could have made these strangers take me in my trouble from that dreadful place, and make me comfortable and take care of me? I said it must be their religion. I said, I want a religion that will make anybody do such a thing as this. They told me many stories about their wonderful friend, Jesus, and what he did and what he said. Then I got to thinking about him, and I kept growing more and more interested. One day I said to myself, 'I will think about my pagan religion to-day, and compare it with this.' It had vanished away! I could not find it anywhere. This blessed gospel of Jesus had taken its place and filled all my soul."

"Moses," said another brother, "what will you do with all your past wicked life and the many sins you have committed?"

"I have left all that with Jesus," said he.

We gave Moses a little prayer in Indian, which he repeated a great many times every day. "O Christ Jesus, help me to believe in thee every day as my Saviour from sin!" We wanted Moses to realize that it was not enough to believe that Jesus saved him once a long time ago from sin, or that he was going to save him by-and-by; we wanted him to believe that he was saved from sin then, every moment, every day, so that he might

know that peace of God which passeth all understanding.

One morning I read to Moses from an Indian
Testament the story of the wheat and tares. " I was
one of those tares," exclaimed he. " The devil had
me. But I belong to Jesus now; the devil had me
long enough, long enough."

" But, Moses, when you walk about among people
again, will you not be tempted to go back to your
pagan dances? "

" No, no! " said he with great emphasis. " I want
to go to meeting; I want to spend my time with
Christian people."

Captain Richard Matthews, of Boston, became interested in the story of this man, and sent him a suit
of clothes. In response Moses dictated to him the
following letter : —

My dear Friend and Brother, — I am very glad to write a few
words to such a kind man as you are. I have been in great
affliction, greatly pressed down with sickness and distress; but the
Lord has raised me up through the kindness of Christian people,
who pitied me in my forlorn condition, taking me into their
keeping and nursing me back into life and strength, so that now
I walk about on the earth once more. Such treatment as this I
have never received from anybody before in my life, and I am
grateful to them and to God who made them what they are.

This wonderful kindness which I received from those who
pitied me and lifted me out of my wretchedness caused me to seek
after the reason for their actions, and when I found it was Jesus,
I wanted Jesus too. So I have repented of my sins, and I have
been baptized. Once I was full of the devil, now I am clothed

and in my right mind. God used this Christian kindness to cause my mind to take a great leap from paganism to Christ. When you think of me I want you to think of my mind as growing stronger all the time.

My brother, I feel very grateful to you for the kindness you have shown me. It is strange, it is wonderful, it is something I cannot understand, that you, so far away, should care for my poor body. I can never forget it. I cannot work yet, but I can walk about, and these warm clothes will keep me comfortable this winter. The boots will protect my feet from the snows, the coat and the vest and the pants will shield me from the chilling winds. Poor Moses Crow, the Indian, can do nothing for you, but his wonderful Friend, Jesus Christ, can, and I shall ask him to bless you always. I think I shall never meet you on this earth, but I know I shall see your face in heaven.

My brother, I want you to think of me as one whom Jesus has saved, and helped to stand up firmly on the Lord's side. I have given myself to Christ wholly, not for a little time, but for ever. I am satisfied; I am glad and happy all the time.

Will you ask those kind ladies who meet at your house to sew and make me some underclothing to wear, to pray for me that I may never fall back into sin and forget what Jesus has done for me? Will you thank them for their kindness to me?

I love to think of you all, and of the bright place where you live, all lighted up with the gospel. This has been a very dark place, but the light is coming here too. I think about you sailing on the great ocean. That is something I have never seen. Your Indian friend,   MOSES CROW.

The illustrious ancestor of Grandmother Destroy-town is known to history as one who, with a fierce band of warriors wiped out a small town of pale faces, including men, women, and children, destroying every house with fire. Grandmother Destroytown lived in the woods in an Indian cabin quite a distance from neighbors. She hated the missionaries and their religion most cordially, and declared that no missionary should ever enter her house.

I was passing this little cabin one day on horseback. I saw the poor deluded woman near the house, gathering sticks. My heart went out to her with a great longing that her old age should be illumined by the light of the gospel. The door of the cabin stood wide open. For the sake of giving her the blessed message I resolved to disregard her wishes and enter the house.

Great was the astonishment of the old woman, who had not seen me, when she came to her door to discover a hated white woman, who was also a hated missionary, sitting in her house. I presently gave her the Indian salutation, " I hope it is well with thee, grandmother?" to which she did not respond.

With a malignant scowl, which has been pictured upon my memory ever since, she passed me, went to the corner of her shanty, took a pail, and went out to the spring. Soon she returned with a pail of water and poured it into a tub. Utterly ignoring me she passed back and forth from the spring to the tub until it was filled with water. I thought, " When the tub is full she will sit down to rest and I will talk with her "; but when the tub was full she dipped the pail into it, and suddenly threw a pail of water into the middle of the room, and seizing a broom began to scrub her floor. Pailful after pailful was thrown, and in every case aimed at me, until my clothing and feet were drenched with water. Thinking I would not irritate the woman if I kept perfectly quiet, and that she would soon be reconciled to my presence, I did not speak a word. When I could not run the risk of sitting there longer, I said : —

"Well, Grandmother Destroytown, I came here with the hope of making you very happy. I have a message for you ; it is a message of good news from heaven, and I greatly long to give it to you, for it would brighten all your last days. When you look back over your life you remember some things that you wish you could forget. There are stains of sin on your soul. I came to tell you about One who could wash away all those black stains and make your soul white and clean before God. This wonderful Being that I came to tell you about loves you more than I can possibly tell you, although you have never cared for him, and feel so bitter in your heart toward his messengers ; but should the time ever come when you want to hear about this wonderful Friend of yours, you may come to me at the Mission House. I shall never come to you again."

While I stood giving this message I was receiving, as fast as she could throw it at me, the water from her pail. Then I went out and mounted my horse, who must have been somewhat surprised at my dripping condition, and imagined that he had forgotten some recently forded stream.

Some months before this episode we had taken into the Mission family two deserted grandchildren of Mrs. Destroytown, who had been converted to the Christian religion, and were children of great promise.

One day a messenger from Grandmother Destroytown demanded that we lend these two little girls to her for two days. The first impulse was to deny her request, for, as one of us remarked, " In two days she will undo our work of months." Another said : —

" These children are in the fold. Will not Christ guard his lambs, and perhaps through them reach the heart of the old pagan woman?"

We decided to send them with united prayer that they might now be messengers of the gospel.

Grandmother Destroytown had prepared an Indian dinner for her guests, and welcomed them with great delight. Could these be the miserable, half-starved creatures that she had cast out and left to perish in the woods nearly a year before? She looked at their bright faces, plump cheeks, shining eyes, smoothly brushed hair, clean clothes, in astonishment, and was very proud of them. As she was about helping them to the dinner, one of the little girls said : —

" Stop, grandmother !   Wait ! "

The child knew that a blessing should be asked as at the Mission table, but having had no experience in this exercise was at a loss how to begin.   Suddenly she remembered her little evening prayer.   She closed her eyes, and folding her little brown hands, said : —

> " Now I lay me down to sleep,
> I pray the Lord my soul to keep.
> If I should die before I wake,
> I pray the Lord my soul to take,
> And this I ask for Jesus' sake."

A novel blessing for a noonday meal ; but the little one had done the best she could, and who shall say that her effort was not accepted?   As the old woman understood not one word of English, the only impression left upon her mind was the child talking to Ha-wen-ni-yu.   During the remainder of the day the little girls played happily together, and the grandmother greatly enjoyed their childish prattle.   At night she was preparing to put them to bed upon a couch of skins in the corner when one of them said : —

" Stop, grandmother !   Wait ! "

They knelt together, and in concert repeated the Lord's Prayer, then clambered upon the couch, and with wide-open eyes watched their grandmother as she moved back and forth about the little cabin, ready for any conversation which she might care to hold with them.   She sat down by the open fire and said :

"Why do you talk so much to Ha-wen-ni-yu? What are you saying to him?"

"Why, grandmother," said the younger, "we belong to Jesus now; we have given ourselves away to him. We are doing everything we can to please him, and we love him very much and we love to talk to him. He is our wonderful Friend, and he loves us more than anybody else in the world does. We always talk to him before we eat and before we sleep. We try to please him when we study, when we wash the dishes, and when we sweep the floor, and we try to please him when we play."

She listened attentively, and muttered, "I suppose that is the reason I have not seen you scratch or bite or strike each other to-day."

The children prattled on to her of their great, loving Friend, and at last said, "Grandmother, will you let us sing you a little hymn?"

She consented and they sang to her in her own language the little hymn which we had prepared for the pagans : —

> Jesus, I come to thee, pity me! pity me!
> I am a poor sinner, oh, pity me!
> As thou art merciful,
> Thrust not aside my soul,
> Pity me, for I am a poor sinner.
> Only thy precious blood

Is able to give me relief.
According to thy mercy,
According to thy lovingkindness,
Wash me in thy blood.
I am a poor sinner,
But thou art able to save me.

When the children finished the song the old grand-mother seemed to have forgotten them entirely as she sat with a far-away look upon her face, gazing into the fire. They soon fell asleep, but she sat there through the long hours of the night, reviewing all her past life in its darkness and ignorance and sin. Here she was, a lonely old woman on the verge of the grave. Had her life been all a mistake? Had she been in error? Were Handsome Lake's teachings a delusion, and might she claim this wonderful Friend of the white man and be cleansed from all sin? She recalled a little verse that one of the children had repeated some time during the day: "The blood of Jesus Christ cleanseth me from all sin"; and the other one had said that if one came to him he should not be thrust aside. The Holy Spirit was doing his work of illumination in that benighted mind.

The next morning the children came triumphantly into the Mission, leading between them old Grand-mother Destroytown. As I met them she said: —

" I remembered your words to me that I was to

come to you if I wanted to hear more about the wonderful Friend.   Tell me more now."

Grandmother Destroytown became a consistent member of the Mission church, and at last died in the triumph of the Christian faith.

The experience of one day among these pagans will tell the story of many days during the following weeks and months.

Mrs. Wright and I began this day with a meeting among the Plank Road pagans.   Mr. Porcupine was very angry with us the week before because we "interfered with the dances."   He sat outside in the wind, saying hard things about us, and took a bad cold.   To-day he came into the house and said these words: "I have been very angry with you, but my mind has been greatly troubled since you were here last.   I am an old man of eighty years.   It is time for me to try to understand the new religion.   Tell me how one so old can come into the Jesus Way."   He listened with great attention while the simple plan of salvation was made known to him.

We called upon Moses Cornplanter.   His young wife, a daughter of Cornstalk, was pretty and interesting.   She looked at us wistfully as though troubled with questionings.   Was she reaching out after light?

She gave us cordial welcome and said, " I have attended your Plank Road meeting twice. It is the first time I have heard of the Jesus Way. I want to know the truth. Have I been taught an error?"

Mrs. Wright explained the " new religion" to her very clearly and read the words of Christ from the Indian Testament. We sang gospel hymns and prayed with her.

Mr. Cornplanter was not pleased and had left the house. She thanked us for our words and said, " My husband is a pagan, but he is not a bad man — he is not cross — he does not drink; but you know the woman must not go ahead. Will you win him so that I may come into the Jesus Way? I will gladly follow him."

Our next call was at Silversmith's, to see poor little Jack Pigeon. He was lying upon a board covered with a bit of soiled blanket. A ragged piece of cotton cloth was thrown over him. Somebody had placed a spray of green leaves in a crack of the log near his board. He directed our attention to this as something very pleasant. A half-starved young robin, a pet, was hopping about on the rough floor. After ministering to the poor boy, we went out and dug worms for the robin. An old woman covered with rags and dirt watched us with interest and expressed surprise that we cared to handle the ugly worms!

On our way back through the woods we heard groans from the vicinity of Porcupine's cabin. While climbing a fence he had fallen and was badly bruised. With the remedies in our missionary bag we were able to bind up his wounds. After making him as comfortable as possible in his poor cabin, we looked up Mother Big-Tree and coaxed her to act as nurse for a time. The promise of a bright red handkerchief, when Porcupine should become convalescent, reconciled Mrs. Big-Tree to this rather uninviting position.

On this day Mrs. Big Kettle, who seemed inclined to favor the gospel, had invited us to hold a meeting at her house. Brother Daniel Two-Guns, a member of the mission church, promised to meet us there and give us his assistance. After a drive of five miles we reached the Big Kettle cabin, to find it empty. A neighbor told us that Big Kettle, who was a pagan, was angry, and had taken his wife and the little Big Kettles away. She further made known the fact that he threatened to leave his wife if we held a meeting in his house. Brother Two-Guns had been there, and was now trying to find an open door for us in this neighborhood. We stepped into Mrs. Blacksnake's cabin to await the return of our Christian brother. As soon as we sat down, the woman, with dark looks, began to wash her floor. She "swashed" the water with such vigor that we were well drenched. We went outside and sat upon a log and sang plaintively, " Where, oh, where is our good old Daniel?"

At last his tall figure emerged from the forest. Without a word he sat down beside us. When ready to report he said that there was no door open to us in this neighborhood, but suggested that we remain upon the log a while and pray and sing there. We were too much chilled with the long waiting in our damp condition, thanks to the Blacksnake deluge, to accept his proposition, and were making arrangements to go home, when Mrs. Johnny John, who was passing, said, " You may have a meeting in my house."

We promptly accepted this unexpected invitation, and followed the woman a half mile over an indescribable trail, making familiar acquaintance with treacherous holes and stumps. Her house of one room, sixteen feet by seventeen, accommodated three beds, a large stove, — red-hot at this time, — a table, and a bench. We blew our tin horn and thirty-two people responded to the call and were packed into this small room. A garment, or section of a garment, was tucked into every air hole by which broken windows and loose cracks might have been a merciful relief.

We endured this sense of suffocation and physical discomfort until half-past ten. Each one had something to say for or against the new religion, and it would have been a breach of Indian etiquette, not easily forgiven, to have closed the meeting earlier. Mrs. Wright and I were asked to sing sixteen times. It required more will power each time to open our mouths in that polluted atmosphere.

At last we started for home. While fording the creek the bottom of our wagon fell into the water and floated down stream. "We ought," said Mrs. Wright, "to be thankful that the wheels are left, for they will take us home." We had never before appreciated the value of the dashboard, upon which our feet were elevated until we gladly dismounted at the Mission home.

Four miles from the Mission House, in the woods of the pagan settlement, stood a small frame house, where lived Miss Sylvia P. Joslin, a missionary teacher. There were no flights of stairs in this house of two rooms. On one side of the partition Miss Joslin instructed all who could be induced to come to her school. On the other side she cooked and ate and slept and read, and prayed for the people for whom she had isolated herself from her world. She had absolutely no companionship but that of these pagans whom she was trying to win for Christ. She worked against terrible ignorance and prejudice, but not without results. They did not drive her away and the children became interested in the school.

It was a blessed custom at the Mission House to send occasionally for these lonely workers at the outstations, and give them the comfort of a day or two of Christian companionship. It becomes my turn to go for our dear, brave Miss Joslin, and Ruhama stands at the door waiting for me. She is attached to a rickety wagon. An old hen is tied under the seat to be left with a sick man on the way. She is making vigorous efforts to extricate herself and is quite likely to succeed during the miles of travel before her. In front is a basket containing an old cat and kittens for Miss Joslin, the unhappy family being kept in place by a well-ventilated bit of carpet. There are sundry packages to be transferred from the mission larder to that of Miss Joslin — beans, pickles, a section of pork, a few vegetables, etc. There is also a bottle of milk and a few flowers from the mission garden. These for a sick woman on the way. Ruhama and I are off.

How many times I have heard Mrs. Wright say,

" The greatest need of these Indians is to be set at work. We have preached to them faithfully, we have sent away many young men and women to be trained intellectually, we have looked carefully after their souls ; but with all the training of heart and head, that training of the hand by which the daily bread must be provided has been neglected. The best way to help anybody, white man or Indian, is to teach him how to help himself. These Indian men should be Christian carpenters, blacksmiths, shoemakers, and these Indian women should be Christian housekeepers, needlewomen, laundresses. These boys and girls should learn how to be Christian workers skilled in all the trades."

After many exhortations to the missionaries and Missionary Board in this matter, Mrs. Wright resolved to make the experiment herself, of industrial work among the pagan women, who with their husbands were far behind the Christians in every respect, being deplorably poor and improvident. One day, with the aid of a good dinner, she brought a company of these women together, and providing them with cotton cloth, flannel, and calico, she gave them their first lessons in cutting and making clothing for themselves and their families. While busily at work with their needles she gave them first the Word of God ; then needful lessons in the matter of housekeeping, bringing up children, etc. This was the beginning of weekly meetings of this character. There was usually an opposition gathering outside, who amused themselves in holding up to ridicule those within. As the number of workers increased they were much cramped for room.

At this time Hon. E. P. Smith, of Washington, Commissioner of Indian Affairs, visited the Reservation. He became interested in this effort of Mrs. Wright, and said : —

"You must have more room. If you will secure a piece of land, you shall have a house for your industrial class."

This greatly alarmed the pagan leaders, who shrewdly said, "This sewing is a ruse to break down our religion. If this house goes up, our religion will go down. We will not give a foot of land in this settlement to set that house on."

They warned Mrs. Wright threateningly to stop the work. After a year of waiting, one brave man, a pagan, came boldly forward and gave the land for the house, which, strange to say, was built without further molestation. Besides the industrial class it has been used for Sunday-schools, temperance meetings, and Christmas festivals.

Mrs. Wright's next step in the plan for the women was to teach them to make garments for sale, and with the money thus obtained buy more material; but the prices paid for the garments were so low that this did not prove a financial success. The women, however, had become thoroughly interested and imbued with the healthful fascination of earning something, and were clamorous for more work.

At this crisis Mrs. Wright was able to secure employment from the Indian Department at Washington, consisting of coats of duck, and red flannel shirts for the western tribes. The government promised to purchase these if she would make them, but could not advance the necessary funds for material. In her anxiety to secure work for the women she accepted the offer, borrowing the money to purchase material for six hundred and fifty garments.

Such was the desire to do this work that many women came miles to get it, some of these poor creatures wading a stream in midwinter rather than lose the opportunity. Several women took machines and learned how to use them, hoping to be able to pay for them in work. This was a welcome season to the women, but a season of great anxiety to their missionary who had incurred a debt of eight hundred dollars. This, however, she was able to pay when, after many weeks, the government paid her for the garments.

CORNPLANTER.

This matter of gospel industrial education is the one step by which as a nation we may right a great wrong in the black records of our dealings with the Indian race.

Allusion has been made to the pagan prophet. His name was Handsome Lake, and he was a half-brother of the famous warrior Cornplanter. Through his constant companions, Blue-Eyes, Big-Tree, and two or three others, the following particulars are well known concerning this curious Indian prophet. He was born in 1735, and had been a very dissipated man. One day, after a long illness, he lay upon his bed of skins very near death. His daughter, who was ministering to him, had stepped to the door to welcome some friends, when she heard a groan and sprang back in season to see her father fall upon the floor. With help she placed him upon the bed.

He opened his eyes and exclaimed, "I heard a voice. It said, 'Come out here.' I started to go and I saw three persons close by the door. They were shining ones. No man ever looked as they did. They were covered with a glory. Their faces were painted a little as we paint our faces. They said, 'The Good Ruler has sent us to you; we have come to call you; there were four of us when we started, but one has gone back to the Happy Home beyond the Setting Sun, where we live. It was important that he be present at a great dance there to-day. You will see him by-and-by. You expect to die soon. You have begged Ha-wen-ni-yu to spare your life. You have promised that if he does this you will repent of your bad life, and hereafter live a new life. Ha-wen-ni-yu hears your prayers and your promise. At noon to-morrow you shall be perfectly restored. At that hour throw away your medicine.'

"The Bright One handed me a strawberry vine covered with the fruit, and said, ' Eat it and be well.' Let Dry Mush and his wife take you into the woods and kindle a fire and care for you; but let no other person be near, or see you for three days. Then call the people together, and we will come to you with the message of Ha-wen-ni-yu for the people.' "

Handsome Lake obeyed these orders, and in three days called the people together and gave the heavenly message as he declared it was given to him by the Bright Ones at his side, who were visible to him alone.

"The Good Ruler," said he, " is displeased with you. You do many things of which he disapproves. He will now, through these Bright Ones who are with me, and for whom I interpret, make known to you his will. You have four great sins of which you must repent: —

" 1. You drink too much fire water. You may drink one cup of fire water in the morning, one at noon, one at night. This is all.

" 2. You sin in permitting witches among your people. Ha-wen-ni-yu is displeased at this. You must repent.

" 3. You break up your families too easily. Ha-wen-ni-yu wishes you to live with your families and take care of them. Death only must separate you. If you leave your families and get other families three times, you will not be admitted to the Happy Home hereafter.

" 4. You sing tunes from other nations at your dances. These are poison. You may dance again and have the kettles boiled, but repent of this."

The Bright One then made a personal remark to Handsome Lake, but we are not told that he made it known to the assembled multitude. It was this: " There are some things which you yourself must repent of if you are to be a prophet to this people. You must not sing at the dances for the dead. It is not right."

" And now," continued the Bright One, " you may tell the people what will please Ha-wen-ni-yu.

" 1. You must give of your abundance to those who lack substance.

" 2. You who have no children must take an orphan

child, and give it the same care and love you would your own.

" 3. If you tie up the strings of the clothes of an orphan child, Ha-wen-ni-yu will notice it and reward you.

" 4. If a stranger comes to your people, welcome him to your home, be hospitable to him, speak kind words to him, and always mention the Good Ruler, Ha-wen-ni-yu."

Then the Bright One spoke to Handsome Lake, and said : —

" What do you see? "

He said, " I see a man bringing a load of meat, and he gives some of it to every person he meets."

Then said the Bright One, " Learn the lesson. This man is blessed; this is pleasing to the Good Ruler; he loves those who are bountiful, but he is displeased with the covetous man. When that man dies he cannot get away. His covetousness sticks to him and is heavy upon him and holds him down, so that he cannot rise toward the Happy Home.

" Those who have charge of the amusements here will be taken out of the hands of death, and will lead the amusements in the Happy Home.

" Those who dance here will also dance in the Happy Home; but those who neglect the dances here will not be happy there, for they will not be permitted to dance there.

"Again, you say, 'Oh! the whiskey is not bad. It touches our food. It is made of our corn.' Go to the council house. Put half the people on one side, and give them whiskey. Put half the people on the other side, and give them bread. You will notice the difference. Those who drink will fight. Those who eat the corn bread will go peaceably away."

After this great meeting, in which Handsome Lake assured the people that the Bright Ones, or angels, had given him all these words, he published to all the people that he was inspired; that the Good Ruler had given him supernatural gifts, and that he was to give them a new revelation.

He claimed to have been taken in a vision to the Happy Home beyond the Setting Sun. It was filled with Indians. The white people were all shut out. George Washington was permitted to look into this paradise from afar, because he had been kind to the Indians.

He claimed also to have visited the House of Torment. There he saw a drunken Indian. The Evil-Minded was pouring a cup of boiling lead down his throat; the flame burst from his mouth, as he screamed with agony. There were a great many kettles of boiling lead, into which people were plunged, who kept moving up and down with the boiling liquid. There were many who were being tormented by a red-hot iron.

When a man died, if he had obeyed the prophet, he would go directly to the Happy Home by a narrow path. If he had not obeyed him, he had to take a long, crooked road, which led him through the various punishments of the House of Torment. He saw an Indian there who had been in the habit of beating his wife. He was obliged to beat a red-hot statue, and the sparks continually flew out and burned him.

Those who had sold fire water to the Indians had the flesh eaten from their arms. Those who sold land to white people would be forever employed in removing mountains of sand, grain by grain.

Lazy women would be employed in pulling up weeds in a large field of corn, which would immediately grow again.

There was an appropriate punishment also for those who were unkind to the aged or children.

The new prophet went from house to house, from village to village, telling of his visions and revelations, and the Indians believed in him.

One day, as Handsome Lake stood before a great assembly of people, he saw David Halftown passing by. He said, "There goes a perfect man. He pleases Ha-wen-ni-yu in all the dances and amusements. He will have a high place in the other world."

Just then the Bright Ones said to him, "Look into the other world; what do you see?"

"I see Red Jacket."

"What is he doing?"

"He is wheeling a load of dirt back and forth."

"Well," said the angels, "so will it be with him forever, because he sold the lands of his people."

When the Quakers came to the Reservation and wished to teach the children, the people asked Handsome Lake what they should do. After a vision he told them that the Good Ruler was willing that the Quakers should do as they pleased, because they had always befriended the Indians; and so the Quakers were among the first to start schools among them.

One day the angels took Handsome Lake to see what befell those who did not obey his teachings. He saw a rope and fetters, and a prison with stone walls. "These things," said the angels, "are for those who do not listen to your preaching."

Cornplanter, a chief of great power among the Senecas, had two children who were taken ill. Notwithstanding all the boasted power of the prophet Handsome Lake, both children died. Cornplanter was furious, and said, "How is this? If you were a true prophet, you could have saved my children. I will have nothing more to do with you!" and he drove him and his followers away from that settlement. From this time the power of the pagan prophet began to wane.

The climax came when he told the people that there was a monstrous serpent a foot underground, on the road to Buffalo. It would be a dreadful thing if this awful serpent should come above ground and devour them all. But by his powers he could hold him in check. Some of the people said, " We will take our shovels and dig for this monster and kill it!" but he solemnly warned them that the most disastrous consequences would attend any such excavation.

Old Sun Fish stood up before the prophet and said, " I believe you are lying to us. I will take my snow shovel and dig him out if he is there."

After this test they applied other tests to his statements, and many left him. Yet there were others who followed him to the end ; and there are even now those who believe in the divine mission of Handsome Lake, and who earnestly exhort the pagans to heed his instructions.

Old Silverheels, a pagan, appeared at the Mission House one day and said, " A messenger tells me that the lady from the land of the rising sun [Boston] likes to listen to the story of our race. Would she like to hear about our feasts?"

Of course she would! But she was not to be gratified until the body of Silverheels should be nourished
by the white man's bread and his spirit comforted by
his favorite tobacco. When these important prelimi-
naries had been suitably adjusted he was ready to
begin. His statements were as follows: —

"My people have six festivals, in which we thank
the Good Ruler, Ha-wen-ni-yu, for the maple tree
which gives us its sweet water and our sugar; for the
wonderful strawberry and for the green corn. At
the New Year's feast we thank him for all his gifts.
We have also the big feather and medicine feasts.
Certain people are elected as 'keepers of the faith,'
and they always get up the feast. We always dance
at our feasts, because it is pleasing to Ha-wen-ni-yu.
We used to have thirty-two dances, and we believe
that we shall dance in the Happy Home beyond the
Setting Sun, and have strawberries to eat every day,
and so we thank Ha-wen-ni-yu for the strawberries."

The strawberry feast in old times consisted entirely
of the wild fruit eaten with maple sugar in bark
trays. Before partaking, the leader returned thanks
for the people to Ha-wen-ni-yu, and also to the earth,
water, air, and fire, for the special blessings given by
each.

"At the green corn festival we thanked Ha-wen-
ni-yu for the corn, beans, and squashes. But the

New Year's festival was our great festival and is so to this day.

At the maple festival, in old times, the leader made this speech : —

Friends: The Sun, the ruler of the day, is high in his path, and we must hasten to our duty. We are here to observe an ancient custom handed down by our forefathers, and given to them by the Good Ruler, Ha-wen-ni-yu. He requires us to give thanks for the blessings we receive. We will be faithful to this command.

Friends: The maple is yielding its sweet waters. We join in thanksgiving to the maple, and also to Ha-wen-ni-yu, who made this tree for the good of the red man.

The services of the day were closed with the "great feather dance."

" When we addressed the Good Ruler directly we threw tobacco on the fire that our words might ascend to him on the incense. We never used incense at any other time. The leader would say : —

Ha-wen-ni-yu, listen now to our words. The smoke of our offering arises. Listen to our words as they arise to thee in smoke. We thank thee for the sweet water of the maple. We thank thee for the return of the planting season. Let our corn and beans and squashes grow. Ha-wen-ni-yu! continue to listen, for the smoke yet arises [throwing on tobacco]. Preserve us from pestilential diseases. Preserve our old men, and protect our young. Ha-wen-ni-yu! thou dost love thy people and hate their enemies. Thou hast given us the panther's heart, the eagle's eye, the moose's foot, and the cunning of the fox; but to our enemies thou hast given the eye of the owl in daylight, the foot of the turtle, the heart of woman, and the stupid brain of the bear in winter.

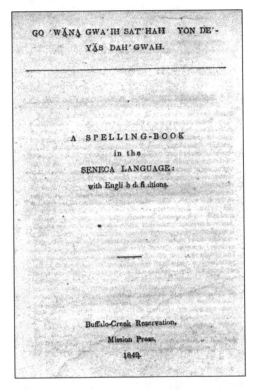

A spelling book in the Seneca language. Printer Benjamin VanDuzee issued this 112-page spelling book in 1842. Rev. Wright obtained a printing press in 1841 and accented type from Boston in 1842. (Private collection.)

At a time of drought they called a council, and prayed to Heno, the Thunderer, for rain : —

"Heno, our grandfather, hear us! Listen to our words. We feel grieved, our minds are troubled. Come and give us rain, that the earth may not dry up, and refuse to support the life of thy grandchildren."

"Silverheels," said I, "why did n't they call on Ha-wen-ni-yu for rain?"

"Because the heart of Heno, the Great Thunderer, would be more easily touched by the pitiful cry of his suffering grandchildren than by an order from the Great Ruler."

When the Indian told us that the green corn feast consisted of succotash, a soup of corn and beans boiled together, our pride in this purely Yankee dish received a shock. It is centuries old and we received it from the Indian! Mr. Silverheels begged for a short recess that he might indulge in that custom of the white man known as "a smoke," and thus gain inspiration to tell us of the most wonderful feast and dance of all : —

THE NEW YEAR'S FEAST AND THE WHITE DOG DANCE.

After the "smoke" the old man stretched himself upon the bearskin in front of the fireplace, and fell asleep. Not being possessed of that troublesome reminder, a watch, and unburdened in mind as to "appointments" or "business engagements," he slumbered on, knowing from past experience of missionary hospitality that he was welcome to the bearskin and the floor for the night, should he choose to occupy it. The fact that the members of the family, passing back and forth upon household errands, were obliged to step over his prostrate form did not in the least disturb his repose.

"All things come to him who waits," and at last the Indian veteran pronounced himself ready to speak of the exciting scenes of the "white dog dance."

"This festival," said he, "in old times lasted nine days. The week before, two grotesque-looking persons called at every house with a message. They were dressed in bearskins fastened about their heads with wreaths of corn husks, and falling loosely over the body or girdled about the loins. Their arms and wrists were ornamented with wreaths of husks, and in their hands they held corn pounders. Upon entering a house they knocked upon the floor to command silence, and then said these words: —

"'Listen! listen! listen! The ceremonies which Ha-wen-ni-yu commands are about to commence. Prepare your houses. Clear away the rubbish. Drive out all evil animals. Should your friend be taken sick and die, we command you not to mourn nor allow your friends to mourn. Lay the body aside. When the ceremonies are over we will mourn with you.'

"After a song of thanksgiving the messengers departed, to repeat this ceremony in every house."

"Did they actually obey the command to lay aside a dead body nine days for this feast?"

"Yes. If any one died during the festival, the body was put away and no evidence of sorrow was visible until afterward, and then the funeral rites were performed as though he had just died.

"On the first day of the feast, a white dog 'without spot or blemish' was chosen and strangled, that no blood should be shed or bones broken. The body was painted with spots of red and decorated with feathers. Around the feet were wound strings of wampum and beads. The dog was then fastened to the top of a pole, about twenty feet from the ground, where he remained until the fifth day. Then they built an altar of wood, upon which the body of the dog was laid and burned. As they did this the great thanksgiving address was made, and tobacco was constantly thrown upon the fire that the prayer might ascend in the clouds of smoke:—

"'Hail! Ha-wen-ni-yu! hail! Listen with an open ear to the words of thy people.' (Throwing on more tobacco.) 'Continue to listen. Give us zeal and fidelity to celebrate the sacred ceremonies which thou

hast given to us. We thank thee that we still live.
We thank our Mother Earth which sustains us. We
thank the Rivers for the fish. We thank the Herbs
and Plants of the earth. We thank the Bushes and
Trees for Fruit. We thank the Winds which have
banished disease. We thank our Grandfather Heno
for the rain. We thank the Moon and Stars which
give us light when the Sun has gone to rest. We
thank the Sun for the warmth and light by day.
Keep us from evil ways that the Sun may never hide
his face from us for shame and leave us in darkness.
We thank thee, O mighty Ha-wen-ni-yu, our Creator
and our Good Ruler. Thou canst do no evil. Everything that thou doest is for our happiness.'

"During this feast there were social hours, and
times for games. On one day all the people went
into each other's houses, each one carrying a wooden
shovel, with which the ashes upon the hearth were
stirred and scattered, while invoking a blessing upon
the household.

"They were allowed to enter the houses and secure
something for a feast without detection. If detected,
they must give up the article and try again. Another
amusement at this time was guessing dreams. They
had a great variety of games during the week.

"The war dance, which was a part of this festival,
is something which I cannot make you see. I have

no words. They acted war. The war song was sung which aroused all the fire of the young warriors — and then the arrows flew thick and fast, the tomahawk was lifted, the dead and dying were upon the battlefield, the scalps were taken ; and then you could hear the shout of victory and the dirge for the slain. It was all done by various devices of paint, false scalps, etc., but it appeared very real and was terribly exciting.

" You cannot understand," said the old man with kindling face, " what a joyful time it was. Nobody knew any trouble during those nine days."

" Silverheels," said I, " do tell us about the Medicine Feast."

" Listen ! " said the old man. " There is a wonderful medicine used by the Iroquois Indians, which they believe will restore a man even though shot through the body, if he can have it in season. They tell us that this medicine is composed of a little of the flesh and blood and fiber of every animal and every herb on this continent. It is prepared by special medicine men, and I will tell you its origin.

" Many, many years ago, a Seneca was killed by some of the southern Indians while upon the warpath. He was shot with an arrow through the body, and left in the woods near the trail. He had been a great hunter, but it was his habit to take only the skin of the animal, leaving the flesh for the wolves and wild bears to eat. As he lay dead upon the ground there came along a wolf who looked upon the dead man with sorrow, and set up a wail which called all the wild animals about him. He then addressed them : —

" ' Can we not in our united wisdom bring this dead man to life, who has been our best friend by always killing the larger animals and leaving their flesh for us to eat?'

" The eagle, vulture, bear, and all flesh-eating animals said, ' We will try.'

" So they set themselves to work to prepare a medicine. Each one was to furnish the most potent remedy with which he was acquainted. An acorn cup contained the whole when it was finished. This they poured down the throat of the dead man. Then they sang to him, each one with his peculiar note, while the birds fanned him with their wings. All night long they surrounded him, making the best efforts they could to restore him. In the morning they discovered some warmth about the heart and the question was raised, ' Who will go after the scalp which the enemy has taken from him?'

" After much discussion the chicken hawk offered to reclaim it. He flew with great speed, soon arriving at the enemy's camping ground. He saw the scalp of his friend stretched on a hoop with many others, suspended on a pole and painted red. The whole settlement were dancing about it and rejoicing over their victory. He seized it with his beak, flew back, and found the man sitting up and almost well. They soaked the scalp until it was soft and then fitted it upon his head. They then taught this man how to make the wonderful medicine which had restored him to life, and which they named Ga-ni-gah-ah (a little liquid). And this is the origin of our famous medicine which will restore the dead to life if taken in season.

" In our day this medicine is made into a very fine powder. Then some one takes a cup and goes to the brook, fills it, dipping toward the way the water runs, and sets it near the fire. A prayer is offered while tobacco is thrown upon the fire, so that the words may ascend with the smoke. The medicine is placed upon a piece of skin near the cup, then taken up with a wooden spoon and dusted upon the water in three places in spots in the form of a triangle. If the medicine spreads itself over the surface of the water and wheels about, it is a sign that the invalid will be healed. If it sinks directly, there is no hope — the sick person will die, and the whole is thrown away."

" But what about the medicine feast?"

" The white woman pushes me," said Silverheels, somewhat annoyed. " I am preparing her mind to understand the feast. The medicine feast is held at the hunting time. As soon as it is dark on the night of the feast, all those who are permitted to attend shut themselves in one room without light or fire. The embers are covered, the medicine is placed near them, and the tobacco by its side. Then they begin to sing something which proclaims that the crow and other animals whose brains form the medicine are coming to the feast. At the end of the song, the ' caw ' of the crow, the howl of the wolf, etc., are imitated. Three times in the course of the night prayer is offered, while throwing tobacco upon the smothered flames. They pray that the medicine may heal the sick and wounded. Through the night the door has been locked, and no one has been allowed to enter or leave the house, or to sleep, as this would spoil the medicine.

" Just before dawn the leader takes a deer's head, and biting off a piece, passes the head to another, who does the same, until all have tasted. A little later the leader takes a duck's bill, and, dipping it full of the medicine, gives it to each one present, who puts it in a bit of skin, and wrapping it in several coverings keeps it carefully until the next feast. The skin of the panther is preferred. Those who take part in these ceremonies are medicine men. These medicine men add pulverized roots of corn and squashes and bean vines to the original powder.

"Perhaps you have been told," said old Silverheels, "that the Indian knows more about the healing herbs than any other race?"

"How can it be?" I asked skeptically.

"I will tell you," said the Indian, "as my grandfather told me. An Indian hunter went forth to hunt. Suddenly he heard a strain of beautiful music. He listened, but could not tell whence it came. He knew it was not from any human voice. When he thought he was approaching the sound it ceased.

"Then came Ha-wen-ni-yu to him in a dream and said, 'Wash yourself until you are purified; then go forth and you will again hear the music.'

"So he purified himself, and went into the thickest woods, and soon his ear caught the sweet strains, and as he drew near they became more beautiful. Then he saw that the wonderful music came from a plant with a tall green stem and tapering leaves. He cut the stalk, but it immediately healed and became as before. He cut it again, and again it healed. Then he knew it would heal diseases. He took it home, dried it by the fire, and pulverized it. When applied to a dangerous wound it no sooner touched the flesh than it was made whole. Thus Ha-wen-ni-yu taught the Indian the nature of medicinal plants, and from that time has directed him where they are to be found."

" Minnie Myrtle " was our guest at the Mission House many weeks, while she studied these Indians and at the same time wrote " The Iroquois," from materials which we secured for her. She says : —

" When we read that the Indian ornamented himself with the husks of his favorite maize and went from house to house with a basket to gather offerings from the people, we call it heathenish and barbarous, while the story of Ceres, the goddess of corn, whose head was surrounded with sheaves and who holds in her hand a hoe and basket, is picturesque and beautiful !

" We listen to the Indian story of the woman in the moon, who is constantly employed in weaving a net, which a cat ravels whenever she sleeps, and that the world is to come to an end when the net is finished ; and we say ' Ridiculous !' But the story of Penelope weaving her purple web by day to be raveled by night, during the prolonged absence of her husband, Ulysses, is a conception worthy of being expanded into a poem of a thousand lines and translated into all languages ! "

WHEN the white people asked the Iroquois for land enough to stretch themselves upon, they consented to give them that much; but discovering after a time that the strip was a mile long they remonstrated, saying, "Why! do you not know that we, the Iroquois, are so powerful that if an enemy attempts to take possession of our territory, we need not to raise our whole hand against him? One finger would destroy him!"

XIV.

O N long winter evenings Mrs. Wright and I sometimes joined a group of Indians gathered about the open fire while the oldest warrior related the historic legends of their race, as handed down through the centuries from fathers and fathers' fathers, and, strange to say, with very slight variation. Will the reader join the group this evening and listen to old "Squire Johnson," who is approaching his hundredth year, with eye and ear and memory unimpaired. I do not know the origin of his English name, but it was probably given him by some friendly white man. He is a member of the Mission church — a consistent and devoted Christian. He lives alone in a small cabin on the shore of Lake Erie. At dawn every Sabbath morning he may be seen starting for the Mission church, seven miles away, to which he regularly walks, through cold, heat, rain, or snow, for the all-day service, returning to his lonely cabin at night to praise God for the privilege.

This evening he will take us back to the creation, as the story has been handed down to him by his ancestors, and bring us gradually down to the present age. He speaks no English, and the story loses much of its vividness in the translation. Will he be able to throw any light upon the mysterious origin of this strange race?

" I will tell you first," he remarks serenely, " the origin of good and evil.

" At one time there was no earth, and all this world was one immense lake, in which great multitudes of water animals amused themselves after their own fashion of diving and playing in the water. It is well known that at that time these animals had the gift of language.

" One day a duck, who was possessed of uncommon intelligence, cried out, ' Some strange being is coming down to us from the sky!' A council of waterfowls was called at once to decide what should be done to prepare for this being who might not be fitted for life in the water. One duck said, ' I will dive, and find out if there is any bottom to our lake, which may be brought up for this purpose.' After some time she came to the surface, shot into the air, and fell back lifeless. The struggle had been too great for her strength. Several others made the same attempt with similar results. At last a muskrat said, ' I will try.' He came to the surface dead, but with a little earth in his claw. This encouraged others to renewed effort, and many were successful in bringing up small quantities of earth. At the suggestion of their chief, this soil was placed upon the back of a turtle, who expressed his willingness to become the foundation of an island. Although small at first, the turtle grew, and finally became the foundation of the great continent of North America.

"The mysterious object in the sky was coming more clearly into view, and at length the waterfowls, flying upward to meet it, found it to be a woman. They received her upon their outspread wings and landed her safely upon the earth. She began at once to explore her new island, and noticed that it took a longer time every day to walk around it. By this she knew it was growing in size. In course of time, the woman from the sky gave birth to twin boys, one of whom, the principle of good, was named Ha-wen-ni-yu, the Good Ruler; the other, the principle of evil, was named the Evil-Minded.

"Immediately after the birth of these boys the mother died. Ha-wen-ni-yu, the Good Ruler, said, 'I will take my mother's face and make a sun; her shining eyes shall give light to the whole earth. Of her body I will make the moon.' Thus was the light of day and night established. From that part of the earth where the beautiful mother died there grew corn, beans, and squashes, the favorite vegetables of the Indians.

" Thus far, there had been no plant or tree on the earth. ' Let the grass grow!' said Ha-wen-ni-yu, and at once the earth was made beautiful with the green grass. He then made the red willow grow on the wet lands and other trees and bushes for the dry land. He soon covered the island with beautiful flowers and herbs and trees and grains and vegetables, and many useful animals. It gave him great joy to do this. He also placed on the island many good people whom he loved.

" When the evil-minded brother saw how powerful Ha-wen-ni-yu was in producing beautiful and useful things, he was filled with envy, and began to thwart him in the good work by trying to spoil everything he had made. He even desired to kill him, but did not know how. One day he asked : —

" ' What would be fatal to you?'

" Ha-wen-ni-yu replied : ' Perhaps the cat-tail flags, whose leaves are so sharp, would kill me if I were pierced by them.'

" So the Evil-Minded took a bundle of the long leaves and thrust at him, but they only bent double. They would not harm him.

" ' What do you fear most of all things?'

" ' The deer's horn,' answered Ha-wen-ni-yu ; ' it is so hard and sharp.'

" Then the Evil-Minded found a cast-off deer's horn

and tried to thrust at him, and chased him a long way in the woods.

"At last Ha-wen-ni-yu rebuked him sharply, and said, 'You must stop this bad work. You must no longer spoil the good things I have made. Look at this crab apple! Taste of its juice! Look at these poisonous plants, these hideous reptiles, and these cruel animals which you have made. If you do not stop, I must punish you, for I have the power. I shall not destroy you; but I shall shut you up in darkness beneath the earth, with the hedgehog and other animals who shun the light.'

"The Evil-Minded replied, 'I have as much power as you, and can make as beautiful and useful things if I wish.'

"'Try and see,' said Ha-wen-ni-yu; 'make a useful dish.'

"The Evil-Minded went to work and made a very good-looking dish; but when water was put into it, it fell to pieces. It was useless.

"Then Ha-wen-ni-yu took of the sand and clay and formed a dish. He dipped water in it and set it down. The dish was whole and useful.

"One day Ha-wen-ni-yu was walking about his island, and he met some giants clothed in stone. They were the first people that lived here, even before the great lake was here. We do not know how they came, nor when. One day, Ha-wen-ni-yu met a strange man walking about by himself. Ha-wen-ni-yu spoke to him pleasantly, and asked him who he was. 'I am He-no, the Thunderer,' said he, 'and I should like to be employed by you in some great work.'

" 'What can you do?' asked Ha-wen-ni-yu.

" 'I can wash the whole island,' said he.

" 'Very well,' said the Good Ruler; 'that would indeed be a good work, and I will employ you to do it for me. You may wash the island as often as you like.' And this was the origin of rain.

" One day Ha-wen-ni-yu saw a man sitting all alone as in a prison. His face was very old and wrinkled. He had a tangle of discordant sounds all about him.

" 'Who are you?' said the Good Ruler.

" 'I am Ga-oh, the spirit of the winds,' said he, 'and I want permission to do what I will on your island.'

" Ha-wen-ni-yu gave him permission under his control, and now when he is restless you hear the rushing noise of the mighty wind, in the forest and on the sea. On his motions depend the rolling of the billows and the fury of the tempest. He can even put the whirlwind in motion, and he can stop it. When he is quiet there is only a gentle motion, a soft, fanning breeze. Ga-oh does not always have his own way, but is subject to the Good Ruler, Ha-wen-ni-yu, and obeys his will.

" There are other spirits who are very beautiful — the spirits of the corn, beans, and squashes. The guardian spirit of the corn is dressed in the long, tapering corn leaves, ornamented with the silken corn tassels, which are also arranged about her head in wreaths. The guardian spirit of the bean has her garments of its leaves, woven together by the delicate tendrils. She has upon her head a crown of the rich pods and blossoms. The guardian spirit of the squash is also clothed with the productions of the vine under its care. These three beautiful spirits are never separated, and for this reason the Indian plants the corn and beans and squashes in one hill. All summer long the three spirits flit about among the plants, taking care of them. But the Evil-Minded has spread over these vegetables his blight, and they are not as easy to cultivate as in the past. If you stand near the cornfields at night, you will hear the sweet spirit of the corn, in her compassion for the red man, bewailing her blighted fruitfulness.

" We Indians have always believed that each one has a protecting spirit appointed by the Good Ruler to take care of him ; and this is also true of everything that is beautiful to the eye or good for food. There is the protecting spirit of fire, of water, of medicine ;

of every healing herb and fruit-bearing tree; there
is the spirit of the oak, the hemlock, the hickory, the
maple; the spirit of the blackberry, the blueberry, the
whortleberry, the raspberry; the spirit of spearmint,
peppermint, and tobacco; there is a protecting spirit
at every fountain and by every running stream; by
every mountain and river and lake."

The following lines from one of our own poets have
reference to this habit of personifying nature, by
these simple children of the forest: —

TO THE SPIRIT OF THE RIVER.

Gwe-u-gwe the lovely! Gwe-u-gwe the bright!
Our bosoms rejoice in thy beautiful sight;
Thou art lovely when morning breaks forth from the sky,
Thou art lovely when noon hurls his darts from on high,
Thou art lovely when sunset paints brightly thy brow,
And in moonlight and starlight still lovely art thou.

Gwe-u-gwe, Gwe-u-gwe, how sad would we be,
Were the gloom of our forests not brightened by thee!
Ha-wen-ni-yu would seem from his sons turned away.
Gwe-u-gwe, Gwe-u-gwe, then list to our lay.

Having completed the story of the creation, and
settled the problems of good and evil, thunder and
rain, corn, beans, and squashes, and all the good and
useful as well as the bad and worthless, our Indian
patriarch places another heavy section of a log on
the fire, which has been producing marvelous pictures
during the strange recital. This fireplace, occupying,

as it does, one entire side of the humble cabin, would strike envy to the heart of the white man. A fresh cut from his beloved tobacco, and the old warrior proceeds to tell of that far-away period before Columbus ever dreamed of America: —

" At that time," said he, " our race were wandering about in small bands like wild animals. They had no knowledge of the true God, although they did believe that there was one powerful being who ruled over all, and whom they called Ha-wen-ni-yu, the Good Ruler. They acknowledged him as the author of all the good things that came to them. They had no mode of worshiping him except to thank him for these good things. They had no knowledge of his real character or of his will. They were guided by their dreams in everything.

" My people then clothed themselves with the skins of wild animals. They kindled their fires by the friction of a pointed stick upon a dry piece of wood, twirling it between their hands after the manner of a drill. They cooked their meat in a bark kettle, which they made by using a flint axe or chisel to separate ·the bark from an elm tree. They tied the large pieces of bark together at the ends with strips of the inner bark, making a dish large enough to hold the meat, with water enough to boil it. This bark kettle was suspended between two sticks over the fire, and by the time the kettle was burned through the meat was cooked.

" The dishes and spoons were also made of bark. The wigwams were made of old bark, one end of which was set up against a fallen tree. The other end was propped up by hickory sticks. They used hickory for their bows and arrows, the latter being pointed with flint. With this weapon they killed game. The beds were skins of the deer and other animals, laid upon the ground or upon piles of hemlock twigs. When so inclined, the community started off in the morning, and at sunset encamped as described, the women making a fire for the comfort of the little children. If the hunting was worth the while, they remained a few days, and even a few weeks. If it suited their fancy, they moved every day.

" In those days the Indian women had to provide all the wood, fetch the water, keep the fires, and do all the work, the men never laboring at all. The wigwams were all huddled together in the encampment. The women had to go a long way into the woods to bring the fuel in bundles upon their backs. Sometimes the snow was three feet deep. Then they used snowshoes. These women took turns in providing fuel for the whole settlement, two or three working at

it all day, only resting at noon to cook and eat. The
men were usually lounging upon their couches of skins
or playing upon the Indian flute. After a while they
would get up, take their guns, and go out for game,
killing a deer or perhaps a bear, thus providing meat
for the household or the whole settlement. This was
their only business. By degrees in later days the men
began to help get in the wood, but their piles of wood
would often run out, and a man would wait until it
was all gone before he would bestir himself to get
more. The houses even later were made of bark. In
my younger days I remember only two log houses.

"A matter of vital interest to my people in those
days was the physical training of their children.
Boys who were smart and brave naturally were
trained to be swift runners. The training began at
the age of ten. The point selected for the race was
one mile away. A company of little fellows were
stripped of their clothing and when fairly started were
pursued by an old man with a whip made of the tail
of the fisher (a fish). If he succeeded in catching
a boy, he plied him vigorously with the whip. The
boys ran and dodged, he following and striking right
and left until they were home again. If a boy succeeded in keeping entirely out of reach of the whip,
he was elected the boy chief.

"The Indian boys were also trained to bear hunger

and fatigue.   When a little fellow reached the age of
six years, he was awakened by this message: 'Up!
Go shooting birds!   Don't come back till sunset!'

" They trained me in that way!" said the old man,
his rugged features lighted by a smile.   "I remember
well the morning I was six years old and aroused from
a sound sleep by that message.   I was sent out in
the early morning without a mouthful of food, to
shoot birds with my little bow and arrow.   When I
returned at sunset they gave me a piece of cold boiled
corn bread and a little hominy, not enough, however,
to satisfy the cravings of hunger.   For days and
weeks I was not permitted to taste of anything warm.
I was thus being trained to endure the fatigue and
hunger incident to our long excursions for hunting,
or war with distant tribes.   In winter they cut a hole
in the ice, and in the early morning forced us to
plunge in and dive and swim, that we might learn
not to fear the cold."

This reminiscence of his childhood brought back
other scenes, I suppose, for the old man sat gazing
with a far-away look into the fire, quite oblivious of
our presence.   At last we gently interrupted his
reverie by a question: —

" Before the white man found your country, what
did the wandering companies do with their dead?"

The Indian started as though suddenly awakened

from sleep, and with a gratified expression at our unabated interest, said, "Let me tell you first of a wonderful thing that happened two hundred years ago.

"At that time the Kah-gwas lived on the eastern shore of Lake Erie along the Niagara River. In history they are called the 'neutral nation.' The Iroquois then occupied the whole length of the state of New York from the Hudson River to Lake Erie. Two Seneca chiefs resolved to go to the Kah-gwa villages to see how strong they were. They found the warriors away on the warpath and no one at home but the women and children. This made them suspicious that the Kah-gwas proposed to make war upon them. They returned immediately to their own tribe and raised the cry, 'Go weh! Go weh!' to let the people know that the enemy was approaching. A large council was immediately called to adopt measures for self-defense. The principal chief proposed that they should go out a distance from home to meet the enemy. He said : —

"'We do not want so many dead bodies to lie about here near our villages. It would make a bad odor.'

"The warriors assembled at Geneva, leaving their women and children there, and sent out spies in every direction to watch the progress of the enemy. They discovered that there were twenty-eight tribes coming against them, a great multitude from the west and the south; they were coming even from the Rockies. The Iroquois warriors encamped on a hill on the Genesee River. The Kah-gwas and their allies came near and halted. The Senecas sent out demanding a parley, the result of which was that four sachems of the Senecas and four of equal rank from the enemy were to meet halfway up the hill. It was the custom to smoke the long pipe together on such occasions. Four were seated on the west side of the fire and four on the east side, and smoked a long time in dignified silence. At length the principal Seneca sachem demanded of the other party: —

" ' What is your business here in such great numbers?'

" They answered, ' We have come to extinguish the Iroquois.'

" The Seneca replied, ' You had better not try it. You will fail and a great many people will be killed for nothing.'

" The Kah-gwas answered, ' We are determined to destroy you.'

" This was repeated three times. As they continued resolute and determined to fight, one of the Senecas arose and deliberately killed three of the other party. He then said to the remaining one: —

" ' Go and tell your people what you have seen.

Tell them to go home while they may safely, and do not trouble us to fight you.'

" As soon as the Kah-gwa came to his friends an immense multitude rushed on in great fury, but the Iroquois met them and stood the shock like men and soon forced them to retreat. The Senecas then called upon the Burnt Knives [young men], of whom there was a large number hidden in the bushes, to engage in the fight. They came down the hill with great speed, armed with heavy clubs, and fought with such desperation that the enemy soon fled to the river, and many attempting to cross were drowned, while others were knocked on the head in the water. Very few of the enemy escaped the rage and fury of the Iroquois. The women and children and old men heard of the defeat of their tribes and rent the air with a howl of despair and grief. They had brought large piles of moccasins to put upon the feet of the captives they had expected to take, and in rage they now threw them away. The Senecas took a large number of the different tribes captive, and said to them : —

" ' We will now do to you as you do to your captives.' So they took the Kah-gwa chief who had headed the expedition, stripped him, bound him to a tree, smeared his body with deer's grease, made a great fire, and burned him up. Then they took a Chippewa chief and proceeded to treat him in the same manner. But when he said, ' I was forced into this fight through fear of death,' they released him and said to the remainder, ' Now you may all go home, but do not try to conquer the Iroquois again.' "

And now the old face is all aglow with pride in the glory of the past; but in our impatience he is soon recalled to the humiliating present as we insist upon the story of the dead.

" My people," he continued, " always buried their dead in the ground. The body was wrapped in skins, with a piece of bark laid above and beneath. Before burial the body of the dead was laid upon a piece of bark elevated a little from the ground. He was dressed in the best he had. The feet were incased in moccasins. Some chief of his clan was appointed to tell of his bravery in war, his skill in hunting, his loyalty to his clan and tribe. He publicly mourned the great loss to the tribe.

" Then," said he, dropping into the present tense, " relatives approach the body, addressing the departed with significant gestures. They thank and praise him for his kindness and virtues. They deplore his loss, while they know he has gone to the Happy Home beyond the Setting Sun. They charge him with messages to the friends who have preceded him to the

Happy Home. After this the whole circle bursts out in a heart-rending wail, which continues a long time and then gradually dies away. The body is then carried to the dwelling place of each relative in turn, where the same ceremony is repeated. Then the upper piece of bark is laid over the body and it is placed in the ground, lying upon the back with the feet toward the west. In the grave are placed articles of ornament, clothing, cooking utensils, and food, also pipes, bows and arrows, and stone knives.

" After the burial a company of ten hired mourners come to the wigwam of the departed and have a season of wailing with the family. Then the wailers go to the grave, build a fire at the head, and spend the night watching the grave. Early in the morning they return to the house of the dead and commence wailing there, in which they are joined by the family. The family feed these wailing women and treat them with great attention. They rest and sleep during the day, and at night return to the grave to watch and wail again. This ceremony continues ten days.

" During these ten days the family and relatives take off all ornaments and clothe themselves in the poorest garments they can find, even to rags. If a garment looks worse on the wrong side, it is worn wrong side out. Even the silver brooches necessary to fasten the clothes are put on wrong side out. The faces are not washed nor the hair combed. The more filthy and disgusting they appear the more sincere the grief. A more abject-looking object than the mother and wife of a dead man during these ten days can hardly be imagined.

" At the end of the days of mourning comes the funeral feast, in which all the clan participate. It consists of the very best provisions that can be obtained. The possessions of the dead man are now distributed among his relatives, and each one of the hired mourners receives a present.

" At this feast a portion of each kind of food is set apart in a secret place for the use of the departed, who during these ten days has been constantly with them taking note of every expression of grief. At the close of the day of the feast he takes his final departure to the Happy Home beyond the Setting Sun.

" It was often the case, months and years after, that some friend was notified by a dream that the departed wished to have assurance that he was not forgotten. Then the friends held another feast, at which they recounted his virtues and reviewed their memories of him. At this feast the wailing and disfigurement of the person were omitted and each was obliged to furnish a share of the provisions."

Squire Johnson was tired and expressed a wish to be left to the solitude of his cabin, but in answer to our inquiry, "What is the distinction between the *clan* and the *tribe* which you have made this evening?" he reluctantly granted us an extension of hospitalities.

"Each tribe of the Iroquois," said he, "is divided into eight clans, known as the Wolf, Bear, Beaver, Turtle, Deer, Snipe, Heron, and Hawk."

"But what tribes do you include in the Iroquois?"

"Your mind is very dark," said the old man, "if you do not know about the five tribes of the powerful Iroquois: the Mohawks, Oneidas, Onondagas, Cayugas, and my own tribe, the Senecas — the wonderful people of the Long House."

"The Long House!" I exclaimed; "you surely cannot mean that all these tribes live in one house?"

The usual attitude of dignified repose, characteristic of the race, gave place to a burst of laughter.

"The Good Ruler," said he, "has given us the night for sleep, and I will tell you about the Long House another evening."

We were forced at last to yield to the inevitable and wait until the "protecting spirit" of the Indian legend should see fit to move our friend to fresh revelations.

After many days a messenger brought the good tidings that Squire Johnson would graciously enlighten our ignorance concerning the Long House. A ride of nine miles over the snow, and we were again seated before a roaring fire in Squire Johnson's cabin, ready for further revelations.

"The Long House extended," said the old man, "from the Hudson River to Lake Erie; and from the river St. Lawrence to the Susquehanna. It was occupied by the five tribes which I mentioned to you. A few years before the white man whom you call Columbus came here, these five tribes formed themselves into a league for protection against the Indian tribes of the west and east and south. We were as one family sheltered by one roof. Each of the five tribes was divided into the eight clans, of which I told you.

"The Onondagas lived in the center of the Long House, on the north shore of Onondaga Lake, and kept the council fire always burning. This means that we acted together. The Mohawks lived at the eastern door, on the banks of the Hudson, to keep watch toward the rising sun. The Senecas had charge of the western door, which was the most important door, because the tribes toward the setting sun were fierce and warlike. The Oneidas and Cayugas dwelt at equal distances east and west of the Onondagas. This tribe, being in the center, kept the council brand and the wampum. They also kept the records by the wampum belt. There were fifty sachemships — all the sachems having equal authority and ruling together over the whole. After this league was formed there was a great improvement in our habits. We did not wander away as before, and we raised great quantities of corn and beans and squashes."

This reminded us of a very old diary of a Frenchman, DeNonville, which we had noticed one day among other musty books in the Mission garret, and we afterward looked up any allusions which he made to this curious confederation of the people whom the French had named "Iroquois." This diary was dated 1607, and confirmed the story of the old man. DeNonville, who was sent by the French with a company to fight these Indians, says he found large villages. In four of these villages he destroyed 1,200,000 bushels of corn, besides great quantities of beans and squashes. He says they had a large fort fifteen miles from the present town of Rochester, of five hundred paces in circumference, built on a high place. These powerful Iroquois, or "United People," were a terror to other tribes.

"By far Mississippi, the Illini shrank
When the trail of the TURTLE was seen on the bank.
On the hills of New England, the Pequod turned pale,
When the howl of the WOLF swelled at night on the gale;
And the Cherokee shook in his green, smiling bowers,
When the foot of the BEAR stamped his carpet of flowers!"

" The Tuscaroras," continued old Johnson, " who had once been with us, living near Niagara Falls, had been driven away ; but after the league was formed (1715) they came back and were admitted. From that time it has been known as the ' League of the Six Nations.' "

The poet tells us : —

"Naught in the woods their might could oppose,
  Naught could withstand their confederate blows.
  Banded in strength and united in soul,
  They moved in their course with the cataract's roll."

" The Oneidas," said the Indian, " used to meet about a great stone. It was very large. There was no stone like it within one hundred miles. You may see the Oneida stone if you wish to in the graveyard at Utica."

" Were the Six Tribes ever called together ? "

" Always," said he, " when there were important matters to be settled. It was done by ' runners.' They were as fleet of foot as the deer. Their trails connected village and village, clan and clan, tribe and tribe — and even reached to the Mississippi and Gulf of Mexico ; and they also reached to the Atlantic Ocean and the northern lakes."

" Johnson," said I, " do you think the trails of those tribes are our great streets and railroads now ? "

" I know they are," said he ; " the trail was a footpath at first, just wide enough for one person, but they were used by so many people that they were worn several inches deep."

" My brother ! " I exclaimed, in a burst of enthusiasm, " it is true indeed, as has been said : ' Not by our great thoroughfares alone will your race be remembered. Your expressive and beautiful names are upon every hillside, in every valley ; in the foaming cataract and upon our beautiful lakes.'

> ' Your name is in our waters,
> We may not wash it out.' "

Not understanding one word of this outburst the Indian received it without demonstration, and silently awaited the next question.

" About the ' runners,' Johnson ; did one runner notify all the tribes ? "

" No," said he. " If anything happened in either tribe that required the advice of the assembled sachems and people, a runner was sent to the tribe nearest, and that one sent a messenger to the next, and so on until all the six tribes had been notified. Do you understand ? " he asked. " Suppose the Senecas wished the council called. The sachems of the Senecas had to meet first and decide whether the matter was of sufficient importance. If it was, then they sent a runner with a wampum belt to the Cayugas. The Cayugas sent the wampum belt to the Onondagas, these to the Oneidas, and the Oneidas to the Mohawks. Then the sachems and chiefs and warriors, with the women and children, gathered about the council fire, coming from the farthest points of the Long House, heeding no toil or danger in their zeal for the common welfare."

" Of what was the wampum belt made? "

" Of small shells strung upon strings of deerskin. The belt was made of several strings woven together; some were black, emblem of war; some white, emblem of peace. They treasured up speeches and events by the belt. ' This belt preserves my words' was a common expression. The orator associated each part of the speech with a portion of the string. No notice was taken of any messenger or of his message unless he could produce the wampum belt."

" One more question to-day, Johnson; what is the ' calumet of peace' that we read about? "

" That was a very sacred symbol," said the old man, " among my people. It was a pipe made of red stone finely polished. The quill was two feet and a half long, made of a strong reed. The red calumets were often trimmed with white, yellow, and green feathers."

This calumet we found out later was a flag of truce

among Indian tribes, and a violation of it as disgraceful as an insult to the white flag among civilized peoples.

> " Whilst high he lifted in his hand
> The sign of peace, the calumet;
> So sacred to the Indian soul,
> With its stem of reed and its dark red bowl
> Flaunting with feathers, white, yellow, and green."

The old warrior was in a good mood this evening, and volunteered an extra crumb of information.

" You may remember I told you that each tribe had eight clans : the Wolf, Bear, Beaver, Turtle, Deer, Snipe, Heron, and Hawk. It is the same with us now ; and no son or daughter of any clan is allowed to marry a person of his clan in any tribe. A Deer of the Senecas may marry a Turtle of his own or any other tribe. But a Wolf may not marry a Wolf or a Bear a Bear. The children belong to the clan of the mother. If she is a Deer, then all her children are Deer. They not only call her mother, but they call all her sisters mother, and they call all her sisters' children brothers and sisters. This is the reason they do not marry in their own clan. The children belong to the tribe of the mother as do the children's children to the latest generation. If a Cayuga mother marries a Seneca father, the children are Cayugas. If the marriage prove unhappy, the parties are allowed to separate, and each is at liberty to marry again. But the mother has the sole right to the disposal of the children."

This talk about marriage reminded us of the Indian's reply to the white man who criticized the matrimonial methods of that race: "You marry squaw; she know you always keep her, so she scold, scold, scold, and not cook your venison. I marry squaw, and she know I not keep her if she not good. So she not scold, but cook my venison, and always pleasant; we live long together."

The offices of sachems, chiefs, etc., were inherited in the line of the mothers. It would seem that women were treated with respect in those days. The emblem of power was a deer's antlers, and if the women disapproved of the acts of a sachem, they had the power to remove his horns and restore him to private life.

It is not recorded that the women ever abused their privileges. They never meddled with that which did not belong to them. They never manifested a desire to become warriors or sachems. They planted corn, dressed deerskins, worked wampum belts, wrought porcupine embroidery for centuries without a murmur! These Indians say to-day: —

" The Long House belonged to the warriors who defended it and to the women who tilled it, and if it had not been for the fire water which degraded the men and left them to be easily bribed to make treaties contrary to the rules of the people and the judgment of their best men and all their women, the glory of the Iroquois would not have faded away."

During our ride home that night we resolved to ask Mr. Parker, the United States Interpreter, this question: " Who were the Kah-gwas?" for the old Indian had mentioned a tribe of whom not even Mrs. Wright had heard before. We give his reply for the benefit of any curious reader: —

" The Kah-gwas," said Mr. Parker, " were a tribe of Indians who emigrated from the south and west untold years ago and settled near the foot of Lake Erie. We find traces of their mounds and fortifications near the shore of the lake. They grew in strength and became very numerous. Then they became proud and challenged the Senecas to a national wrestling match.

" The Senecas accepted the challenge and with twelve picked athletes met the Kah-gwas on their own grounds. The condition of the match was that whoever was vanquished should be immediately dispatched by the victor. The Kah-gwas were defeated. The tribe was indignant and decided to exterminate the Senecas. A large company of Kah-gwa women, laden with immense packs of moccasins with which to shoe the captives who were to be so easily taken, joined the expedition against the Senecas.

" But the Senecas, ever on the alert, discovered the plan of their enemies and prepared to meet them. Not believing it the best policy to await the attack, they marched to meet the foe. The young braves were put in the advance and the middle-aged men in the rear. The tribes met in Livingston County, upon a stream near Honeoye Lake, and there the fiercest battle ever fought by Indians took place. The foes for four successive days swayed back and forth over the stream until it literally flowed with blood.

" The Kah-gwas, finding themselves nearly exterminated, retreated to their homes; from thence to the Alleghany River, down that stream to near Pittsburgh, where they encamped for the night. A few of the Seneca braves followed their trail until they discovered their enemies. Being very few in number, the Senecas resorted to strategy to deceive the foe. They floated down, passed the encampment, until out of sight, then landed their canoes, transported them across the point of land above the camp, and floated down again. They went through this operation again and again until midnight, and then encamped for the night. The trick had its effect. Before daylight the Kah-gwas fled to parts unknown and no vestige of them has been seen to this day."

It was an evening in spring. Our story-teller, Johnson, was visiting us at the Mission. "The sound of the frog which we hear to-night," said the old man, "reminds me of a strange thing that happened long ago : —

"In one of the raids of the Senecas upon the Cherokees a brave Seneca warrior was taken prisoner. It was the custom of the southern Indians to put their prisoners to death by burning ; not so with the Iroquois. Well, these Cherokees had a long account to settle with this prisoner, for he had slain many of their people. They at last determined that he should be burned. They had a place prepared for such purpose. In the midst was an elevation so that all the people could see where the prisoner was bound to the post. The time was fixed and a great multitude assembled. The Seneca warrior was bound firmly to a post and the fagots piled up around him. The fire was kindled into a blaze, the flames circled around him and burned him about the mouth and chest and legs and feet ; but just then there was a terrible clap of thunder, the rain poured down, the people fled to their wigwams, the fire was extinguished, and the darkness of the shower was followed by the darkness of the night. They supposed he was so firmly bound that escape was impossible and did not take the trouble to look after him.

" Pretty soon the prisoner began to feel green frogs crawling and squirming upon his burned feet and ankles and creeping up so as to cover the burned places all over his body. This relieved him so much that he could move a little and was soon able to release his feet. The next effort was to slip the bands from his hands. But when released he found he could not walk; so he crept away into the woods and finding a hollow log crawled in and concealed himself. At dawn of day the Cherokees missed him and sent scouts in every direction to hunt him up. They surrounded his log without discovering him.

" The green frogs followed him into the log; all day long they were busy relieving his burns. At night he crawled out and, not yet being able to walk, crept again as far as he could to another hollow log. Here again the frogs came to his relief and so nearly cured him that the next night he was able to walk and soon found himself beyond reach of his pursuers. But he did not leave his reptile friends without expressing to them his thanks. The frogs said, ' We are only repaying your kindness to us, for whenever you noticed that a snake had caught us by the legs and heard our squeal for help, you always killed the snake and let us go free. And it is in gratitude for this that we have followed you and given you the healing power of our bodies.' "

"And now," continued the old man, "you shall hear how there came to be peace between the Iroquois and their enemies, the Cherokees. I have the story from one who was present at the council fire : —

"Upon a certain occasion a large number of Iroquois warriors started on a long journey for the Cherokee country. On the way they sang the night and morning war songs to secure success to the expedition. The night song was sung in the place of encampment; the morning song was sung by the leader of the march as they started again upon the journey. They had other songs which were used upon their arrival at their destination. When they arrived at the enemy's country, knowing that the Cherokees were always on the lookout, they stopped upon a distant high hill overlooking one of the villages of the plain. At night they came cautiously down and surprised the village, killing all the inhabitants and burning the houses.

"During the night the Cherokees of another settlement heard the cry of alarm — 'Go weh! go weh!'[1] but when they came to the thick bushes it stopped. They could see nothing, but they sent two men to lie in wait and discover what it meant. By-and-by these men heard the cry again — 'Go weh! go weh!' As

[1] Go weh is an exclamation signifying that some great calamity has befallen a war party, or some distinguished sachem has fallen. It is said that this exclamation has such a charm that it can be heard for miles before the runner or messenger has reached a settlement. This word is used only on such occasions as the above. — *N. H. Parker.*

they came near they saw a hedgehog approaching who stopped and stood upon his hind feet and cried out, ' Go weh! go weh! ' They killed the hedgehog and went back to tell their people.

" The Cherokees were alarmed and sent at once to see what had befallen the neighboring village. They found it burned and the people slain. Not one had escaped to tell the story. They looked for traces of the enemy, and discovered five paths all converging on the hill and a wigwam marked with black paint. Then they said, ' It is our old enemy, the Iroquois.'

" They sent messengers to notify their people of what had happened and called a general council. The chiefs came together and the question was laid before them : ' What shall we do? At this rate our enemy will soon exterminate us.' One chief said, ' I can see but one course for us, and that is to make peace with the Iroquois.' The others answered, ' We will do it.'

" Accordingly they sent four men to the Iroquois telling them of their proposition of peace and asked to have it done at the Cherokee council. The Iroquois consented and decided that a large company should go armed for any emergency or treachery on the part of the Cherokees. And so a large band of the Iroquois arrived at the Cherokee country fully armed, arrayed in all their gorgeous costume of feathers, beads, paint, etc., in order that their large numbers and imposing appearance might lead the Cherokees to suppose that they were not obliged to make peace, but simply consented to their request as an act of condescension. On taking their seats in council and receiving the pipe of peace the Cherokee chief said to them :

" ' It is our wish to make peace if possible. We are exceedingly anxious that this war should cease.'

" A distinguished Seneca sachem replied, ' We are willing on our part, only we wish all grievances to be buried, and buried so deep that not one shall ever come above ground again ; but if from any cause difficulties should arise and trouble show itself again, we will do then as we have done now ; we will bury it so deep that it can never even sprout again, and I for my part promise, and I will keep it, that when our troubles are buried and we are at peace again I will not heed any proposals from other nations to break our peace with you. If one from another tribe shall come and entice me to join with him in war upon you, I will not be tempted by him. I will maintain our covenant with you.'

" The Cherokee chief replied : ' I will do so too. If any of the neighboring nations shall say to me, ' Come, let us exterminate the Iroquois ! ' I will refuse. I will only look to and strictly observe the covenant which we are now making.'

" After full discussion both parties declared themselves satisfied and proceeded to shake hands in ratification of friendship. The Cherokees took hold with the right hand of the hand of the Iroquois and each reaching forward the left hand grasped the shoulder of the other, thus pledging permanent fidelity to the compact. This was their custom, and this mode of shaking hands made the promise securely binding. The Senecas said : —

" ' Henceforth we will be brethren as if of one blood.'

" The Cherokee added, ' If one of your people shall come here and wish to be at home with us, and desire to marry among us and become a Cherokee, he may do so. Now this agreement is enforced this day.'

" When all parties were satisfied the Cherokee chief said, ' It is finished ; and now let us have sport together. We have a swift runner who beats all the rest of our people. Let us have a foot race.' The race was about twenty rods. A Seneca volunteered to run with the Cherokee and defeated him. This is the last important war of the Iroquois with the western Indians."

The next morning Johnson gave us a reminiscence of his boyhood. " When I was a boy ten years old, I lived with my grandfather. A chief of the Cayugas came to visit him. One day I was sitting on a log where this chief had called a council. I heard him say these words : —

" ' I have called you together to take into consideration the condition of our people. We are losing all our Indian traits and privileges and we cannot perpetuate them, and we can do nothing to prevent this change. The whites will overpower us. We sided with the British against these whites and the British are overcome, and the whites will drive us before them if we continue our Indian mode of living. We cannot go west; the Indians there will consider us intruders and will drive us back. What shall we do? My judgment is that we must stay where we are and adapt ourselves to the coming changes. We must adopt the white man's life. We must give up our old ways. We must drop our pagan feasts and dances. We must learn to work like the white man, and get our living from the soil. We must wear clothes like a white man. We must have our children educated. We must adopt the religion of the white man. There is nothing left for us to do. There is no other help remaining. We shall soon lose everything peculiar to the Indian. We cannot live unless we endure these changes and become like the white man.'

" The chief was silent. My grandfather then spoke : —

" ' I will add to these words. What has been said is true, but we do not yet see this change. My grandson, who sits there on the log, will perhaps live to see it accomplished, but we old men are yet free and will probably die as we are. Still it is coming to our children, and we cannot prevent it. We have lost our power. We must let these old things all go which we have prized so highly: our painted faces, our tufts of feathers, our ornaments in the laps of our ears, our dances and ceremonies must all disappear. But these things must go because they are not of the Good Ruler. They are the contrivance of man, who pretended that the Good Ruler ordained them. This is not so. If it were, these things could not be destroyed by man. It is the human works that perish. No man can destroy what the Good Ruler ordains. Our Indian customs, rights, and ceremonies perish because he did not appoint them. They are mortal — the work of man. The Good Ruler could have kept the whites from crossing the ocean if it had been his will, and would have done so to preserve us and our customs if they had been ordained by him. But he chose to bring the white man here and to let us fall and perish before him because our way was not his way. And thus it is true that our fate is inevitable. We cannot prevent it. Before the white man came here, while we were yet alone in this country, we had nothing with which to help ourselves. We made no progress. We made no improvement in our condition. They came here, and brought the flint and steel for striking fire. It was a good thing. They brought knives and axes; we liked them; and we liked their guns; and we have been glad to use all their improvements. They brought money here, and we have been glad to get it. We have begun, through their help, to make progress, but they are all about us and we cannot stand up against them. We must adopt these other things which they bring, some of which we shall also find good for us. Their books and learning are good. Their laws are good for us as well as for them. Perhaps we shall like their religion. It will be better for us to embrace it. It will not avail us to resist and provoke them. If we are good, they will treat us kindly and we can remain where we are. Brothers, let us beware of one thing the white man has brought here. Let us beware of his strong drink. We have seen how that often causes death. If we use it, it will certainly destroy us. Let us be good and peaceable, and adopt all the good ways of the white man and avoid his evil ways. Thus only will it be well with us.'

" Another chief arose, and said : ' My brother's words are true. He has spoken like a prophet. His words will come to pass. This boy on the log will

live to see it. The things which the white man brings
to us are as good for us as for him. It will be for our
advantage to make use of them. Let us adopt the
religion and customs of the white man that we may
be preserved when no power is left us for maintaining
the old ways of our forefathers.'

" I often wonder," said Johnson, " at the foresight
and wisdom of these old men and at the exact fulfillment of their predictions. They spoke from the
heart and the people felt that their words were true."

IROQUOIS SASH

SHOULD the Indian be entirely banished from this land the memory of him cannot die.

> Their names are on our waters,
> We cannot wash them out.

The dialects of the Six Nations of the Iroquois resemble each other, although there are differences which mark them as distinct. The Mohawk and Oneida strongly resemble each other, as do the Seneca and Cayuga. The Onondaga is considered by the Iroquois as the most finished and majestic, while to our ears it is the most harsh and the Oneida the most musical. In Mohawk the sound of *l* is prominent and in Tuscarora the sound of *r*. The Senecas and Cayugas can talk all day without shutting their lips, and there are no oaths in their language. Metaphors are in constant use in the speeches and conversation of the Indian. When the weather is very cold he says, " It is a nose-cutting morning"; of an emaciated person, " He has dried bones "; a steamboat is " the ship impelled by fire"; a horse is " a log carrier"; a cow is " a cud chewer." In old times they kept warm by covering themselves with boughs of hemlock, and now if an Indian is about to repair his cabin he says, " I will surround it with hemlock boughs," meaning, " I will make it warm and comfortable." When a chief has made a speech he finishes with saying, " The doors are now open, you can proceed." The Iroquois call themselves " the older people," and the white man " our younger brother."

THE Seneca sachems used to plead with the governors of colonies to prevent the sale of fire water to the Indians. This was their plea: "It destroys our old and young. We have great fear of it. Our hearts tremble, our minds are deeply concerned. We entreat you, forbid the sale of this poison to our people!"

RED JACKET.

XV.

IT may be of interest at this point to give a few specimens of the old-time Iroquois eloquence, as compared with Iroquois eloquence to-day.

In 1805 a missionary came to the Iroquois and asked permission to teach them his religion. A council was called to decide whether he should be received. He was invited to state his plan and to explain his religion. Red Jacket made the following reply : —

" Friend and Brother : It was the will of the Good Ruler that we should meet together this day. He has taken his garment from before the sun and caused it to shine with brightness upon us. For this we thank him.

" Brother : This council fire was kindled for you. We have listened in silence to what you have said. You ask us to speak our minds freely. We stand ready before you to speak what we think. We speak as one man.

" Brother : Listen to our words. There was a time when our forefathers owned this land. Their seats extended from the rising to the setting sun.

Ha-wen-ni-yu made this land for the use of the Indian. He created the buffalo, the deer, and other animals for our food; he made for us the bear and the beaver; their skins served us for clothing. He caused the earth to produce corn for our bread. All this he did for his red children because he loved them. But an evil day came upon us; your fore-fathers crossed the great water and landed here. Their numbers were small. They found in us friends, not enemies. They told us they had fled from their own country because of wicked men, and had come here to enjoy their religion. They asked us for a small seat. We took pity on them — granted their request; they sat down among us. We gave them corn and meat. In return they gave us — poison [rum]!

"Brother: The white people had now found our country. Tidings were carried back and more white people came, yet we did not fear them. They called us brothers, and we believed them to be friends. At length their numbers had greatly increased; they wanted more land; they wanted our whole country. Our eyes were opened and our minds became uneasy. Wars took place. The white people hired the Indians to fight against each other, and many of our people were thus destroyed. The white people brought to us the fire water. It was strong and powerful, and has slain thousands.

" Brother: Our seats here were once large and yours were small. You are now a great people, and we have scarcely a place left to spread our blankets. You have got our country, but you are not satisfied. You now wish to force your religion upon us.

" Brother: Continue to listen. You are here to instruct us how to worship the Good Ruler according to his mind. You say you are right and we are lost. How do we know that your words are true? You say your religion is written in a Book. If the Book was intended for us too, why did not Ha-wen-ni-yu give the book to our forefathers? We know only what you tell us about this Book. How shall we know when to believe you who have so often deceived us?

" Brother: You say there is only one way to worship the Good Ruler; then why do the white people differ so much about this way? As the Book was sent to you and you can all read it, why do you not all agree?

" Brother: We do not understand these things. You tell us that your religion was given to your forefathers, and has been handed down from father to son. Our religion was given to our forefathers and has been handed down from father to son. It teaches us to be thankful for what we receive; to love each other and to be united. We have never quarreled about our religion.

" Brother : You tell us that you have been preaching to white people in this land. We will wait a while and see what your religion does for them. If it makes them honest, if they tell the truth, and no longer cheat the Indian, we will consider again these words that you have said.

" Brother : Now we will part; we take you by the hand and hope the Good Ruler will protect you on your journey and return you safe to your friends."

From the same remarkable orator is the following : —

" We first knew you, a little feeble plant, which wanted a little of our earth on which to grow. We gave it to you, and when we could have trod you under our feet we watered and protected you. Now you have grown to be a mighty tree, whose top reaches the clouds, whose branches overspread the whole land ; while we who were once the tall pine of the forest have become the little feeble plant, needing your protection. When you first came here you clung around our knee and called us father. We took you by the hand and called you brother. You have grown so great that we can no longer reach up to your hand, but we now cling around your knee and beg to be called your children."

A lady, who knew that Red Jacket had lost several

children, asked if he had any living. He fixed his eyes upon her with a mournful expression and replied : —

" Red Jacket was once a great man and in favor with Ḥa-wen-ni-yu. He was a lofty pine among the small trees of the forest; but after years of glory he degraded himself by drinking the fire water of the white man. Ha-wen-ni-yu has looked upon him in anger, and his lightning has stripped the lofty pine of all its branches."

Red Jacket gave these last instructions to his daughter : —

" When I am dead it will be noised abroad through all the world, ' Red Jacket, the Indian orator, is dead ! ' White men will come and ask you for my body. Do not let them take me. Put upon me my simplest dress ; put on my leggins and my moccasins, and hang the cross which I have worn so long around my neck and let it lie upon my bosom.[1] Then bury me among my people. The missionary who has come here says the dead will rise; perhaps they will; if they do, I wish to rise with my Indian friends. I do not wish to rise among pale faces. I wish to be surrounded by red men."

After these words Red Jacket laid himself upon his

[1] This large cross, which he always wore, was a very rich one of stones set in gold. No one knew by whom it was given to him.

couch and never rose again. He lived several days but was most of the time in a stupor. Occasionally he would unconsciously utter, " I do not hate the missionary ; he thinks I hate him, but I do not. I would not hurt him although he accused me of being a snake and trying to bite somebody. This was true, but now I wish to repent of it."

Chief Logan was another noted Indian orator.

In 1774 a deputation was sent from the government to treat with the sachems and chiefs of the Iroquois, and to endeavor to appease their revenge upon their oppressors, the white people. Chief Logan was a long time in yielding. He would not talk with the white men of peace. At last he said : —

" There is no hope for the Indian but to flee before the white man who oppresses him ; but I will never be his friend."

General Gleason followed Logan into the depths of the forest, and there, seated upon a fallen tree, with the aid of Cornstalk, a venerable chief, he was at last induced to sign the treaty, which all the other sachems had signed. But before he did it he uttered the following heart-rending story of his wrongs and the wrongs of his people. It was like wringing out his heart's blood to see them thus wasting away, and while he said these words the tears ran down his furrowed cheeks and he seemed to be a victim of intense suffering: —

" I appeal to any white man to say if he ever entered Logan's cabin hungry and he gave him no meat; if he ever came to him cold and naked, and he gave him no clothes. During that long and bloody war, Logan remained in his cabin urging his people to peace. Such was my love for the white man that my people pointed as they passed, and said in scorn, ' Logan is the friend of the white man.'

" Last spring, Colonel Cresap, in cold blood — unprovoked — murdered all the relatives of Logan. He did not even spare my women and my children. There runs not one drop of my blood in any living creature. This called on me for revenge. I have sought it; I have killed many white men. I have fully glutted my vengeance for my race; I rejoice at the beams of peace, but do not harbor a thought that mine is the joy of fear. Logan never knew fear. He will not turn on his heel to save his life. Who is there left on this earth to mourn for Logan? Not one ! "

This man wandered about for many years from settlement to settlement, restless, moody, and unhappy, and finally laid himself down in the woods to die of a broken heart. Very truly Jefferson remarks, " There were none left to mourn for Logan, but his talents and his misfortunes have attached to him the respect and commiseration of the world."

These extracts are taken from addresses given in English by educated Indians, who during my missionary life were still living among their people. The following was made before the Historical Society of New York by Peter Wilson, a Cayuga. The Cayugas, who had been driven from the " Long House " (New York State) and sent beyond the Mississippi River, were reduced to such extreme suffering that many of them died in less than a year. Peter Wilson obtained ten thousand dollars for the purpose of bringing back the remainder, five hundred of which was given by a Quaker in Baltimore.

" The honorable gentleman has told you that the Iroquois have no monuments. Do you not know that the Empire State, as you love to call it, was once laced by our trails from Albany to Buffalo — trails worn so deep by the foot of the Iroquois that they have become your own roads of travel? Your roads bind one part of the Long House to the other. The Empire State, then, is our monument, and we wish its soil to rest above our bones when we shall be no more. We shall not occupy much room in living ; we shall occupy less when we are gone ; a single tree of the thousands which sheltered our fathers — one old elm under which the representatives of the tribes were wont to meet —

will cover us all. But we would have our bodies twined in death among its roots on the very soil where it grew. Perhaps it will last the longer from being thus fertilized.

" Have we, the first holders of this prosperous region, no longer a share in your history? Glad were your forefathers to sit down upon the threshold of the Long House ; rich did they then hold themselves in getting the mere sweepings from its doors. Had our forefathers spurned you from this end of our house when the French were thundering at the opposite end to get a passage through to drive you into the sea, whatever has been the fate of other Indians, the Iroquois might still have been a nation; I — I — instead of pleading here for the privilege of lingering within your borders, — I — I — even I — *might have had — a country !* "

M. B. Pierce, a chief of the Senecas, gave utterance to the following : —

" It has been said, and frequently repeated, that it is the doom of the Indian to disappear — to vanish like the morning dew, before the advance of civilization.

" But why are we thus doomed? Why must we be crushed by the arm of civilization? Why must the requiem of our race be chanted by the waves of the

Pacific, which is destined at last to engulf us? Say, you, into whose lap fortune has poured her brimful horn so that you enjoy the highest and best of spiritual and temporal blessings, should some superior race, to whom you open the hospitality of your dwellings, claim the right to your possessions — the right to hunt you like wild beasts from your long-anticipated doom, how ready would you be to be taught of them? How cordially would you open your minds to the conviction that they would not deceive you further and still more fatally, in their proffers of pretended kindness? How much friendship for them and esteem for their manners and customs would you feel? Would not the milk of human kindness in your breast be turned to the gall of hatred toward them? I believe that every person who hears me to-day wonders that the hatred of the Indian has not burned with tenfold fury against the white man, rather than that they have not laid aside their own habits and religion to adopt those of this civilized nation. Blot out these terrible pages of your nation's history in connection with our people before you rise up to call the Indian treacherous or cruel.

"Tell me whether

> The poor Indian, whose untutored mind
> Sees God in clouds and hears him in the wind,

is not capable by cultivation of rationally comprehending the true God, whose pavilion is the clouds, and who yet giveth grace to the humble?

" I ask, then, in behalf of the New York Indians, that our white brethren will not urge us to do that which justice, humanity, religion, not only do not require, but condemn. Let us live where our fathers lived, that we who are converted heathen may be made meet for that inheritance which our Father hath promised to give his Son, our Saviour; so that the deserts and waste places may be made to blossom like the rose, and the inhabitants thereof utter forth the high praises of our God.

" Let me tell you our condition when the pale faces landed on the eastern shores of this great island. Our government then, many centuries ago, was remarkable for its wisdom, and adapted to the condition of our nation. It was a republican and powerful democratic government, in which the will of the people ruled. No policy or enterprise was ever carried out by the council of the Grand Sachems of the Confederacy of the Long House without the sanction and ratification of the people, and it was necessary that it should receive the consent of every one of the Six Tribes. The consent of the warriors alone was not deemed sufficient, but the women, the mothers of the nation, were also consulted. By this means the path of the wise sachems was made clear; their hands were strong, their determinations resolute, knowing that they had the unanimous support of their great constituency. Hence the confederacy of the Iroquois became great and strong, prosperous and happy; by their wisdom they became statesmen, warriors, diplomats; by their valor and skill in the warpath they became formidable; they conquered and subdued many tribes, and extended their territory.

" Our territory, which once required the fleetest runners to traverse, is now spanned by the human voice. Our possessions are so reduced that now when we put the seed of the melon into the earth it sprouts, and its tender vine trails along the ground until it trespasses upon the lands of the pale face."

Asher Wright Memorial Presbyterian Church, ca. 1930s. Dedicated in October 1857, this building served the combined congregations from the Lower Mission Station and the Upper Mission Station. Still in use today, this historic structure is located on Route 438, Cattaraugus Territory. (Calvin E. Lay Collection, Cattaraugus Territory.)

XVI.

"A WEDDING LIKE WHITE PEOPLE."

SEVENTEEN happy years of missionary life with Mrs. Wright among these Indians — and the call came to return to the New England home and friends, and enter a new life as the wife of a business man, Lemuel E. Caswell, of Boston. When the plans were nearly matured they were made known to the unsuspecting Indians.

"This cannot be!" they said. "Your father, the man with two pairs of eyes" (he wore spectacles), "brought you here when you were a young girl. He gave you to us. We have adopted you into our tribe — you belong to our Deer clan. You belong to us — and you have not asked our consent!"

After considerable discussion the announcement was made that they would feel satisfied if the wedding ceremony might be performed on the Reservation, exactly as it would be in Boston, that they might see "a real wedding." Consent was given to this, provided the bridegroom elect did not object. Contrary to expectation, the bridegroom was greatly taken with the novel plan, and promised to come to the Indians, and bring with him a company of friends. This company included the late Lawson Valentine, publisher of The Christian Union, and his wife; the late B. F. Whittemore and wife, of Boston; Dr. J. B. Clark, of Boston, with other relatives and friends. The party came within nine miles of the Reservation by rail, and at two o'clock in the morning were met by Indians who had volunteered their teams and services to bring them into Indian land. The procession made its way through dense woods, over indescribable roads, in darkness which could be felt; but, although some of the ladies were a little " nervous," they bore this bit of pioneering with commendable fortitude. The city pale faces were entertained at the Mission House and Orphan Asylum, and heroically adapted themselves to the accommodations at hand. On the day following their arrival they were taken by their Indian charioteers to the various out-stations, to the pagan dance house and its surrounding cabins, and to the well-tilled farms and comfortable houses of the Christian Indians. A pagan chief offered Mr. Valentine two cows, three pigs, twelve strings of corn, and a cabin, if he would remain. A similar offer was made to Mr. Caswell.

On the Sabbath, the party attended the Mission church in the forenoon and visited the out-stations among the pagans in the afternoon.

Mr. Caswell had secured a hack from a town thirty miles away for the comfort of the guests who were unable to endure the rough wagons. This hack, including team and driver, became the center of attraction upon the Reservation.

The wedding ceremony was to take place on Monday evening. The Indian committee of arrangements consisted of a Bible class of thirty young men, who from boyhood had known no teacher but the one now leaving them forever. These young men spent the day decorating the walls of the Mission church with boughs of the hemlock and clusters of red berries. The effect was very artistic and the guests watched these children of nature during the process with keen interest. On the platform below the pulpit, they erected a bower of the same green, brightened by the red, over which they placed the words woven from the delicate sprays of the hemlock : —

> "The Lord bless thee and keep thee;
> The Lord cause his face to shine upon thee,
> And give thee peace."

The marriage ceremony was to be solemnized under this bower. During a sudden shower in the afternoon one young Indian said to another in English: "The sky weeps for the red man, because he loses a friend."

The anticipated hour arrives at last, and from all parts of the Reservation the Indians make their way

to the Mission church. The haughty pagan for once
humbles his pride and enters the Christian church. A
promise had been given that upon this occasion the
wishes of the Indians should be consulted, when prac-
ticable, and the first request comes from the mothers :
" May we take our babies to the wedding ? " This
privilege was promptly granted.

When the bride and groom reach the church, in the
famous hack, the Indian committee are at hand to
escort them to the steps. They have taken up the
carpet from the church aisle and spread it upon the
ground for the use of the missionary bride. Who told
them to do this? No one. The committee divide
into two sections, one half preceding the bridal pair,
the other half following, until they are escorted to the
bower which has been prepared for them.

Dr. Clark, brother of the bride, steps forward at
once, and with his usual brevity upon such occasions, pronounces the words which make the couple
husband and wife. Thus joined they are about to
leave the church when a sensation is noticeable in
the audience.

Is this all? Have we worked weeks to make suitable costumes and walked miles this very day to see
only this? Brevity is odious to the Indian.

" We do not understand ! " they say. " Let us
have it in Indian ! " Then the venerable missionary,

Rev. Asher Wright, steps forward and repeats the ceremony in their own language, taking three times the amount of time. This is satisfactory so far. But wait. Mr. Two-Guns is slowly walking up the aisle, followed by Mrs. Two-Guns and the baby — the latter resplendent in a bright yellow calico dress. There is absolute silence until he says, " We wish our child baptized by the brother, and named for the husband, of our departing friend." And then Dr. Clark performs the rite of baptism, and the infant receives his name — Lemuel Caswell Two-Guns.

" And now," said one, " as we have had a promise that our wishes are to be gratified on this occasion, we ask that the bridal pair may stand where they are under the bower until we shake hands with them."

All the people in the church, in the most perfect order now pass up one aisle and down the other, stopping to shake hands and give us a word of congratulation. When the first mother appears in the procession, the black-eyed, plump-cheeked baby proves too great a temptation to a baby-lover, and Mr. Caswell stoops and kisses the child. After this every baby in the house is presented with the emphatic word " Gwah ! " (here !)

The bridal pair, with their guests, and two hundred special friends among the Indians, now adjourned to the Indian Orphan Asylum two and a half miles away, and passed a few hours very pleasantly while an Indian program was carried out for the entertainment of those from abroad.

A voice was heard saying these words: "Alas! alas! our sister! What shall we do for our sister? We adopted her into our tribe, we made her as one with ourselves. She has broken the law, she has married out of her tribe. She cannot join us in the Happy Home beyond the Setting Sun! Alas! alas! our sister! What shall we do for our sister?"

Second voice: "Let me speak; I will tell you what we will do for our sister. We will adopt the man she has chosen into our tribe. Thus we will save our sister. Then she may join us in the Happy Home beyond the Setting Sun."

Two lines of men were then formed. A sachem took Mr. Caswell by the arm and led him up and down, between the lines, while the men clapped their hands and shouted, "Yip! yip! yip!" and sang the war song. He was then named Sa-go-ye-ih after Red Jacket.

Dr. Peter Wilson, a tall, powerful-looking Indian, a Cayuga, now stood before the newly wedded couple and addressed them as follows: —

"Once upon a time there was in New York City a poor boy who had no home, no friends. He slept upon doorsteps or in boxes at night and begged by day. A kind lady saw him one day and invited him to enter her Sunday-school class at the Mission. He accepted the invitation and a new world was opened to him. He was very grateful. He wanted to give the lady something all his own; but he had nothing.

"One day a boy gave him half his 'chew of gum.' After chewing it a while the little waif suddenly thought of the lady. 'There!' he exclaimed, 'at last I have something all my own to give her!' And on the next Sabbath the presentation was made.

"Now," continued Peter Wilson, suddenly placing a book of Indian photographs in the hand of the bride, "this book which we give you is worth no more to you than the chew of gum was to the lady, but it is all we have. We have done our best."

The Indian choir, which had been singing in eastern cities for the benefit of the Orphan Asylum, now gave some of their songs in Indian and English, and after a bountiful supply of wedding cake "all the way from Boston" the wedding feast broke up at midnight.

The next morning, the friend who had been with them so many years bade them good-by with sorrow that the happy life with them had closed, her grief being mingled with joy in the prospect of the glad life opening before her.

During these days of sore trial to Mrs. Wright she smiled bravely through her tears and said, "It is

all right.   These seventeen years of close companionship have been very precious, and I must not rebel.
God will surely raise me up another helper, another
companion."

But her heavenly Father was leading her in ways
she could not understand, yet evermore leading her, in
the days and weeks and months of loneliness on that
Reservation, to draw nearer to him as her only refuge
and help and comfort.   One by one the workers with
whom she had been associated left her.   They were a
noble, consecrated band.   The memory of their spiritual companionship was very precious to her.   She
loved to recall the words and ways of their little ones ;
she loved to repeat the list of names so dear to her :
Rev. Messrs. Thayer, Bliss, Gleason, Hall, Curtis,
Ford, and the honored teachers who had so faithfully
coöperated with them ; and in addition to those
already mentioned in these pages, she ever held in
loving remembrance Mary Jane Thayer, Caroline
Fox, Martha Stevens, Jane Shearer, Mary Gleason,
Laura Raymond, Eleanor Jones, and other valued
helpers.   Then the companion of her youth and old
age, and by whose side she had labored for these
Indians fifty years, was laid to rest in the Indian
graveyard, and she was left to carry the burden alone.
Her faith was tested as by fire ; trial succeeded trial ;
but in childlike submission she said, " It is the Lord.

Let him do what seemeth unto him good." Her
favorite lines at this time were : —

> "When through fiery trials thy pathway shall lie,
> My grace all-sufficient shall be thy supply —
> The flame shall not hurt thee — I only design
> Thy dross to consume — thy gold to refine."

And indeed the gold of her character *was* refined —
until it reflected the face of the Master.

At last Rev. M. F. Trippe and his lovely wife were
appointed by the Presbyterian Board [1] to this mission,
for which she was deeply grateful. They were a comfort and inspiration ; but all too soon they were withdrawn and she pursued her journey alone, — as to any
helpful companionship, — giving every hour of her life
to these Indians, until, on the morning of January 21,
1886, God suddenly called her home.

[1] This Indian Mission had already been transferred from the American Board to the Presbyterian Board of Missions, who still have it in
charge.

BARK CANOE.

XVII.

To Mrs. Leroy Oatman, Buffalo, — Mary Shanks came to-day to tell me that she had no stove. I gave her two dollars, and must try and get an old stove for her somewhere. That family is suffering. Mary was ever so thankful for the sewing machine, and you are the good angel who got it for her, because you put me on the track. How thankful I am for all the kindness shown me by you and your husband! May God reward you! And he will, because you give the cup of cold water in Christ's name and for his sake, even though I am such a poor unworthy creature, not fit to be called his disciple; but I do long to know the things which are freely given to us of God. I have an indefinable yearning for something to which I have not yet attained.

We have little fruit, for which I greatly long at times, but we do have tomatoes, and how thankful we ought to be for them!

I intended to go to Buffalo next week, but alas! I have had a blow on the temple from my horse's head, while I was arranging his bridle. It did not hurt me much, but blackened my eye so that I am a fright! The pony did not do it in malice, only in restlessness. How I want to see you! I feel the gnawings of hunger for companionship congenial to my soul. There is a good reason why I am hindered from going to you now. God knows, and it is all right.

We are having some hopeful signs of revival interest at one of my out-stations, and I am experiencing some agonizing desires for a blessing in my own soul, and upon this people. I am studying the promises. I am more and more convinced that the promises are for us, only we don't appropriate them by faith.

(1) " Thy faith hath saved thee." (2) " O thou of little faith, wherefore didst thou doubt?" (3) " O woman, great is thy faith." (4) " He could not do many mighty works there because

of their unbelief." Setting these opposite each other, what do you understand by them? I am sure it is the lack of taking hold of the promises which makes us unprofitable and fruitless. Is it not so? We need the illuminating power of the Spirit to help us to grasp them. We need the intercession of the Spirit. We need the sanctifying power of the Spirit. God helps us to come humbly on account of our sins to the throne of grace, but boldly on account of God's infinite condescension and great love for this lost world.

I send you a package of mosses and leaves, which will serve to remind you of the autumn of my life; but I still find in my heart a loving, tender regard for friends long endeared. I am very busy — crowded with work of every kind and pressed on every hand. Oh, how we need more laborers here!

That dear lady is in all respects a jewel of the first water, but the setting is wrong. We may make mistakes sometimes, but God knows just how to deal with us. I often say, What a pity he or she should have taken this or that step! but how do I know but God permitted it for good, and perhaps took that course to save? Oh, the depths, both of the riches, wisdom, and knowledge of God! How unsearchable are his judgments and his ways past finding out! But how safe to trust all our interests entirely in his hands! How restful! God help us always to look to him in faith and hope and love, knowing that he is able to do exceeding abundantly above all that we can ask or think. Let us shout, " Begone, unbelief!" and go on our way rejoicing in God always, trusting implicitly in his wisdom, faithfulness, power, and love.

We are passing through some trials. The enemy roars upon us sometimes. It seems as though he would swallow us up. Oh, for overcoming faith! Sometimes I cry out many times in a day, "O Lord, have mercy upon us! Undertake for us!" Will you pray that my faith in God may be unwavering, and that we missionaries may be delivered from unreasonable and wicked men; that, notwithstanding our mistakes, we may not be left to be devoured of the adversary?

An Indian mother called to-day to tell me of the illness of her only daughter. She said: " I do not think she will ever be any better, for she is in a decline; but I am so thankful that she has come to me, and that I can make her comfortable in her last days. When she left me many years since, she was a member of the church, and I thought a true Christian — but she has been living since at the door of hell. I have prayed all these years that she might be brought back from her wanderings, for she had lost all her religion. There were no good influences around her. Now she has come home to me to die. Will you pray for her that before she leaves me I may know that she has asked and received forgiveness?" I gave such counsel and comfort as I could under the circumstances, and left such medicines as were needed for her temporary relief.

A few days later the mother came again to the Mission House and said, "I have been watching and praying very earnestly for a change in my daughter's mind. A few nights ago, after I had retired and all was still, I lay awake praying for her all by myself, when I thought I heard her speak. I rose immediately and went to her bedside and said: —

"'Do you want anything?' 'Oh, no!' said she; 'I was praying here all by myself; I did not know that I spoke.'

"Oh, how thankful I was to hear her say that! My tears streamed down my cheeks and when I could speak I said: —

"'Daughter, I thank God for this answer to my prayer. I too was praying in my bed and pleading with God that you might return to him, and that I might hear your voice in prayer once more. And now I will kneel down here by your bed and we will pray together.' And so we did, and from that time my daughter has been clear and happy in her mind."

This state of mind continued till her death. Christian friends visited her from time to time and found her in a humble, penitent, and believing state of mind. After all was over the mother came again to see me and said: —

"I never can be thankful enough that our daughter was brought back to Christ before she died. While she lived in that dreadful place it seemed to me she could not repent; the temptations were so thick around her, and I used to lie awake nights, praying, praying for her. It was God's hand that brought her home to die. 'His will be done.'"

To a Former Associate, — Spiritual darkness thickens all around us. Watchman, what of the night? The door is open, but the people are stupid, sleepy, dead, like dry bones in the valley. They need the breath of the Spirit to blow upon them; they need to awake to their condition. God help us!

I am making a special effort for the women and children among the pagans at Newtown. I have invited the mothers to come together and make garments for their children. I am satisfied that this is a good thing to do, and I am able thus to reach both mothers and children. Samuel Morris, a good Quaker of Philadelphia, has sent me one hundred dollars for this work; and this with the money from Boston will help me through.[1]

Humanly speaking, there never was a time on this Reservation when things looked so dark. May God have mercy upon us! is my prayer. Once in a while I meet some old woman who really sheds tears over the spiritual desolation here, and this encourages me. You cannot know how utterly alone I feel here now. There is no one left who can fully and intelligently sympathize with me. Sometimes the loneliness oppresses me so that I am in danger of breaking down. I cannot speak to any one of my fears and my discouragements. I have no one to whom I can communicate my anxieties. I am sorry I have been tempted to send you such a piteous wail.

I have received some wonderful intimations that God favors the effort I am making to raise funds for my gospel industrial work. A Quaker lady in New York City promised me two hundred and fifty dollars for this work. Last week she wrote that she could send me only twenty-five dollars of the money promised. I was stunned, and lay on my face before God in great distress and darkness of mind. Saturday evening I received another letter, in which she told me she felt impelled to send the two hundred and fifty dollars in addition to the twenty-five. I was rebuked for my unbelief, and with a thankful heart went on rejoicing.

I am so thankful for the help that comes to me from Boston! I could not live without it. The drought has been a terrible thing, and the crop of corn and potatoes almost useless. Strong drink is doing a dreadful work all over the Reservation. It was never so bad before, and you know that in itself means poverty and suffering and every evil to which flesh is heir. Mr. Trippe, our new missionary, is working bravely and his sweet little wife is helping with all her might.

[1] An appropriation from the Society for the Propagation of the Gospel among the Indians.

You will be surprised to hear from me in Buffalo. I came here a week ago to-day to solicit money from the good people of this city to help repair our Indian church. It is in a deplorable state. You know it was always shaky. The plastering was loosened all around and it leaked, and the chimneys were very bad. The Indians are very enthusiastic about repairing it. A large company of men have been at work drawing lumber and shingling, and doing something for two weeks. The men have raised one hundred dollars in cash; the women seventy dollars; and the Council has given one hundred dollars. Now I am trying to get Christian people here to help. I have received thus far eighty dollars, but, oh, it is such hard work! I have called on ladies here who have hundreds and thousands of dollars at their command, who are surrounded with every luxury, who tell me they cannot afford to give anything. Some frankly say, "I have no interest in this matter." If I did not feel it to be my duty to raise the money, I would never go through this torture. If I did not feel that the Indians have really done all they can, I would not ask a white man for one cent. I have received encouraging words from Rev. Mr. Lowell and Rev. Mr. Hubbell, which have greatly strengthened me.

I am struggling to-day and every day to find access to God, by prayer. I am not satisfied with my piety. There must be more for us to know. We certainly have not yet come to the perfect stature of Christian life. I have not. How can I be willing to live out the remainder of my life, poor and worthless as all has been, without a deeper experience of the power and love and faithfulness of God? I want to know the things that are freely given to us of God. Even these longings are filled, I fear, with doubt and unbelief, unreconciliation and ignorance, and even rebellion. I long to get into the light of faith and perfect trust. Oh, such burdens as I feel with regard to this people and the people of the neighboring white communities! So much ignorance and apathy on a subject which should lie so near the heart of every disciple! Oh, for a revival of religion among the white people who surround this Reservation of Indians!

I want you to pray that I may be baptized with the Spirit of God, whom Christ said should come and lead his people into the truth. I am sure this is what I need, and what all Christians need at the present day. I long for a mighty effusion of this divine life in my own soul to fit me for divine service. Would that I might be permitted to do some good before I die!

It seems to me I never saw the vanity of living to make money as I see it now, except as it can be used to forward the interests of Christ's kingdom. What poor trash it is! How it leads men to death, present and eternal! Will you pray that I may be enabled to do some good to certain people on this Reservation who are led captive by Satan at his will? There are those here who have not relapsed into outrageous sin; but any sin unrepented of does so sear the conscience and harden the heart! Very few bear us on their hearts to the mercy-seat now, and the number grows less every year, because our old friends are dying off. Do you realize that I am on the last half of my semi-centennial year of service among these Indians? Poor service! Next January I shall have been with them fifty years.

My heart is full of sad thoughts about the state of affairs here. The corn is cut off this year, as you know, but you cannot imagine how the whole people feel it, especially the poor. Last week seventy persons came to us for meal or flour; that which we have is almost gone. There are so many suffering ones about us that I cannot enjoy eating my food. Sometimes more than thirty people in one day come to tell us the story of their wants and to get me to beg for them. There has been an article in the papers telling the need of help, and asking the benevolent to send contributions. This distress will be likely to increase until spring opens.

I have passed through the horrors of cholera and smallpox and malignant typhoid fever, with these Indians, when a hundred died within a year, but I never saw anything like this. It takes all my vitality to see and talk with the multitude of people who come here with their pitiful stories, and not be able to help them.

Do you know we are entirely destitute of fruit this year? No apples, peaches, or grapes. I am nearly starved for fruit. I do not have tea or coffee, and do not eat much meat, so I am somewhat "hard up" to get anything that relishes; but the Lord is good to me, and I have great reason to be thankful. My greatest anxiety is to see this people converted. Must I die and leave them in rebellion against God? How can I bear the thought?

I cannot tell you much that is encouraging about our spiritual interests. The people have not raised the amount that was asked of them, and so Mr. Trippe has been withdrawn from this station and placed in charge of all the other Reservations. So we have preaching only once a month. The people are very much discouraged. They thought they did all they could. The crops were poor last year, the roads almost impassable all winter, so that they could do nothing in the woods. You know there are only a few who can do very much. The rich members of the church have died. There are only two left, and they are old men, who live a long distance from the church. Last year nobody was able to lay up any corn or potatoes. You know the Indians cannot be driven; they will follow if they can be made to believe that you really love them. They will not bear scolding.

I confess that I am constantly praying that the Lord will bring you back here just for a few weeks. It has seemed to me lately as though you might walk in any minute. Perhaps it is because we have been cleaning house, and fixing up, and arranging the many things which you have sent us to make the Mission House more attractive. More and more I feel what a blessing it would be to these people if you could come here just a little while. May God in his great mercy grant us this, the desire of our hearts! He has done great things for us, whereof we are glad, but giving does not impoverish him. He is able to do exceeding abundantly more than we can ask or even think. How little we know of the things which are freely given to us of God! and therefore we are lean and unprofitable in our service. How we toil and strive in vain, when we might live in the sunlight of God's love!

I am conscious of making a daily struggle towards the possession of simple, trusting faith in God's Word. This is not unattainable — but I am so earthly, so human, so slow of heart to believe that God is willing to do such good things for us, that nothing shall be impossible to us. How wonderful is God's forbearance to us!

I cannot help clinging to the hope that the way will be open for you to come to us. I cannot bear to think that this blessing will not come to this people. Will not your husband for Christ's sake, for the sake of this people, spare you to us a little while?

Her request is granted, and her friend, to whose husband the following letter of grateful appreciation was addressed, was permitted to spend one month at the Mission.

To the Husband of her Former Associate, — I feel constrained this afternoon to write to you. My heart is so full I must speak. I want you to know that I shall feel grateful to you as long as I live, and I think I may say through all eternity, for letting your dear wife come to see us. I cannot tell you how I have longed to see her these years, and how I have choked down the dreadful feeling of disappointment as each summer has passed away and I have failed to see her. I had come to think that it would never be on this side the pearly gates, and have often found myself anticipating the meeting on the other side. I have felt lately that her coming was a delusive dream, something which it must be wrong to hope for, something not to be thought of.

When she really did come I could hardly believe the evidence of my senses for some days; but now I know that her visit is a reality. I have tested her living presence and enjoyed it to the full. Now I count the days and the hours of her stay, and I bless you every time I do so. It is so kind of you to let her stay here a whole month! You can never know what her presence is to this people, and to me; I shall go in the strength of this meat many days, if my life is spared.

There has never been a time since she left us when she could have done so much for us. Every circumstance has been ordered by the loving Father's hand. She has been constantly at work, but I do not think she has suffered from it. I have watched her with the deepest anxiety, but all mountains have been leveled before her, and the rough places have been made smooth, and no accident has cast a gloom over our rides day and evening, upon the wretched roads and broken bridges and through the swollen streams of this Reservation. We have gone out and come in as we used to do in the blessed years of the past.

She has sung and played on our old broken-down melodeon to the exquisite satisfaction of our Hemlocks, Big Kettles, Cornplanters, Yellow Blankets, Green Blankets, Halftowns, and Silverheels. I only wish you could have seen the smiling faces, and the brown hands stretched out in happy greeting as they came around her at the close of every meeting. You see they did not expect her really to come any more than I did.

Well, I cannot express what I feel, and so I stop here, as I hear her voice calling from below, "Auntie Wright, there is a man here who wants some medicine." So farewell, dear brother; God bless you in soul and body for time and for eternity. Your ever grateful friend,   LAURA M. WRIGHT.

XVIII.

CATTARAUGUS RESERVATION, January 14, 1886.

FROM F. E. Parker : —

Auntie Wright is very, very ill with pneumonia. The doctor thinks she will not get well. Will you pray for her that she may be spared to us a little longer, that her prayers may yet be answered for our people?

From Mrs. Trippe : —

. I have been sitting with Auntie Wright for a time and she has requested me to write to you. She is no better, but the doctor says if she lives twenty-four hours she may possibly recover. Her brother Henry came yesterday. She was so glad to see him. She threw her arms around his neck and drew him close to her pillow, and whispered, "Glory to God!" Her voice is strong at times. The doctor does n't wish her to talk or sit up, even in bed, but she has a strong will and is very restless. Your letter is most fitting to be the last to her if she must go. Your words of encouragement concerning the results which must follow her earnest, constant prayer were a great inspiration to her. I trust you will not be overcome in view of the possible loss of this dear one to whom your own life has been so closely attached. Let us think only of her joy, her blessed entrance into the Beyond, her release from all the trials and anxieties of life; for as you well know she bears the burden of every one.

From her niece, Miss Ella Sheldon : —

The dear sick one is sleeping now, but may arouse at any minute. Her mind is very active. She knows every one who speaks to her.

301

It does not seem possible for her to recover. The doctor gives us no hope. Dear friend, what shall we do without her?

When your letter to young Parker came, cousin Helen Mixer sat down very close to Auntie Wright and said, "Auntie, here is a message for you. Shall I read it to you? Can you hear me?" "Yes," said she. And then cousin Helen read it very slowly and distinctly, just as you would have liked her to read it. Then for a full minute, it might have been a longer time, Auntie Wright kept perfectly quiet. It was so long that we feared she had not heard or comprehended, when she exclaimed, " No one knows — no one knows but God — what a comfort these words are to me."

From her brother, Mr. Henry Sheldon : —

January 21, 1886.

We have been up through the night with the sick one. She is now unconscious, except when aroused to take medicine or milk. It is hard to say it, but we have given up all hope, although we are doing all we can to save this precious life. What will become of this people when she leaves them, God only knows!

Later. I have the sad news to impart to you that Mrs. Wright breathed her last at one o'clock P.M. to-day. In the house and all about it are groups of bereaved Indians in tears. The funeral services will be held at the house and at the Mission church a half hour later. Of her it is surely recorded above, "She hath done what she could."

Thus did Mr. and Mrs. Wright give their lives to these Indians, not by a tragic death, but by long years of unremitting ministry, the outline of which is summed up in the following page. The power of this influence in the spiritual kingdom is known to Him only for whom they " counted not their lives as dear unto themselves that they might accomplish the ministry which they received from the Lord Jesus to testify the gospel of the grace of God" to the people.

Rev. Asher Wright was born in Hanover, New Hampshire, in 1803. He made a profession of religion at sixteen and from the very first cherished the idea of becoming a missionary. He graduated from Andover Seminary in 1831, and went to the Seneca Indians under commission of the American Board of Commissioners for Foreign Missions. He remained with these Indians fifty-seven years, dying in 1875, aged seventy-three.

Mrs. Wright was born in St. Johnsbury, Vermont, in 1809. She labored among these Indians fifty-three years, surviving her husband eleven years. She died January 21, 1886, on the anniversary of her wedding day, aged seventy-seven.

These two missionaries translated the Four Gospels and several other portions of Scripture into the Seneca language. In the same language they published two editions of hymns, many of them of their own composition. They also prepared a vocabulary of the Seneca language and published many Indian leaflets.

Through the efforts of Rev. M. F. Trippe a monument has been placed in the Mission graveyard at the spot where lie the remains of these lamented and honored missionaries.

XIX.

THE testimony of Henry Silverheels : —

I will say a few words. Our sister, Mrs. Wright, who is through with her work, was a believer. She believed God when he said " Go preach my gospel." We all witness that she did that here. She has labored faithfully among our people ; every day we have seen her doing good. She has instructed all — old men and women, young men and maidens, and even the little ones ; she has cared for their souls and for their bodies. We have seen her in church every Sabbath, and she has spoken to us all some word, or gently whispered about Jesus Christ.

What shall we do now? We shall never more hear her voice. Shall we believe her words or not? Shall we take her advice? Shall we repent of our sins and believe the gospel? She has gone to the world of happiness. Many things troubled her here, but now she is free, in that world of joy. I cannot mourn over her death because she is so happy now in heaven praising God. I urge you, my people, to be faithful unto death, and you shall meet her in heaven, and with her be forever happy.

Her husband, Mr. Wright, gave the best strength of his early manhood to us, and he continued to work for us until the very last. He was always kind and patient with us. He never talked hard when we did not do right; he never scolded us; he was like a good, wise father to us all. He would take as much pains to speak to a poor man, or a very wicked man, as he would to a good man, or a rich man. He loved us all, and he tried to do us all good. We all believed and knew that he was our friend. Sometimes we quarreled about our political affairs and there were very hard words between us. Mr. Wright always acted as a peacemaker. Sometimes we found fault with him and blamed him, but he never said anything back to us, or reproached us. He was like Christ. He always returned good for evil.

From Daniel Two-Guns : —

This brother expressed his gratitude that the Great Father had fulfilled his promise to send messengers, bringing the " good tidings " in which all mankind are participants. He spoke with a full heart of Mr. Wright, whom he mentioned by his Indian name, " Gai-wi-yu," meaning " Good News."

" Good News," said he, " was a good doctor as

well as a Christian worker. He was ready at all
hours to respond to any calls made upon him, and his
health at last broke down under the hardships of his
self-imposed task. He was one of the truest friends
the Indian ever had ; he could speak our language
as well as a native, and frequently delighted us with
a sermon in our own tongue."

F. E. Parker, a Seneca, whose mother, a niece
of Mrs. Wright, married N. H. Parker, the United
States Indian Interpreter, spoke with much feeling
of the devotion of Mr. and Mrs. Wright, with whom
he had resided for several years. "I have often
seen them," said he, "in the early morning, while
all the household were asleep, kneeling in supplication
for the people they loved. Their hearts and hands
were always open for the benefit of our nation.
When cholera and smallpox half ravaged our Reservation, when no one would go near those who
were sick, Mr. and Mrs. Wright went to their homes
and ministered to them. They were truly angels of
mercy."

From Major Cole, an evangelist, of Michigan : —

I once visited the Seneca Indians on the Cattaraugus Reservation.
I found there an aged sister, Mrs. Wright, who had been laboring
among them for many years. All the missionaries who had been
associated with her were dead, or removed to other fields. As soon

as she found I had come to preach the gospel to these Indians, she praised the Lord, saying he had answered her prayers.

"I have prayed," she exclaimed, "that the Lord would send somebody to preach to these people among whom I have worked as well as I could, and for whom I have prayed constantly that they might be saved."

I said, "How long have you been working here, sister?"

"More than fifty years," she replied. She was full of faith that the Lord would send a blessing upon this beloved people.

Well, we went to the little chapel among the pagans, and she said:—

"I will call them to the meeting." She took hold of the bell rope, and with all her strength began to ring the bell. I went up to her and said:—

"Let me do that."

She said, "No, you pray. You must save all your strength for the people. Pray hard that the Lord will give you souls to-day."

We waited five minutes, but no one came; still she kept ringing the bell. Ten minutes passed, yet we were alone. Finally, I began to think we should not have an audience, and that we might as well go back to the Mission.

"Brother Cole," said she, "I have waited nearly fifty years. You won't leave them, will you, until you have preached to them?"

I was reproved, and said, "I will not leave this place until I have seen some of these Indians saved."

She continued to ring the bell, but no one came.

She said: "Brother Cole, you stay here and pray. Pray hard. I will go to every house and bring them in."

So she ran down a little footpath through the woods, and soon a tall Indian came stalking in and took his seat, while she started off down another trail, and presently came back with three more. She kept on until we had quite an audience, and were able to begin the meeting. She interpreted my English into Indian, and such a meeting as we had that afternoon in that little house! God met us there, and thirteen precious souls were saved at that time. This fruit was the result of her faithful seed-sowing.

From Rev. M. F. Trippe:—

Mrs. Wright *literally* bore these people upon her heart. She knew them all. No one will ever live who will know them so well. Every child born since the year 1833 has been tenderly watched by her from infancy to old age or death. She knew their sorrows, successes, hopes, disappointments, failures; their mental, moral, and physical characteristics. Every case of soul-wrecking came as a personal calamity upon her grieving heart. She keenly felt all the bitter curses heaped upon this race by her own. She recognized one thing as essential to the safety and salvation of the people, and that was their full and hearty acceptance of Christianity. For this end she labored, prayed, and wept. Side by side, Mr. and Mrs. Wright toiled, and their holy purpose was to save this people for Christ and heaven.

I wonder if you realize that the intense, persistent, unfailing purpose of this woman was to save your race. Your coming doom as a race and as individuals, if you did not accept Christ, drove sleep from her eyes. She would weep and pray the night through. I cannot tell you how greatly she loved you, how she robbed herself of ordinary comforts to keep you from suffering. Her nature was love. I never knew her to hold resentment for any wrong inflicted upon herself. She never bore ill-will when ill-treated, yet she never forgot a wrong committed against a poor Indian. She was always watchful of your interests, always on the alert to defeat the wicked schemes of unworthy persons who would make you their prey. Denied children of her own, she adopted you all. Never was a more fitting word spoken than the remark made by one of your prominent men on the day of her death: "*The Indians are all orphans now.*"

The death of Mrs. Wright is a loss irreparable to the people to whom she has given all the strength, freshness, and wisdom of a long life. There is no one able to fill her place. As a dear friend said of her, "It is only her body that failed. Her spirit was fresh, young, and helpful to all who came within the sphere of her influence."

One can hardly realize the extent of the sacrifice to persons of the intelligence, gifts, and education of Mr. and Mrs. Wright, to isolate themselves from the stimulus of an active and intelligent community, and conform their lives to the lives of a less-favored people. Mr. Wright was an accomplished Oriental scholar, and a master of seven languages. It will be long ere the Indian race finds other teachers and pastors so superior and so devoted.

From Hon. William P. Letchworth, of Buffalo : —

In the summer of 1854 unusual destitution and suffering prevailed among these Indians. Mr. and Mrs. Wright, who were so active in seeking out and relieving the wants of the distressed, were appalled at the amount of sickness and privation around them, and almost disheartened over their inability to extend anything like adequate relief to the afflicted and dying Indians about them. Early and late through these sad days these good people labored on through the summer, imploring aid from such friends as they could reach; but with tne approach of winter they saw that still greater suffering must ensue. Then more earnest appeals went out both far and near. One of these reached Philip Thomas, a Friend, of Baltimore, who had previously shown a deep interest in their work. Encouraged by promises of liberal aid from him, they redoubled their exertions.

At this time Mr. and Mrs. Wright brought into their family several suffering Indian children, thus assuming in addition to their labors a load of care equal to their utmost capacity. Dwellers in princely mansions, lovers of fashion, luxury, and ease, what think you of this sacrifice?

This was the nucleus and real beginning of the Thomas Indian Orphan Asylum. By the aid of Philip Thomas and a small state appropriation, and the council of the Seneca nation, which gave the land for the home, and benevolent people, the Thomas Indian Orphan Asylum was permanently established.

In 1875, by the enforcement of a recent amendment to the Constitution, all state aid was cut off. This would have resulted in closing the asylum had not Mr. Wright and Dr. Pettit, of Fredonia, another warm friend of the Indian, and president of the board of trustees, gone to Albany and laid the situation before the legislature.

Their petition was at first denied, to the great dejection and sorrow of poor Mr. Wright. Eventually, however, his earnestness and persistency prevailed. A plan was devised whereby the state took the asylum property and assumed control of the institution, supplying all the means for its support, and Mr. Wright returned home in buoyant spirits. This was his last opportunity to present the claims of the Indian children to the legislature, Though in feeble health, nothing could deter him from making this journey, and he never recovered from the fatigue and exposure consequent upon it.

From Secretary Bamuna, of the Buffalo Historical Society : —

I spent three summer days at the Indian Mission House. I left the train at the nearest point to the Cattaraugus Reservation and took a wagon to the Mission House. In this neighborhood the Indians have embraced Christianity. They are intelligent, and somewhat educated; their houses are neat, their farms and gardens well tilled.

Mrs. Wright took me to the settlement of the pagans. These people have refused to embrace Christianity, and a large portion of them are most pitiably drunken, debased, utterly shiftless and worthless. They have no good farms, no gardens, and are miserable objects of charity. The influence of the selfish white man and his fire water could not be more terribly or more truthfully depicted. The contrast between these two settlements could not be more marked.

I found Mrs. Wright a very pleasant woman, and I formed a most favorable opinion of her character as well as of her influence for good among the people about her. She was constantly being consulted by them on all sorts of subjects, and always entered fully into everything that concerned them. A young girl came into the room having on shoes with the toes worn out. She showed her bare toes to Mrs. Wright, who at once gave her some money to buy new shoes. I learned that she always gave in this way all the money she could possibly spare from her salary. She was entirely devoted to this people, and ready to make any sacrifice for them. Hers was not a labor of duty alone, but one of love.

From Miss Ella Sheldon (a niece), Canton, Pennsylvania : —

What a great, loving heart she had! How sure we were of her sympathy in every particular with all our little plans! We ought to rejoice that she is at last at rest. She was almost broken-hearted over that people. When she died what a load must have fallen from her heart! She always cared for others before herself. The day she was taken sick she went out to the barn and nailed a **board over a hole in the wall** so the wind wouldn't blow in on poor Nellie, the missionary horse. In her last hours she said, "God is so good to me, and I do praise his name!" Sleeping or waking, her lips were constantly moving. When we bent over her to listen it was always a word of grace or a breath of prayer which came to our ears. Was it not beautiful that she could go home on the anniversary of her wedding day?

From Mrs. Leroy Oatman, Buffalo, New York: —

I once passed through some silver-refining works, and when a piece of silver came from the furnace after its very last refining, it was perfectly free from all dross. The character of Mrs. Wright seemed to me to have passed this, its last needed refining fire. I could not see why or how she needed the last terrible process, but since she has gone it has been made plain to me. She needed to be made more perfectly like her Pattern. How she did try to imitate him! Her every breath seemed to be in harmony with God's way and God's will. I think I never knew any one so afraid that justice would not be done to everything. Her face was once badly bruised by her pony, but she "did n't believe he meant to hurt her." She never meant to think evil of any one. She was precious, pure metal.

From Miss Sylvia P. Joslin, a missionary teacher: —

My most frequent memory of Mrs. Wright is the expression of her face in my schoolroom at Newtown, when pagan women came in to have a little talk with her before the exercises began. Although I could not understand the language, I knew by the patient, sad look upon her face how sorry she felt for the poor benighted soul who was vigorously blowing her up, as she so frequently allowed them to do.

I would exclaim, "Oh! the miserable ingrates!" but she, dear, patient, forgiving soul, as she listened, was praying for wisdom to reply to these unreasonable charges, and reports of scandal. How gently and wisely she would hold up better things to them! How patiently she would explain these petty matters which had so enraged their small souls!

Do you remember her faithful and delicate ministrations to the sick? How often she gave them the necessary medicines with her own hand through fear of some mistake! And when there was no longer an appropriation granted her for medicine for these people, she furnished it just the same from her own small salary. She would go to Buffalo and buy medicine and groceries and flannel, etc., for these people, and for herself one pair of cheap, congress cloth boots. Her own needs were forgotten in the sore need of these suffering people.

I have often slept in the same room with her. Her first waking thought was a prayer. Every morning I would see that dear hand placed over the eyes while her lips moved in prayer. During my last years with her it seemed as if every breath was a prayer, when she was not talking to some one.

From Rev. W. C. Dewey, a nephew of Mr. Wright, now a missionary in Mardin, Turkey in Asia : —

My earliest remembrances of Auntie Wright are as she appeared on one of her visits with Uncle Wright to the West about thirty years or more ago. At that time I stood quite in awe of her, she seemed so stately and almost austere. It seems to me now, as my memory runs back, that she had changed but very little in all these subsequent years. And yet I remember that even then her innate kindness was as active as ever. I have somewhere among my papers now, I presume, a little hymn which she wrote for me, and another for my younger sister, Mary. This was all, except occasional references in letters and in the family talk, till that winter twenty-one years ago, when we two young " Suckers" from Illinois dropped in at the Mission House one evening.

I was not altogether unappreciative at the time of her kindness to me that year on the Reservation; but it has grown on me more and more as the years have gone by. Ah, how many pictures rise as memory casts her glance backward over the intervening years! Perhaps my own missionary experience helps me to a fuller understanding of what she really was and did in that household and among the people. How dependent our dear uncle was upon her!

I fear I used sometimes to try her patience sadly, as when one time in my simplicity I filled that big box stove in the sitting room with green beech wood! I believe she never actually reproved me but once, and that was, I need not say, most richly deserved. It occurred soon after a visit of the Quakers. We were all in the sitting room one evening and had been speaking of them, when I made some light remark about "the Spirit moving them." It was intended on my part to be simply humorous, and without the smallest thought of disrespect; but I remember as well as though it had been only yesterday her look and manner as she said, "Don't, Willis; I can't endure to hear such good people ridiculed." It was a most salutary lesson to me, putting the subject before me in an entirely new light.

You remember our trips to Newtown, when we sometimes had to build our own bridges across the creeks. But I cannot begin to speak of her constant, unwearying, far-reaching labors of love for that people.

She was ever "as one that served." Well did we choose for the motto on the stone last fall: "They pleased not themselves." When the stone came, and she noted the inscription, she turned and spoke reproachfully: "Why, Willis! why did you put it *they?*"

It was the next time I was there, three years later, in 1868, when I went on and took charge of the Indian Orphan Asylum during my summer vacation, that I began to have a little truer conception of what she really was. I remember thinking at one time that she was not pleased with my course in regard to some of the boys. So I was deeply touched when she spoke to me one evening just before I was going away. She was in the yard at the west end of the house taking in clothes from the line; I had happened over there for something and she stopped me. I do not recall now just what she said, but she spoke in a way that made me feel, as I never had felt before, that she appreciated the difficulties under which I had been laboring and looked upon the work there in no critical, fault-finding spirit.

When next I saw her was the summer of 1875, which I spent there just after Uncle Wright's death; and then I came to know her still better, especially after Phinie [a niece of Mrs. Wright] and I began to draw together — I do not believe there was ever the first selfish thought in her heart in regard to that matter. As I have come to understand since how much this young girl was to her, it would have seemed the most natural thing in the world if she had discouraged anything as likely to take her away. Almost her first words to me on the subject, when she found that the attachment was mutual, were the expression of thanksgiving, and as the tears sprang to her eyes, she said she was sure nothing in the world would have given so great gratification to Uncle Wright had he been living. I was much impressed while among the Senecas last fall, to note the ripening — mellowing of her character — the growing in grace.

THE BELOVED MISSIONARY PHYSICIAN.

He was humble, kind, forgiving, meek;
Easy to be entreated, gracious, mild;
And with all patience and affection taught,
Rebuked, persuaded, solaced, counseled, warned,
In fervent style and manner. All
Saw in his face contentment, in his life
The path to glory and perpetual joy.

Mr. Wright was a man of rare tact and ability, and had acquired an extraordinary influence with the tribe. — *Rev. Dr. Hubbell, Buffalo.*

Although by his talents he might have filled the pulpit of any of the leading churches, he resisted all such temptations to labor for the Indian. He had selected a task more difficult than that of going among the heathen of distant lands; but from that task he never shrank, he never turned back. Nor did he ever regret that he had made this his life work. By the remarkable gentleness that characterized his nature he was often selected to play the part of peacemaker when troubles arose among the pagans as well as among the Christians. — *Rev. Dr. Chester, Buffalo.*

The literary work of both Mr. and Mrs. Wright, the Thomas Indian Orphan Asylum, the cultivated fields of the Reservation, and the prosperity of the Senecas constitute their enduring monument; but the crowning excellence in the character of both was their humble piety and consecration to the Master. — *Colonel J. B. Plumb, Westfield, New York.*

Mr. Wright was energetic, yet quiet; genial in conversation, careful in giving his opinion, and by his sound judgment held great influence with the Indians, with whom he was a recognized counselor and friend. His knowledge of business made him practically useful to his Indian friends in urging them to adopt agricultural pursuits and to form habits of industry. — *Hon. W. P. Letchworth.*

The whole story of his life may be summed up in the single statement: he was Christlike. He had a kind word for everybody, and rarely closed a conversation without a word for God. — *Rev. William Hall.*

It was his nature to avoid, rather than to seek, conspicuous position. He had that happy balance of faculties, that round-about common sense, that quick discernment of the best means to gain the best ends, which we call wisdom. His strong native endowments were subjected to a broad, generous, and continuous culture. He excelled as a naturalist, a linguist, a medical practitioner, as well as a theologian and preacher; and yet he could tell the story of the cross so simply and effectively as to meet the wants of those who were entirely unskilled in human learning. — *Rev. Chalon Burgess, D.D.*

Mr. Wright loved study, but would instantly and cheerfully drop any interesting line of research with books or chemicals to listen to a tale of distress and to relieve suffering. Among his papers was found a scrap yellow with age, the ink faded, upon which was written in his own hand: "Resolved, to let no day pass without speaking with some one on the matter of his soul's salvation." — *Rev. Willis C. Dewey, Mardin, Turkey in Asia.*

XX.

THE foregoing pages present the Reservation life of the Iroquois in his Long House, under the influence of over a half century of Christlike patience and self-sacrificing effort on his behalf. I cannot close this record without adding my tribute to those already given; for to Mrs. Wright I owe a debt of gratitude which can be redeemed only by passing on the story of her saintly life for the inspiration of other Christian workers.

During the many years that I was a member of Mrs. Wright's family, I was impressed by her untiring devotion to the interests, temporal and spiritual, of the Indians. She had acquired a perfect command of the language, and the people, old and young, felt free to come to her with their joys and sorrows and perplexities of every description. She never turned one away without a word of sympathy or advice. Material assistance was also given when needed. If any poor wretch was too repulsive to gain the hospitality of the Indian fireside, she was sure to find some snug corner at the Mission House, where, provided with

a blanket, he might be sheltered from the cold.   But
with all the comfort and relief she was sure to give
a word of gospel truth, praying always that the constant seed-sowing might in time bring forth fruit.
While her ears were open to their varied experiences,
her hands were often busy at the same time preparing
and distributing medicine for the sick.   If the need
were urgent, she never hesitated to give her personal
ministrations in the most wretched of homes, where
lives were saved and suffering lessened by her medical
skill and careful nursing.

With the care of a large house, and constant inter-
ruptions from the lame, maimed, halt, and blind, and
in fact all who could find any excuse to throng her,
Mrs. Wright found time to assist her husband in
translating the Scriptures into the Indian language.
She it was who furnished translations of some of our
choicest hymns for the Indian hymnal.

Although a center of sunshine and good cheer for
missionaries and people, she impressed all who lived
with her as spending much time in prayerful intercession for the people to whom she had given her life.
Often when she thought herself alone I have heard her
pleading with God that this and that sin might not be
laid to their charge.   Many a time I have heard her in
the quiet night hours wrestling with God in agonized
prayer for the salvation of these beloved Indians.

Mrs. Wright had a habit of using odd moments for intellectual culture. In this way she kept abreast with the times. Her mind was unusually active, her intellect keen and clear to the last; her views of the vital questions of the day were expressed with rare insight and intelligence. Public men from Washington, Albany, and New York City, who came to the Reservation upon official matters, considered it a privilege to secure an hour's uninterrupted conversation with this woman. They were never able to solve the mystery of her intelligent comprehension of the outside world, of which she had only occasional glimpses.

When Mrs. Wright took those half-starved Indian children into her family in 1855, and resolved to found an Indian Orphan Asylum, the plan met with very little encouragement from her friends; but in this, as in all other efforts, she never permitted herself to be discouraged by difficulties. Obstacles aroused a more fixed determination to press on. The Indian Orphan Asylum, with its cultivated acres and fine buildings, an ornament and a blessing to the whole Reservation, stands to-day as a memorial of two consecrated lives. Because of the prayers and patient persistence of Mr. and Mrs. Wright, hundreds of Indian children have been sheltered, trained in useful habits, and brought into the fold of Christ.

Before the popular wave of " industrial education "

had begun to sweep over our land, Mrs. Wright had already inaugurated this movement among the Seneca Indians; in connection with religious instruction, she commenced the experiment among the Indian women, who still clung to the pagan faith of their fathers. She gathered them about her and won their confidence by furnishing material which they were allowed to cut and make into garments for themselves and their children under instruction. While pleasantly occupied with their work she read and explained the Scriptures in their own language. She next procured government contracts to make garments for the western tribes. For this work, carried on under the same gospel influences, the Indian women received some compensation.

In her old age she matured her last grand plan for the benefit of these people, for whom she had lived and toiled and prayed, over fifty years. The new plan was a "Gospel Industrial Institute," to include a high school, where the young people might complete their education at home. This plan included classes for boys in the various trades, and instruction for young girls in useful and domestic occupations. These classes were to be placed under the care of competent and Christian teachers, working in full harmony with the missionaries. The institute was to include accommodations for the Young Men's and

Young Women's Christian Associations, with a reading room and a well-selected library for the use of all Indians who could read English. She hoped by these means not only to save the young people, but to elevate them to a higher standard of living and to prepare them for citizenship in the near future. It was in the midst of this supreme effort that she heard the summons bidding her rest from her earthly labors and enter into the joy of her Lord.

Is it not evident to every thoughtful friend of the Indian that such a plan of GOSPEL INDUSTRIAL EDUCATION, thoroughly carried into effect on every Reservation in our land, would solve the Indian problem which confronts this nation to-day?